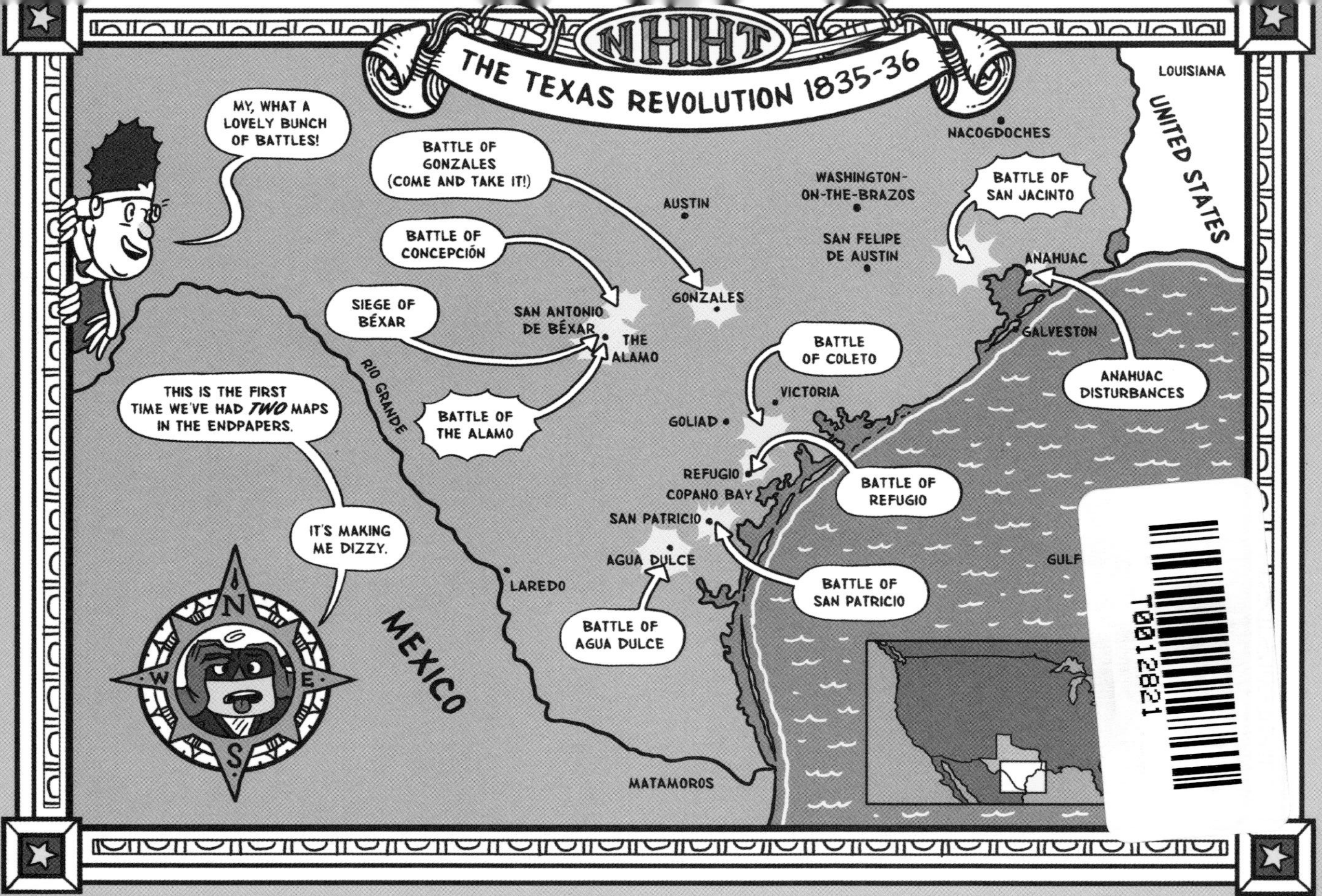
NHHT
THE TEXAS REVOLUTION 1835-36
MY, WHAT A LOVELY BUNCH OF BATTLES!
BATTLE OF GONZALES (COME AND TAKE IT!)
BATTLE OF CONCEPCIÓN
SIEGE OF BÉXAR
BATTLE OF THE ALAMO
THIS IS THE FIRST TIME WE'VE HAD TWO MAPS IN THE ENDPAPERS.
IT'S MAKING ME DIZZY.
N
E
S
W
MEXICO
RIO GRANDE
LAREDO
MATAMOROS
SAN ANTONIO DE BÉXAR
THE ALAMO
AUSTIN
GONZALES
WASHINGTON-ON-THE-BRAZOS
SAN FELIPE DE AUSTIN
NACOGDOCHES
LOUISIANA
UNITED STATES
BATTLE OF SAN JACINTO
ANAHUAC
GALVESTON
ANAHUAC DISTURBANCES
BATTLE OF COLETO
VICTORIA
GOLIAD
REFUGIO
COPANO BAY
BATTLE OF REFUGIO
SAN PATRICIO
AGUA DULCE
BATTLE OF SAN PATRICIO
BATTLE OF AGUA DULCE
GULF

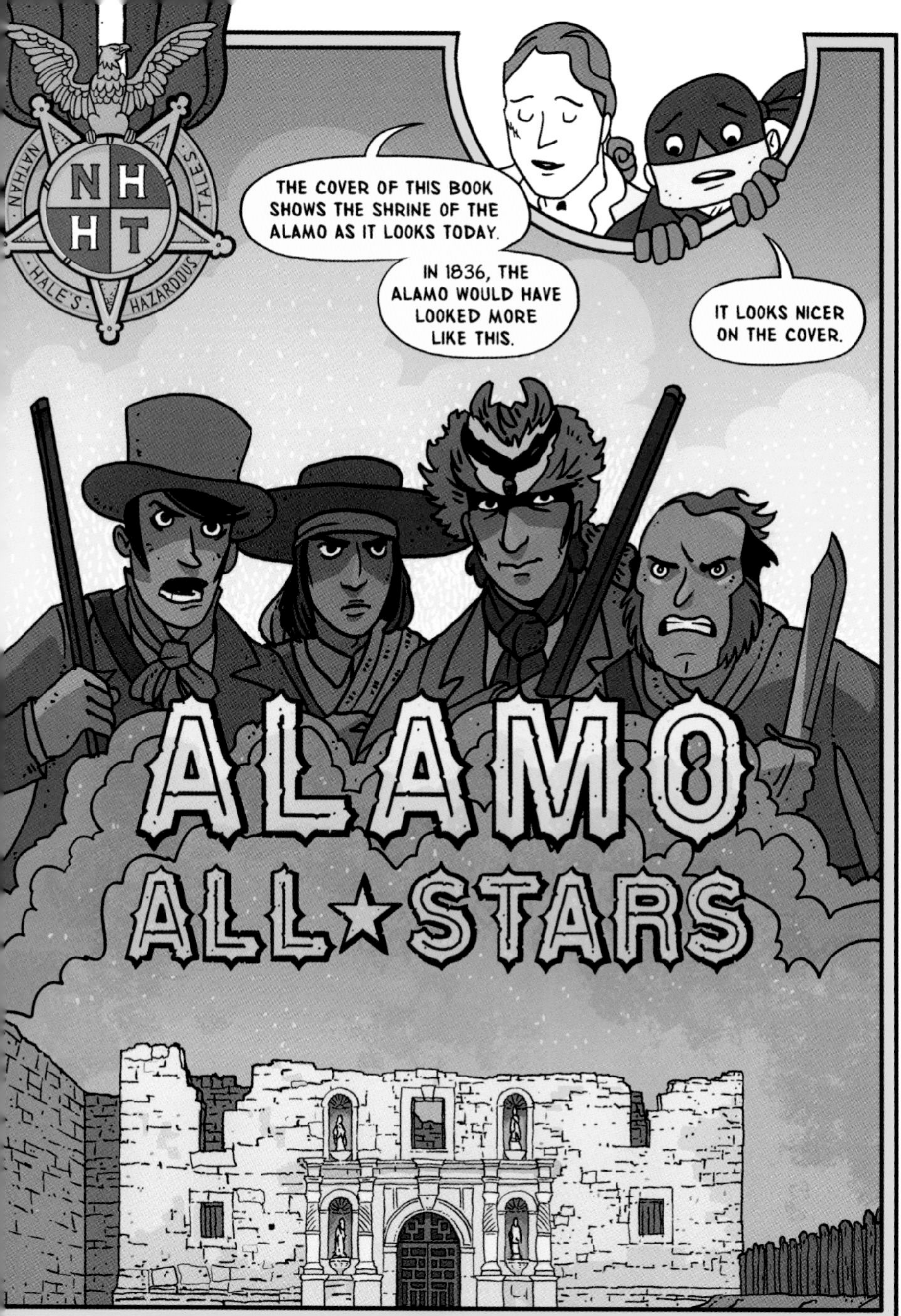
NATHAN HALE'S HAZARDOUS TALES
NH HT
THE COVER OF THIS BOOK SHOWS THE SHRINE OF THE ALAMO AS IT LOOKS TODAY.
IN 1836, THE ALAMO WOULD HAVE LOOKED MORE LIKE THIS.
IT LOOKS NICER ON THE COVER.
ALAMO ALL★STARS

AMULET BOOKS, NEW YORK

CATALOGING–IN–PUBLICATION DATA HAS BEEN APPLIED FOR
AND MAY BE OBTAINED FROM THE LIBRARY OF CONGRESS.

LIBRARY OF CONGRESS CONTROL NUMBER: 2015916055
ISBN: 978–1–4197–1902–8

TEXT AND ILLUSTRATIONS COPYRIGHT © 2016 NATHAN HALE
BOOK DESIGN BY NATHAN HALE AND CHAD W. BECKERMAN

PRINTED AND BOUND IN CHINA
16 15

ABRAMS The Art of Books
195 Broadway, New York, NY 10007
abramsbooks.com

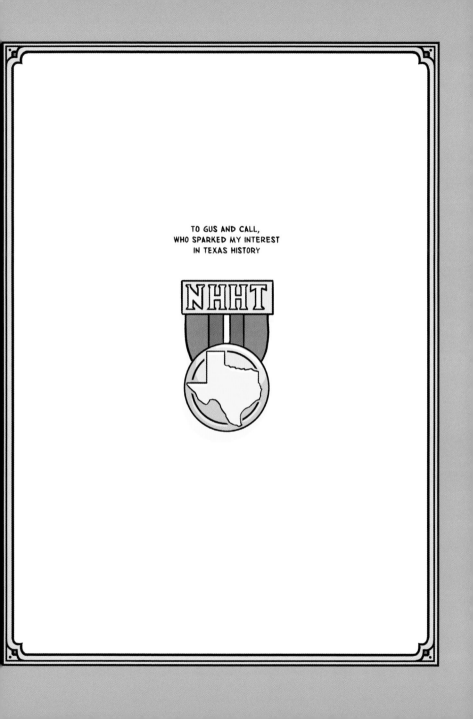

TO GUS AND CALL,
WHO SPARKED MY INTEREST
IN TEXAS HISTORY

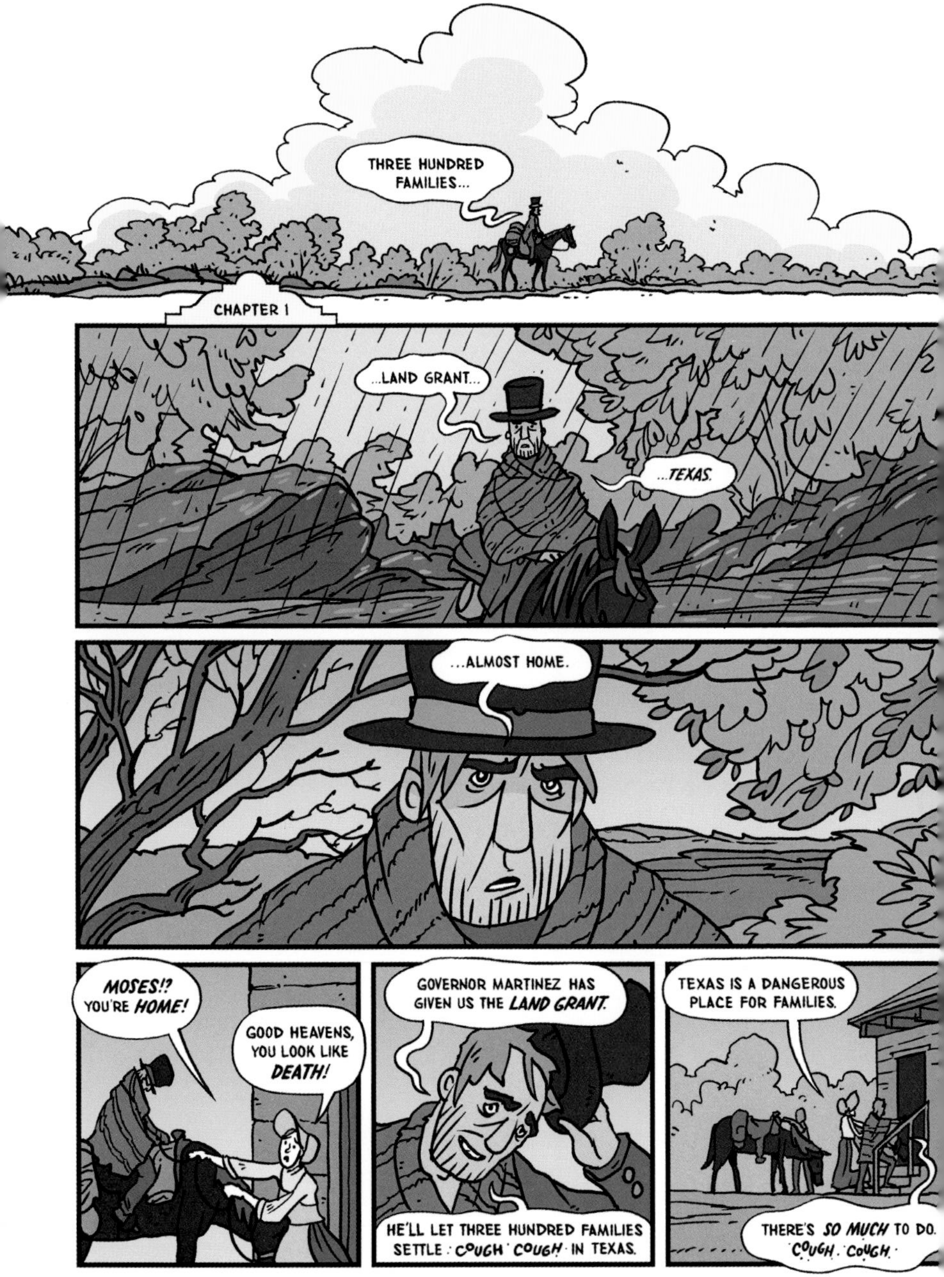
THREE HUNDRED FAMILIES...
CHAPTER 1
...LAND GRANT...
...TEXAS.
...ALMOST HOME.
MOSES!? YOU'RE HOME!
GOOD HEAVENS, YOU LOOK LIKE DEATH!
GOVERNOR MARTINEZ HAS GIVEN US THE LAND GRANT.
HE'LL LET THREE HUNDRED FAMILIES SETTLE COUGH COUGH IN TEXAS.
TEXAS IS A DANGEROUS PLACE FOR FAMILIES.
THERE'S SO MUCH TO DO. COUGH. COUGH.

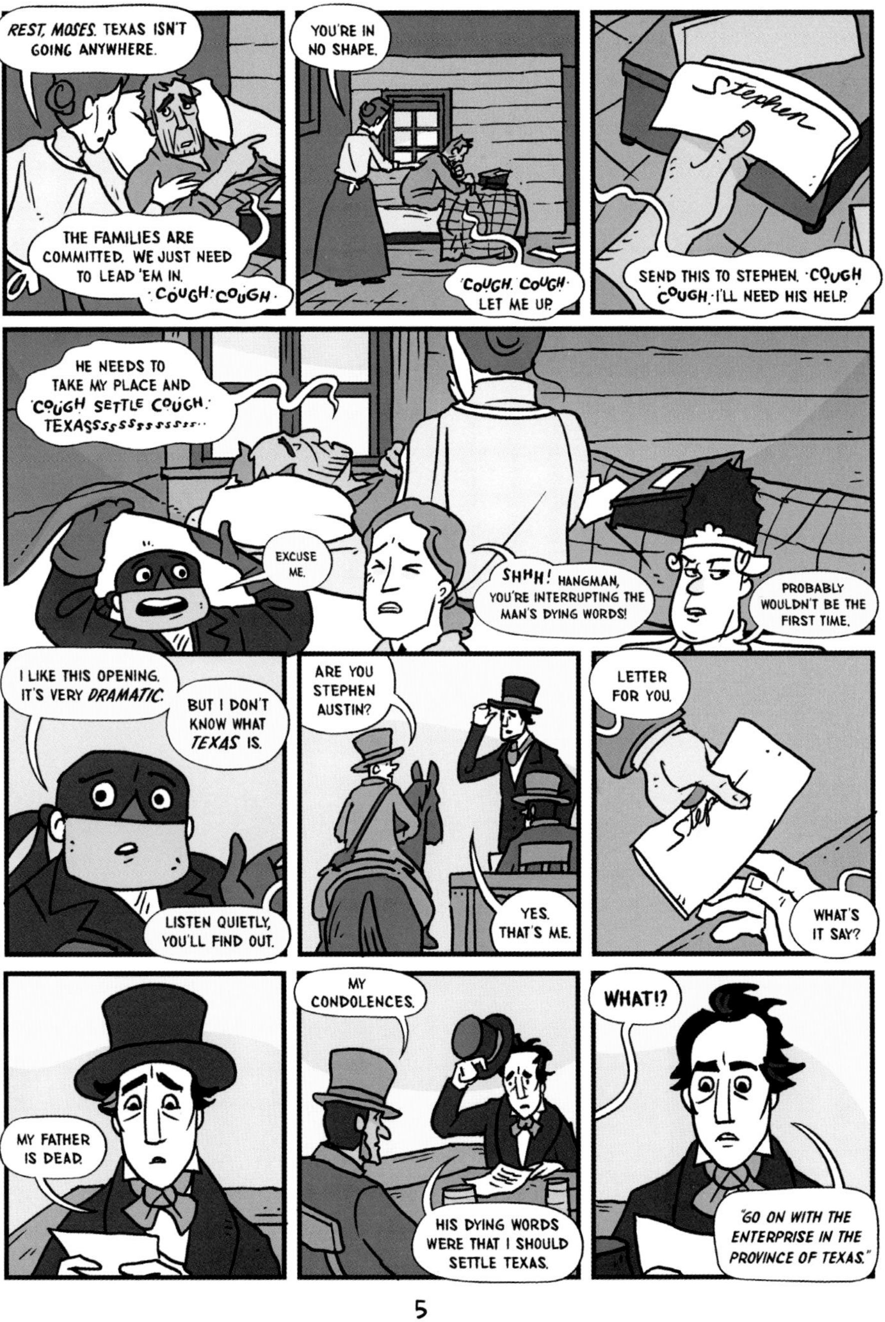
REST, MOSES. TEXAS ISN'T GOING ANYWHERE.
THE FAMILIES ARE COMMITTED. WE JUST NEED TO LEAD 'EM IN. ·COUGH· COUGH·
YOU'RE IN NO SHAPE.
·COUGH· COUGH· LET ME UP.
Stephen
SEND THIS TO STEPHEN. ·COUGH COUGH· I'LL NEED HIS HELP.
HE NEEDS TO TAKE MY PLACE AND ·COUGH SETTLE COUGH· TEXASSSSSSSSSSSS...
EXCUSE ME.
SHHH! HANGMAN, YOU'RE INTERRUPTING THE MAN'S DYING WORDS!
PROBABLY WOULDN'T BE THE FIRST TIME.
I LIKE THIS OPENING. IT'S VERY DRAMATIC.
BUT I DON'T KNOW WHAT TEXAS IS.
LISTEN QUIETLY, YOU'LL FIND OUT.
ARE YOU STEPHEN AUSTIN?
YES. THAT'S ME.
LETTER FOR YOU.
WHAT'S IT SAY?
MY FATHER IS DEAD.
MY CONDOLENCES.
HIS DYING WORDS WERE THAT I SHOULD SETTLE TEXAS.
WHAT!?
"GO ON WITH THE ENTERPRISE IN THE PROVINCE OF TEXAS."

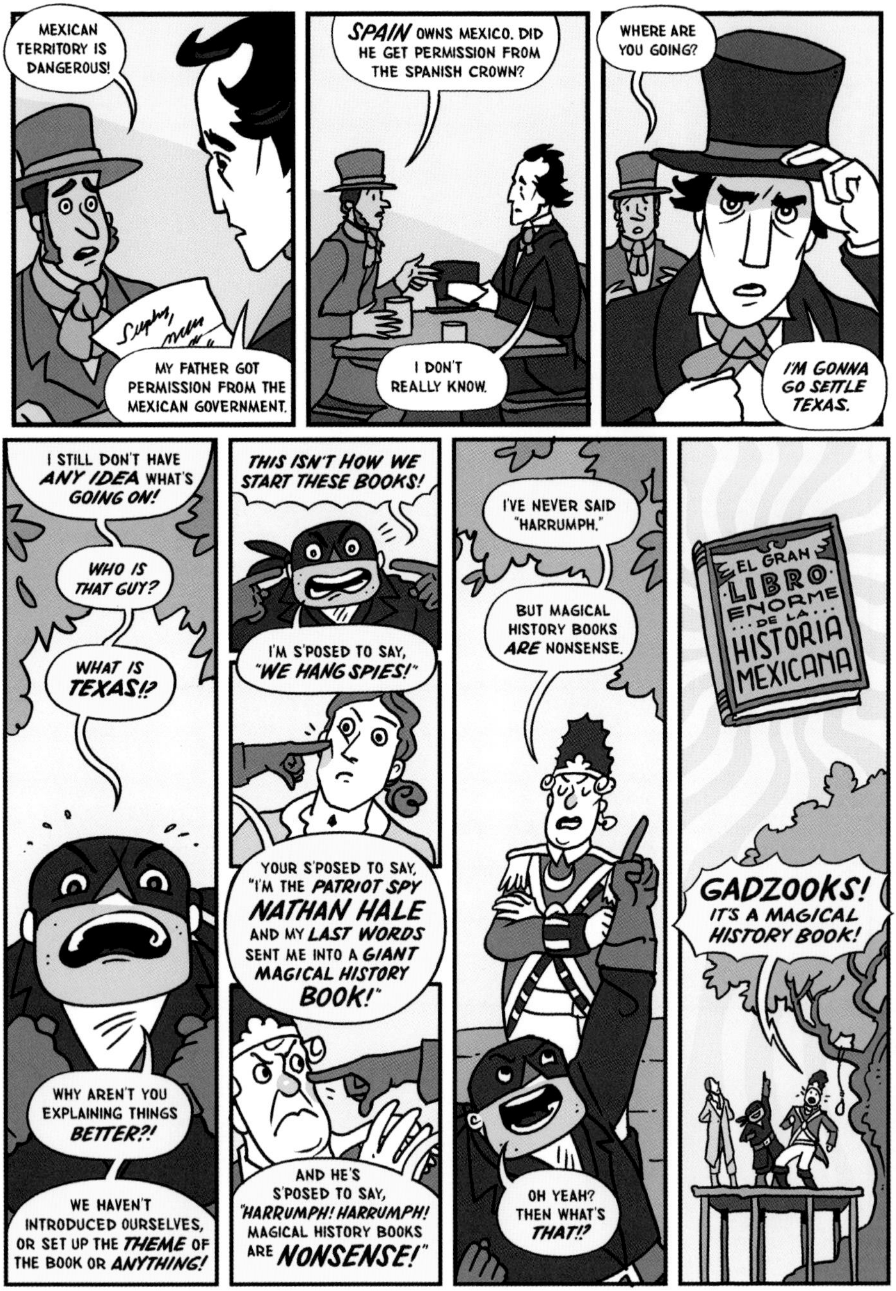
MEXICAN TERRITORY IS DANGEROUS!
MY FATHER GOT PERMISSION FROM THE MEXICAN GOVERNMENT.
SPAIN OWNS MEXICO. DID HE GET PERMISSION FROM THE SPANISH CROWN?
I DON'T REALLY KNOW.
WHERE ARE YOU GOING?
I'M GONNA GO SETTLE TEXAS.
I STILL DON'T HAVE ANY IDEA WHAT'S GOING ON!
WHO IS THAT GUY?
WHAT IS TEXAS!?
WHY AREN'T YOU EXPLAINING THINGS BETTER?!
WE HAVEN'T INTRODUCED OURSELVES, OR SET UP THE THEME OF THE BOOK OR ANYTHING!
THIS ISN'T HOW WE START THESE BOOKS!
I'M S'POSED TO SAY, "WE HANG SPIES!"
YOUR S'POSED TO SAY, "I'M THE PATRIOT SPY NATHAN HALE AND MY LAST WORDS SENT ME INTO A GIANT MAGICAL HISTORY BOOK!"
AND HE'S S'POSED TO SAY, "HARRUMPH! HARRUMPH! MAGICAL HISTORY BOOKS ARE NONSENSE!"
I'VE NEVER SAID "HARRUMPH."
BUT MAGICAL HISTORY BOOKS ARE NONSENSE.
OH YEAH? THEN WHAT'S THAT!?
EL GRAN LIBRO ENORME DE LA HISTORIA MEXICANA
GADZOOKS! IT'S A MAGICAL HISTORY BOOK!

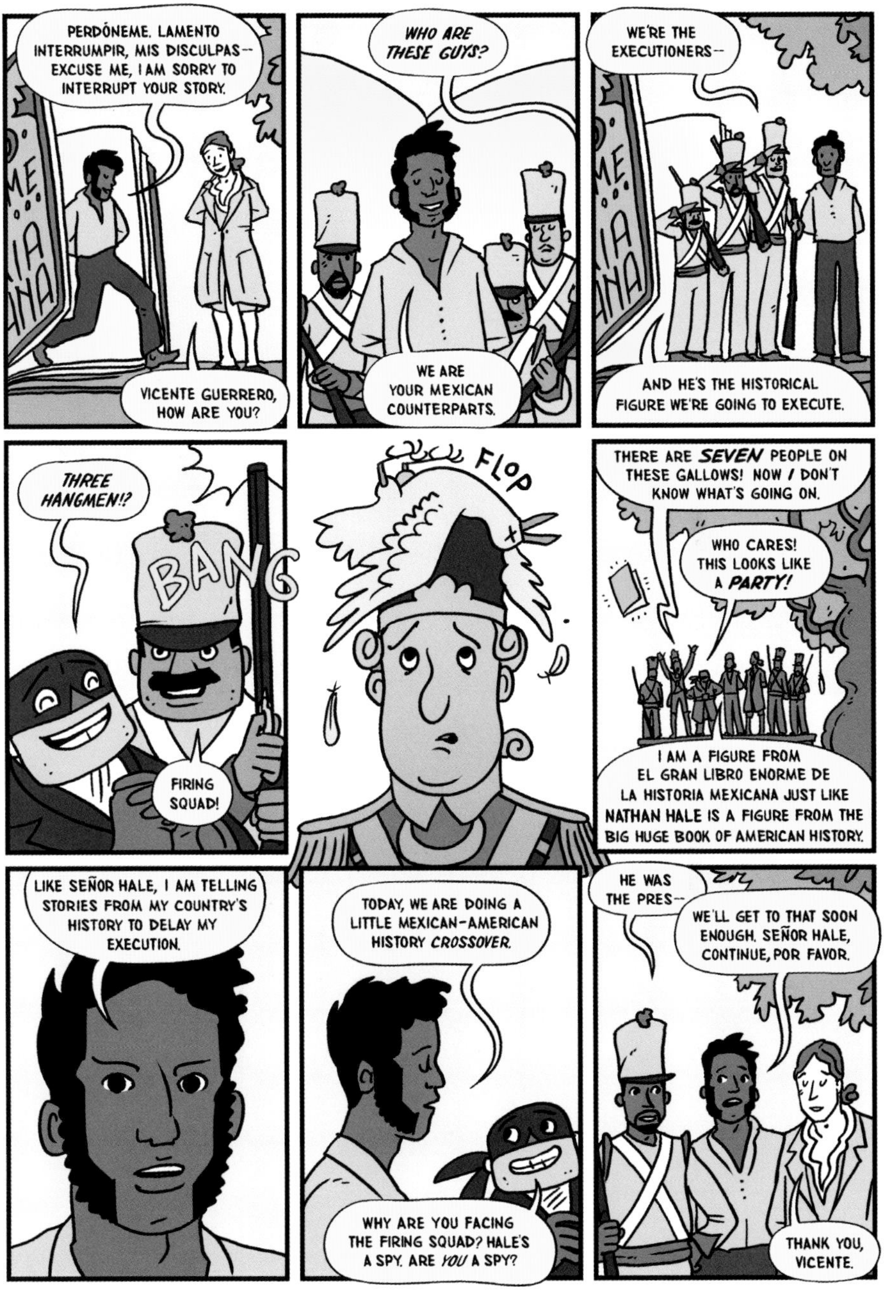
PERDÓNEME. LAMENTO INTERRUMPIR, MIS DISCULPAS-- EXCUSE ME, I AM SORRY TO INTERRUPT YOUR STORY.
VICENTE GUERRERO, HOW ARE YOU?
WHO ARE THESE GUYS?
WE ARE YOUR MEXICAN COUNTERPARTS.
WE'RE THE EXECUTIONERS--
AND HE'S THE HISTORICAL FIGURE WE'RE GOING TO EXECUTE.
THREE HANGMEN!?
BANG
FIRING SQUAD!
FLOP
THERE ARE SEVEN PEOPLE ON THESE GALLOWS! NOW I DON'T KNOW WHAT'S GOING ON.
WHO CARES! THIS LOOKS LIKE A PARTY!
I AM A FIGURE FROM EL GRAN LIBRO ENORME DE LA HISTORIA MEXICANA JUST LIKE NATHAN HALE IS A FIGURE FROM THE BIG HUGE BOOK OF AMERICAN HISTORY.
LIKE SEÑOR HALE, I AM TELLING STORIES FROM MY COUNTRY'S HISTORY TO DELAY MY EXECUTION.
TODAY, WE ARE DOING A LITTLE MEXICAN-AMERICAN HISTORY CROSSOVER.
WHY ARE YOU FACING THE FIRING SQUAD? HALE'S A SPY. ARE YOU A SPY?
HE WAS THE PRES--
WE'LL GET TO THAT SOON ENOUGH. SEÑOR HALE, CONTINUE, POR FAVOR.
THANK YOU, VICENTE.

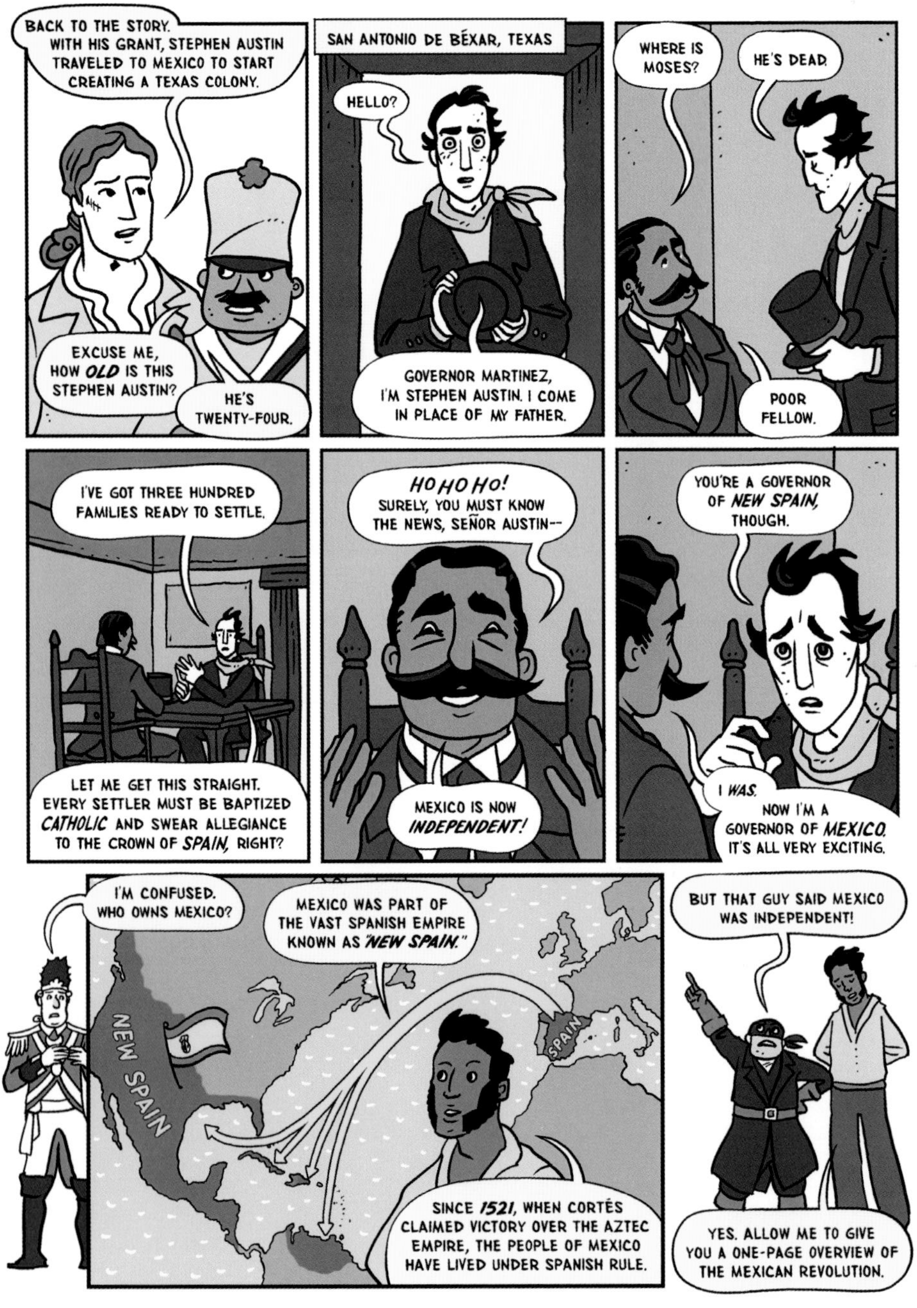
BACK TO THE STORY. WITH HIS GRANT, STEPHEN AUSTIN TRAVELED TO MEXICO TO START CREATING A TEXAS COLONY.
EXCUSE ME, HOW *OLD* IS THIS STEPHEN AUSTIN?
HE'S TWENTY-FOUR.
SAN ANTONIO DE BÉXAR, TEXAS
HELLO?
GOVERNOR MARTINEZ, I'M STEPHEN AUSTIN. I COME IN PLACE OF MY FATHER.
WHERE IS MOSES?
HE'S DEAD.
POOR FELLOW.
I'VE GOT THREE HUNDRED FAMILIES READY TO SETTLE.
LET ME GET THIS STRAIGHT. EVERY SETTLER MUST BE BAPTIZED *CATHOLIC* AND SWEAR ALLEGIANCE TO THE CROWN OF *SPAIN*, RIGHT?
HO HO HO! SURELY, YOU MUST KNOW THE NEWS, SEÑOR AUSTIN--
MEXICO IS NOW *INDEPENDENT!*
YOU'RE A GOVERNOR OF *NEW SPAIN*, THOUGH.
I *WAS*. NOW I'M A GOVERNOR OF *MEXICO*. IT'S ALL VERY EXCITING.
I'M CONFUSED. WHO OWNS MEXICO?
MEXICO WAS PART OF THE VAST SPANISH EMPIRE KNOWN AS *"NEW SPAIN."*
NEW SPAIN
SPAIN
SINCE *1521*, WHEN CORTÉS CLAIMED VICTORY OVER THE AZTEC EMPIRE, THE PEOPLE OF MEXICO HAVE LIVED UNDER SPANISH RULE.
BUT THAT GUY SAID MEXICO WAS INDEPENDENT!
YES. ALLOW ME TO GIVE YOU A ONE-PAGE OVERVIEW OF THE MEXICAN REVOLUTION.

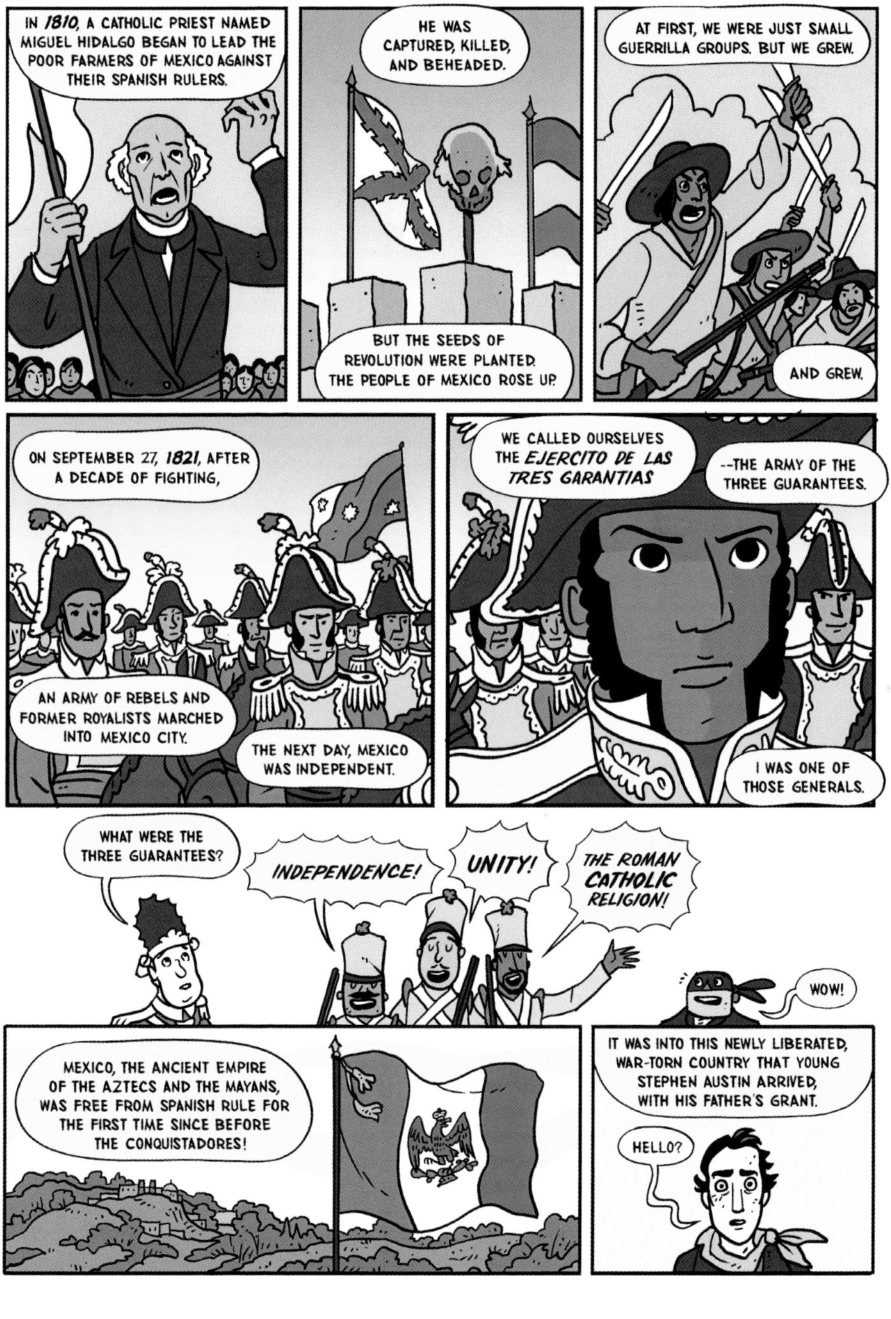
IN 1810, A CATHOLIC PRIEST NAMED MIGUEL HIDALGO BEGAN TO LEAD THE POOR FARMERS OF MEXICO AGAINST THEIR SPANISH RULERS.
HE WAS CAPTURED, KILLED, AND BEHEADED.
BUT THE SEEDS OF REVOLUTION WERE PLANTED. THE PEOPLE OF MEXICO ROSE UP.
AT FIRST, WE WERE JUST SMALL GUERRILLA GROUPS. BUT WE GREW.
AND GREW.
ON SEPTEMBER 27, 1821, AFTER A DECADE OF FIGHTING,
AN ARMY OF REBELS AND FORMER ROYALISTS MARCHED INTO MEXICO CITY.
THE NEXT DAY, MEXICO WAS INDEPENDENT.
WE CALLED OURSELVES THE EJERCITO DE LAS TRES GARANTIAS
--THE ARMY OF THE THREE GUARANTEES.
I WAS ONE OF THOSE GENERALS.
WHAT WERE THE THREE GUARANTEES?
INDEPENDENCE!
UNITY!
THE ROMAN CATHOLIC RELIGION!
WOW!
MEXICO, THE ANCIENT EMPIRE OF THE AZTECS AND THE MAYANS, WAS FREE FROM SPANISH RULE FOR THE FIRST TIME SINCE BEFORE THE CONQUISTADORES!
IT WAS INTO THIS NEWLY LIBERATED, WAR-TORN COUNTRY THAT YOUNG STEPHEN AUSTIN ARRIVED, WITH HIS FATHER'S GRANT.
HELLO?

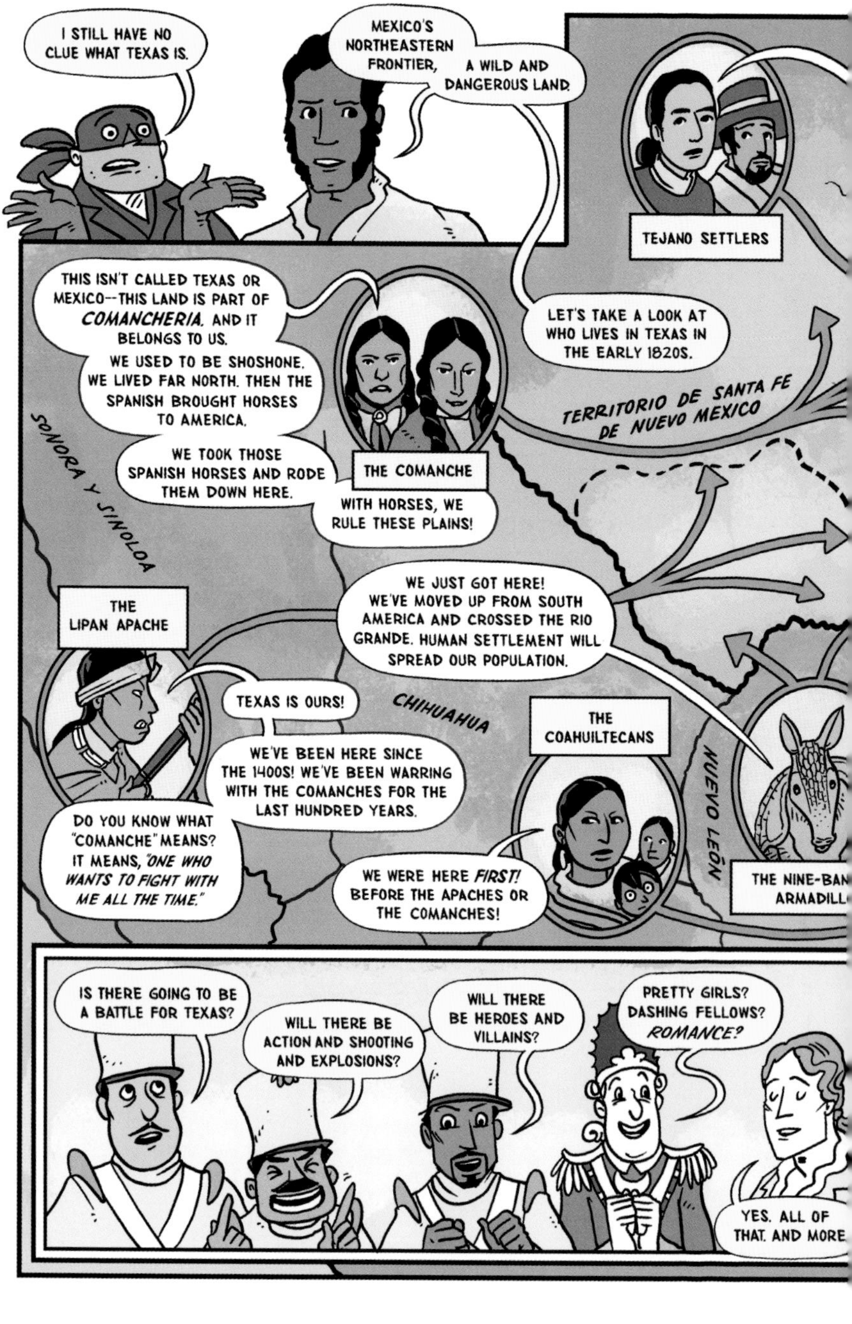

I STILL HAVE NO CLUE WHAT TEXAS IS.
MEXICO'S NORTHEASTERN FRONTIER,
A WILD AND DANGEROUS LAND.
TEJANO SETTLERS
LET'S TAKE A LOOK AT WHO LIVES IN TEXAS IN THE EARLY 1820S.
THIS ISN'T CALLED TEXAS OR MEXICO--THIS LAND IS PART OF *COMANCHERIA,* AND IT BELONGS TO US.
WE USED TO BE SHOSHONE. WE LIVED FAR NORTH. THEN THE SPANISH BROUGHT HORSES TO AMERICA.
WE TOOK THOSE SPANISH HORSES AND RODE THEM DOWN HERE.
THE COMANCHE
WITH HORSES, WE RULE THESE PLAINS!
TERRITORIO DE SANTA FE DE NUEVO MEXICO
SONORA Y SINOLOA
THE LIPAN APACHE
WE JUST GOT HERE! WE'VE MOVED UP FROM SOUTH AMERICA AND CROSSED THE RIO GRANDE. HUMAN SETTLEMENT WILL SPREAD OUR POPULATION.
TEXAS IS OURS!
CHIHUAHUA
WE'VE BEEN HERE SINCE THE 1400S! WE'VE BEEN WARRING WITH THE COMANCHES FOR THE LAST HUNDRED YEARS.
DO YOU KNOW WHAT "COMANCHE" MEANS? IT MEANS, *"ONE WHO WANTS TO FIGHT WITH ME ALL THE TIME."*
THE COAHUILTECANS
NUEVO LEÓN
WE WERE HERE *FIRST!* BEFORE THE APACHES OR THE COMANCHES!
THE NINE-BAN ARMADILL
IS THERE GOING TO BE A BATTLE FOR TEXAS?
WILL THERE BE ACTION AND SHOOTING AND EXPLOSIONS?
WILL THERE BE HEROES AND VILLAINS?
PRETTY GIRLS? DASHING FELLOWS? *ROMANCE?*
YES. ALL OF THAT. AND MORE.

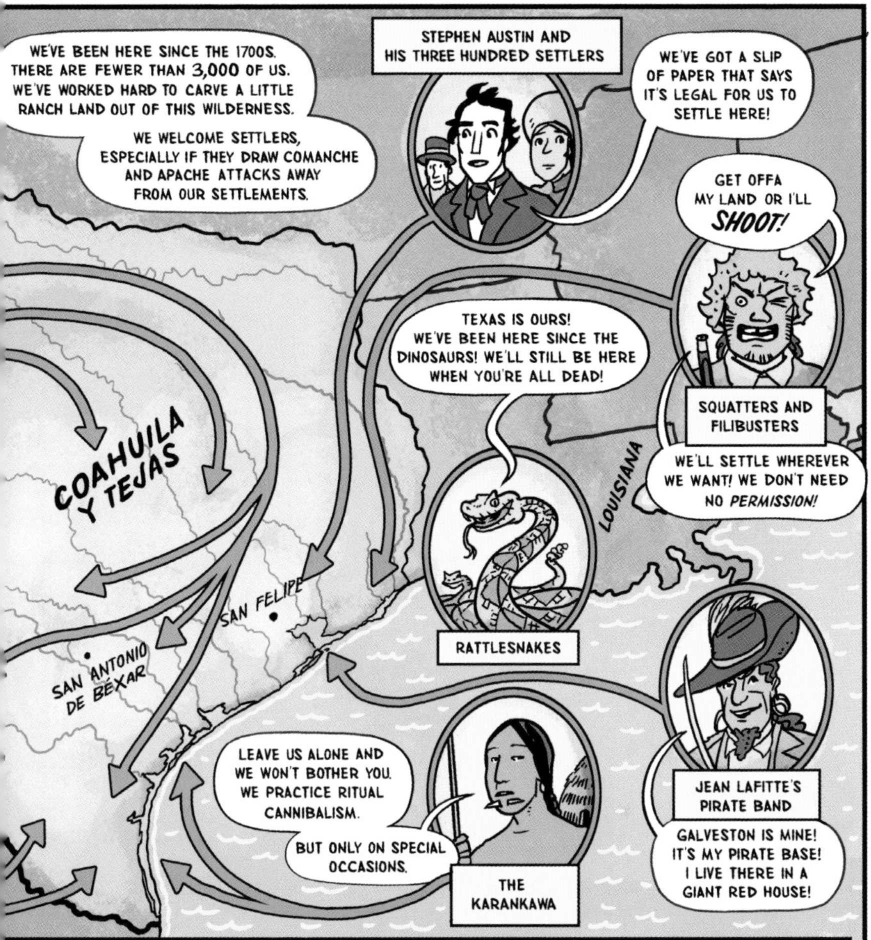
WE'VE BEEN HERE SINCE THE 1700S. THERE ARE FEWER THAN 3,000 OF US. WE'VE WORKED HARD TO CARVE A LITTLE RANCH LAND OUT OF THIS WILDERNESS.
WE WELCOME SETTLERS, ESPECIALLY IF THEY DRAW COMANCHE AND APACHE ATTACKS AWAY FROM OUR SETTLEMENTS.
STEPHEN AUSTIN AND HIS THREE HUNDRED SETTLERS
WE'VE GOT A SLIP OF PAPER THAT SAYS IT'S LEGAL FOR US TO SETTLE HERE!
GET OFFA MY LAND OR I'LL *SHOOT!*
SQUATTERS AND FILIBUSTERS
WE'LL SETTLE WHEREVER WE WANT! WE DON'T NEED NO *PERMISSION!*
TEXAS IS OURS! WE'VE BEEN HERE SINCE THE DINOSAURS! WE'LL STILL BE HERE WHEN YOU'RE ALL DEAD!
RATTLESNAKES
COAHUILA Y TEJAS
LOUISIANA
SAN FELIPE
SAN ANTONIO DE BÉXAR
JEAN LAFITTE'S PIRATE BAND
GALVESTON IS MINE! IT'S MY PIRATE BASE! I LIVE THERE IN A GIANT RED HOUSE!
LEAVE US ALONE AND WE WON'T BOTHER YOU. WE PRACTICE RITUAL CANNIBALISM.
BUT ONLY ON SPECIAL OCCASIONS.
THE KARANKAWA

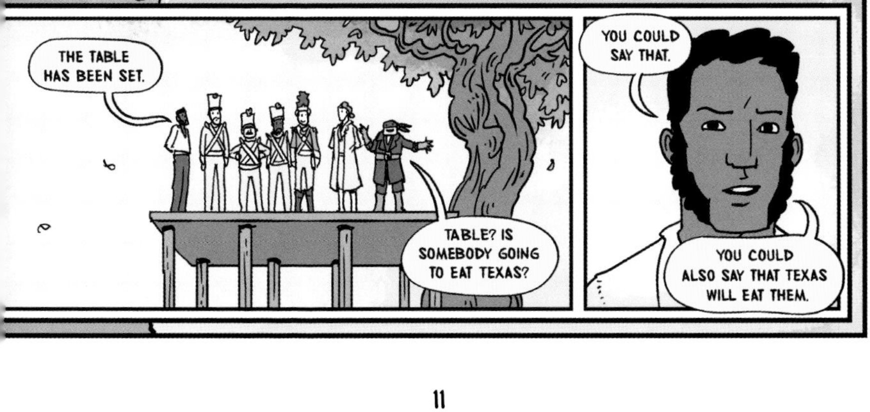
THE TABLE HAS BEEN SET.
TABLE? IS SOMEBODY GOING TO EAT TEXAS?
YOU COULD SAY THAT.
YOU COULD ALSO SAY THAT TEXAS WILL EAT THEM.

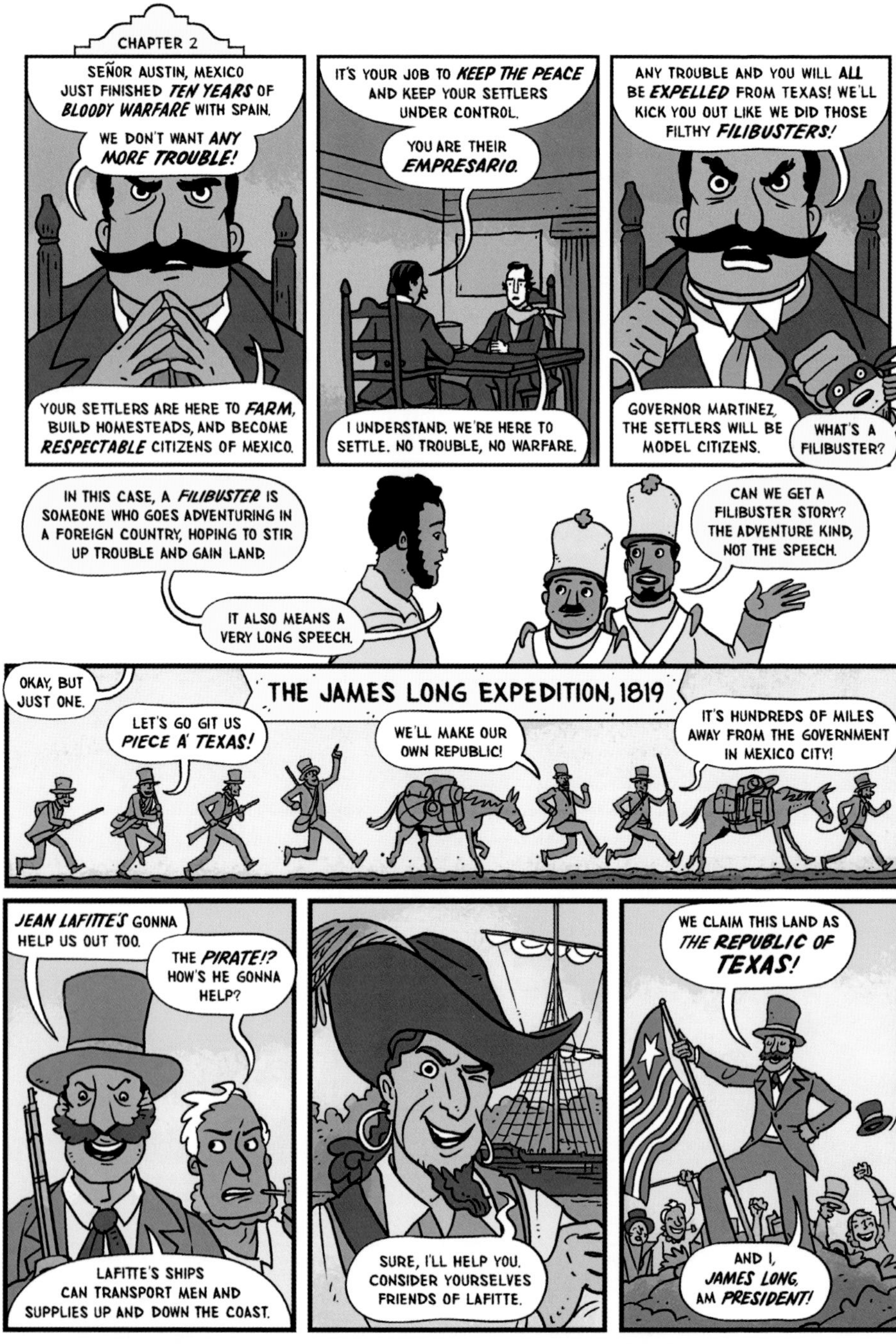
CHAPTER 2
SEÑOR AUSTIN, MEXICO JUST FINISHED TEN YEARS OF BLOODY WARFARE WITH SPAIN.
WE DON'T WANT ANY MORE TROUBLE!
YOUR SETTLERS ARE HERE TO FARM, BUILD HOMESTEADS, AND BECOME RESPECTABLE CITIZENS OF MEXICO.
IT'S YOUR JOB TO KEEP THE PEACE AND KEEP YOUR SETTLERS UNDER CONTROL.
YOU ARE THEIR EMPRESARIO.
I UNDERSTAND. WE'RE HERE TO SETTLE. NO TROUBLE, NO WARFARE.
ANY TROUBLE AND YOU WILL ALL BE EXPELLED FROM TEXAS! WE'LL KICK YOU OUT LIKE WE DID THOSE FILTHY FILIBUSTERS!
GOVERNOR MARTINEZ, THE SETTLERS WILL BE MODEL CITIZENS.
WHAT'S A FILIBUSTER?
IN THIS CASE, A FILIBUSTER IS SOMEONE WHO GOES ADVENTURING IN A FOREIGN COUNTRY, HOPING TO STIR UP TROUBLE AND GAIN LAND.
IT ALSO MEANS A VERY LONG SPEECH.
CAN WE GET A FILIBUSTER STORY? THE ADVENTURE KIND, NOT THE SPEECH.
OKAY, BUT JUST ONE.
THE JAMES LONG EXPEDITION, 1819
LET'S GO GIT US PIECE A' TEXAS!
WE'LL MAKE OUR OWN REPUBLIC!
IT'S HUNDREDS OF MILES AWAY FROM THE GOVERNMENT IN MEXICO CITY!
JEAN LAFITTE'S GONNA HELP US OUT TOO.
THE PIRATE!? HOW'S HE GONNA HELP?
LAFITTE'S SHIPS CAN TRANSPORT MEN AND SUPPLIES UP AND DOWN THE COAST.
SURE, I'LL HELP YOU. CONSIDER YOURSELVES FRIENDS OF LAFITTE.
WE CLAIM THIS LAND AS THE REPUBLIC OF TEXAS!
AND I, JAMES LONG, AM PRESIDENT!

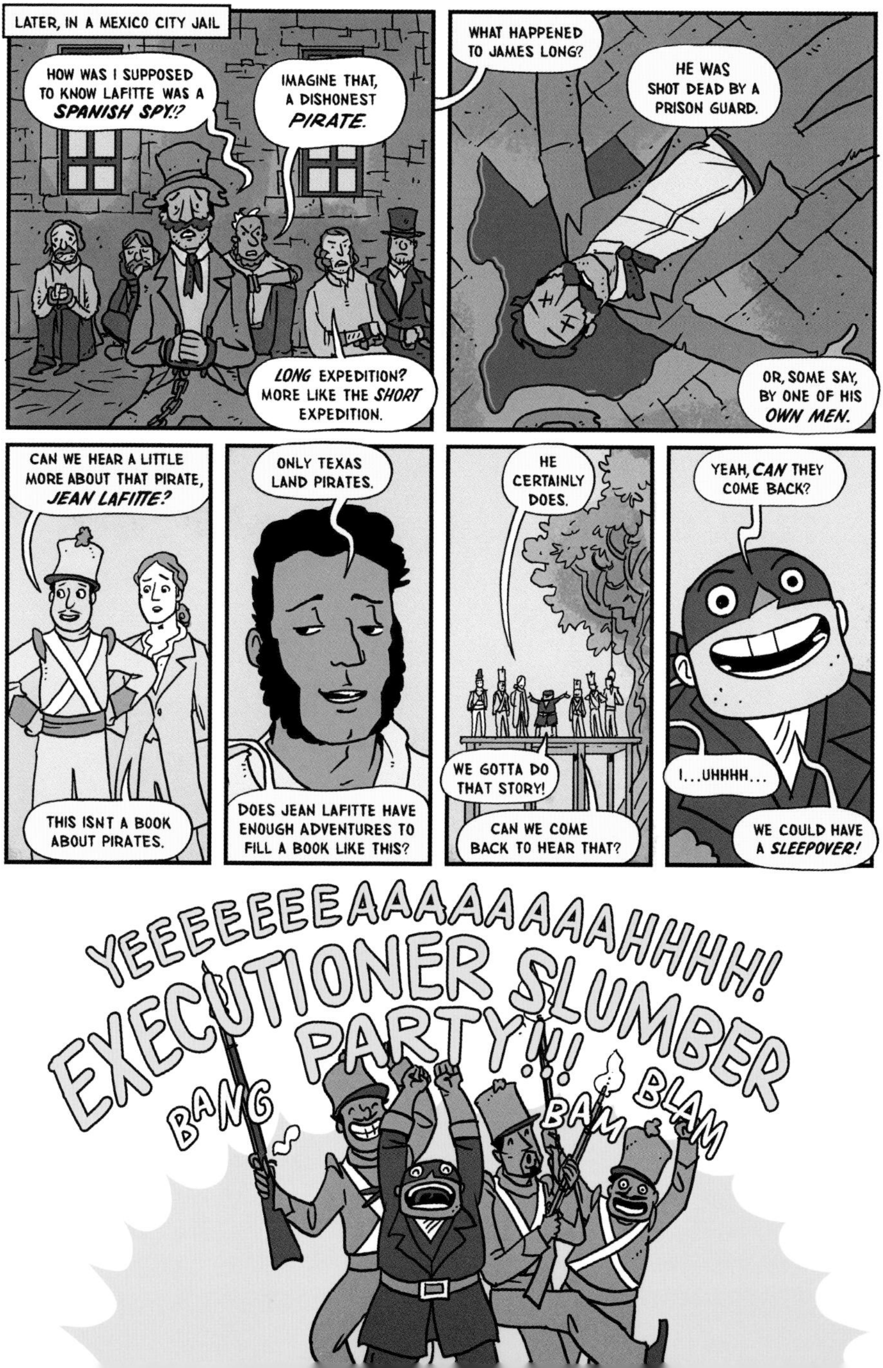
LATER, IN A MEXICO CITY JAIL
HOW WAS I SUPPOSED TO KNOW LAFITTE WAS A SPANISH SPY!?
IMAGINE THAT, A DISHONEST PIRATE.
LONG EXPEDITION? MORE LIKE THE SHORT EXPEDITION.
WHAT HAPPENED TO JAMES LONG?
HE WAS SHOT DEAD BY A PRISON GUARD.
OR, SOME SAY, BY ONE OF HIS OWN MEN.
CAN WE HEAR A LITTLE MORE ABOUT THAT PIRATE, JEAN LAFITTE?
THIS ISNT A BOOK ABOUT PIRATES.
ONLY TEXAS LAND PIRATES.
DOES JEAN LAFITTE HAVE ENOUGH ADVENTURES TO FILL A BOOK LIKE THIS?
HE CERTAINLY DOES.
WE GOTTA DO THAT STORY!
CAN WE COME BACK TO HEAR THAT?
YEAH, CAN THEY COME BACK?
I...UHHHH...
WE COULD HAVE A SLEEPOVER!
YEEEEEEEAAAAAAAAAAHHHHH!
EXECUTIONER SLUMBER PARTY!!!
BANG
BAM
BLAM

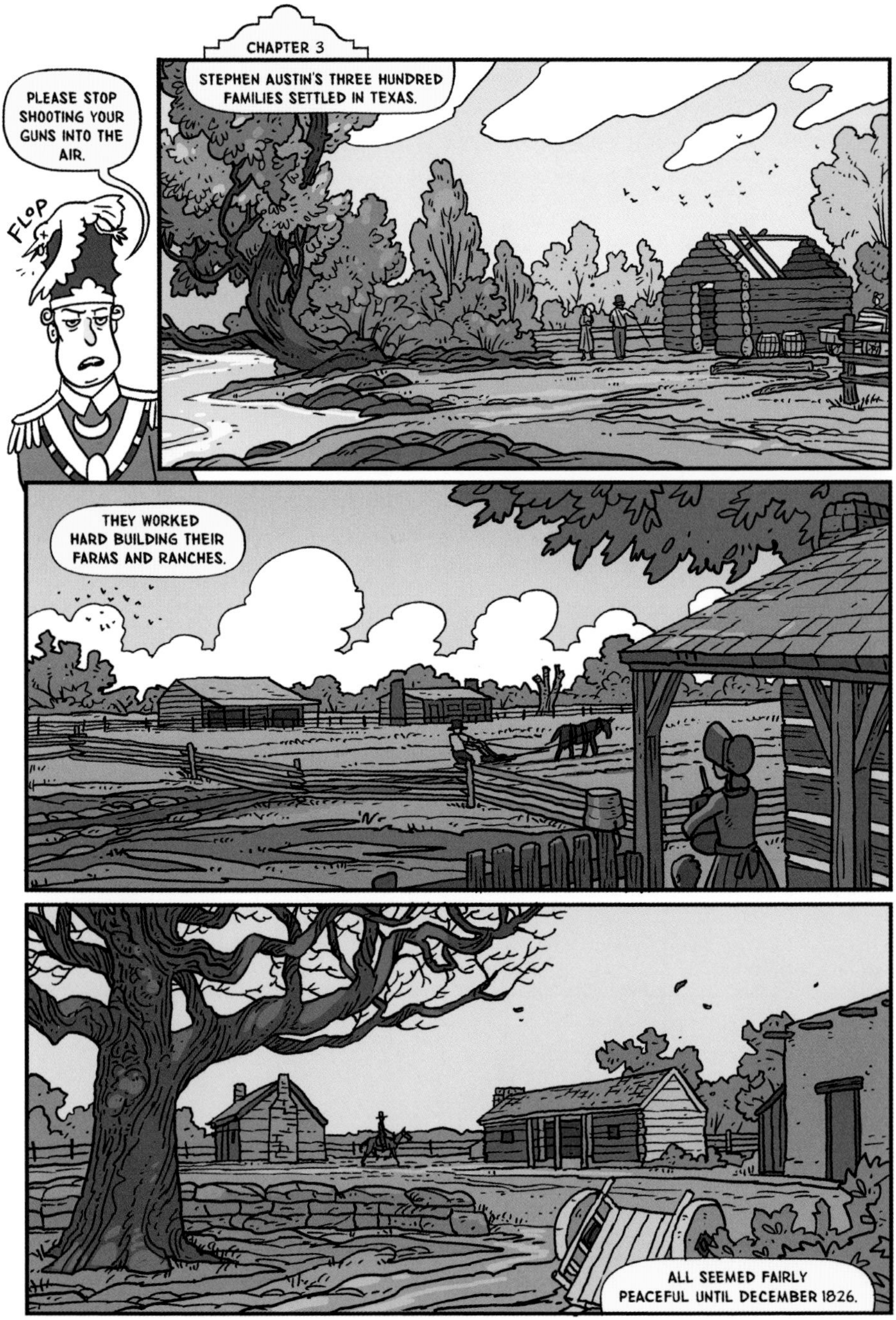
CHAPTER 3
PLEASE STOP SHOOTING YOUR GUNS INTO THE AIR.
FLOP
STEPHEN AUSTIN'S THREE HUNDRED FAMILIES SETTLED IN TEXAS.
THEY WORKED HARD BUILDING THEIR FARMS AND RANCHES.
ALL SEEMED FAIRLY PEACEFUL UNTIL DECEMBER 1826.

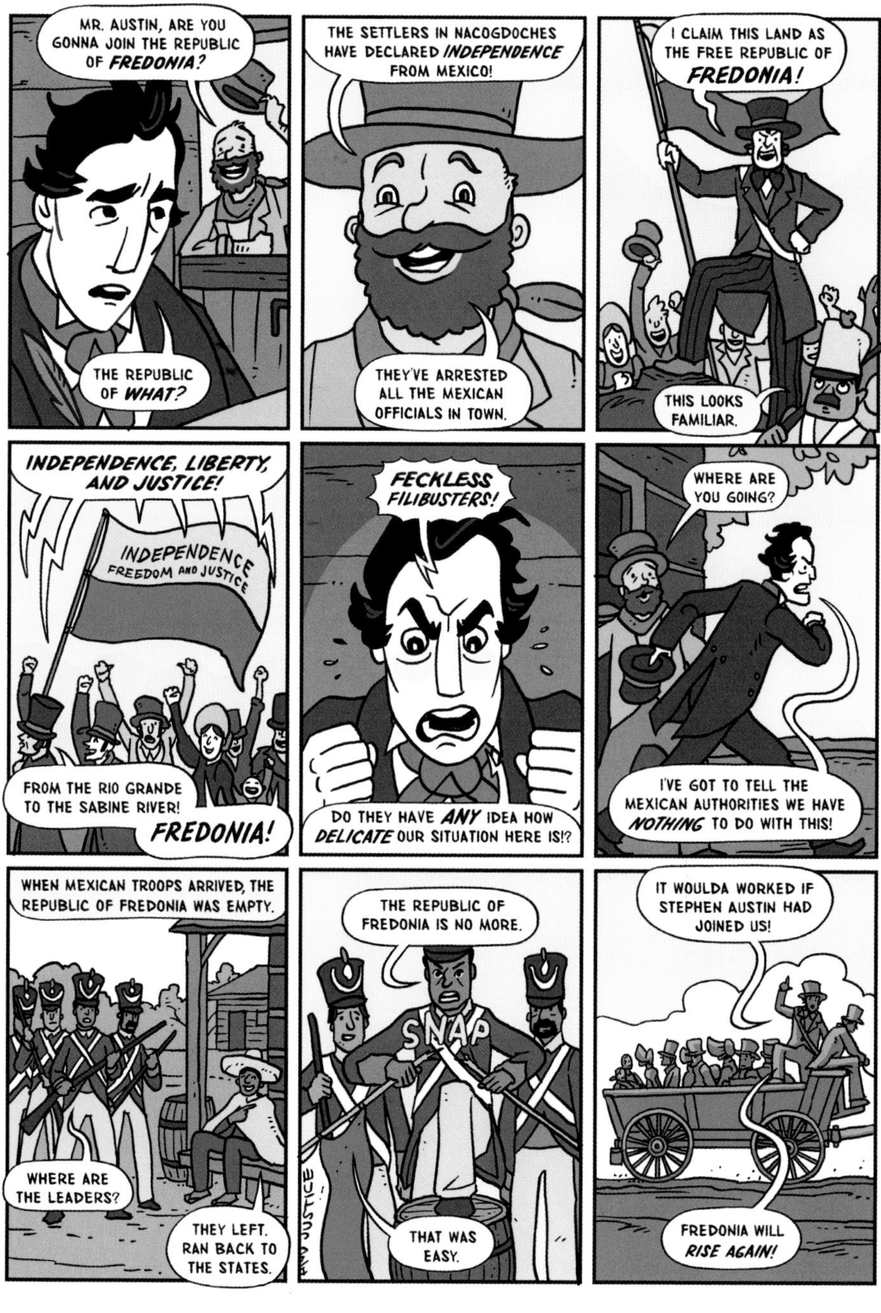
MR. AUSTIN, ARE YOU GONNA JOIN THE REPUBLIC OF FREDONIA?
THE REPUBLIC OF WHAT?
THE SETTLERS IN NACOGDOCHES HAVE DECLARED INDEPENDENCE FROM MEXICO!
THEY'VE ARRESTED ALL THE MEXICAN OFFICIALS IN TOWN.
I CLAIM THIS LAND AS THE FREE REPUBLIC OF FREDONIA!
THIS LOOKS FAMILIAR.
INDEPENDENCE, LIBERTY, AND JUSTICE!
INDEPENDENCE FREEDOM AND JUSTICE
FROM THE RIO GRANDE TO THE SABINE RIVER!
FREDONIA!
FECKLESS FILIBUSTERS!
DO THEY HAVE ANY IDEA HOW DELICATE OUR SITUATION HERE IS!?
WHERE ARE YOU GOING?
I'VE GOT TO TELL THE MEXICAN AUTHORITIES WE HAVE NOTHING TO DO WITH THIS!
WHEN MEXICAN TROOPS ARRIVED, THE REPUBLIC OF FREDONIA WAS EMPTY.
WHERE ARE THE LEADERS?
THEY LEFT. RAN BACK TO THE STATES.
THE REPUBLIC OF FREDONIA IS NO MORE.
SNAP
THAT WAS EASY.
IT WOULDA WORKED IF STEPHEN AUSTIN HAD JOINED US!
FREDONIA WILL RISE AGAIN!

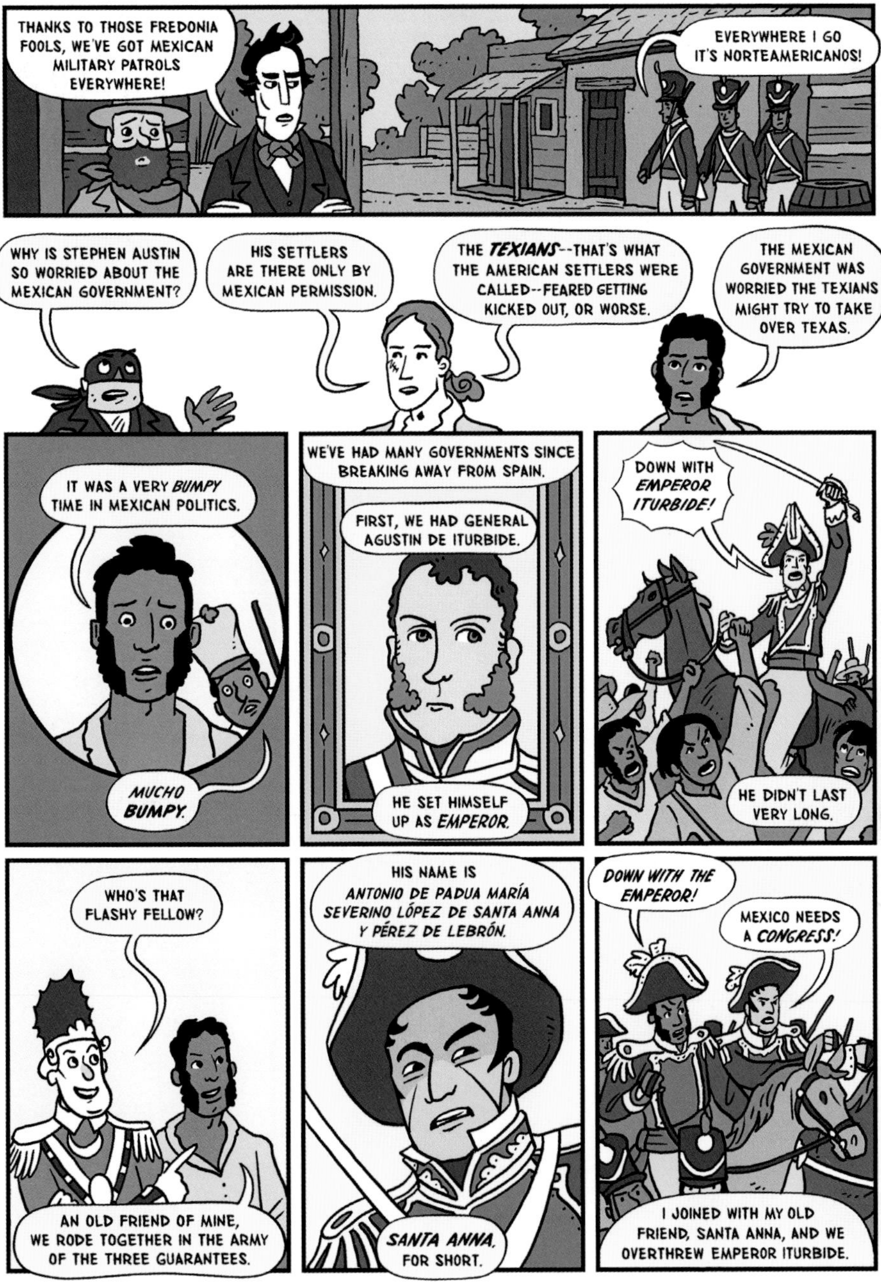
THANKS TO THOSE FREDONIA FOOLS, WE'VE GOT MEXICAN MILITARY PATROLS EVERYWHERE!
EVERYWHERE I GO IT'S NORTEAMERICANOS!
WHY IS STEPHEN AUSTIN SO WORRIED ABOUT THE MEXICAN GOVERNMENT?
HIS SETTLERS ARE THERE ONLY BY MEXICAN PERMISSION.
THE *TEXIANS*--THAT'S WHAT THE AMERICAN SETTLERS WERE CALLED--FEARED GETTING KICKED OUT, OR WORSE.
THE MEXICAN GOVERNMENT WAS WORRIED THE TEXIANS MIGHT TRY TO TAKE OVER TEXAS.
IT WAS A VERY *BUMPY* TIME IN MEXICAN POLITICS.
MUCHO BUMPY.
WE'VE HAD MANY GOVERNMENTS SINCE BREAKING AWAY FROM SPAIN.
FIRST, WE HAD GENERAL AGUSTIN DE ITURBIDE.
HE SET HIMSELF UP AS *EMPEROR.*
DOWN WITH EMPEROR ITURBIDE!
HE DIDN'T LAST VERY LONG.
WHO'S THAT FLASHY FELLOW?
AN OLD FRIEND OF MINE, WE RODE TOGETHER IN THE ARMY OF THE THREE GUARANTEES.
HIS NAME IS *ANTONIO DE PADUA MARÍA SEVERINO LÓPEZ DE SANTA ANNA Y PÉREZ DE LEBRÓN.*
SANTA ANNA, FOR SHORT.
DOWN WITH THE EMPEROR!
MEXICO NEEDS A *CONGRESS!*
I JOINED WITH MY OLD FRIEND, SANTA ANNA, AND WE OVERTHREW EMPEROR ITURBIDE.

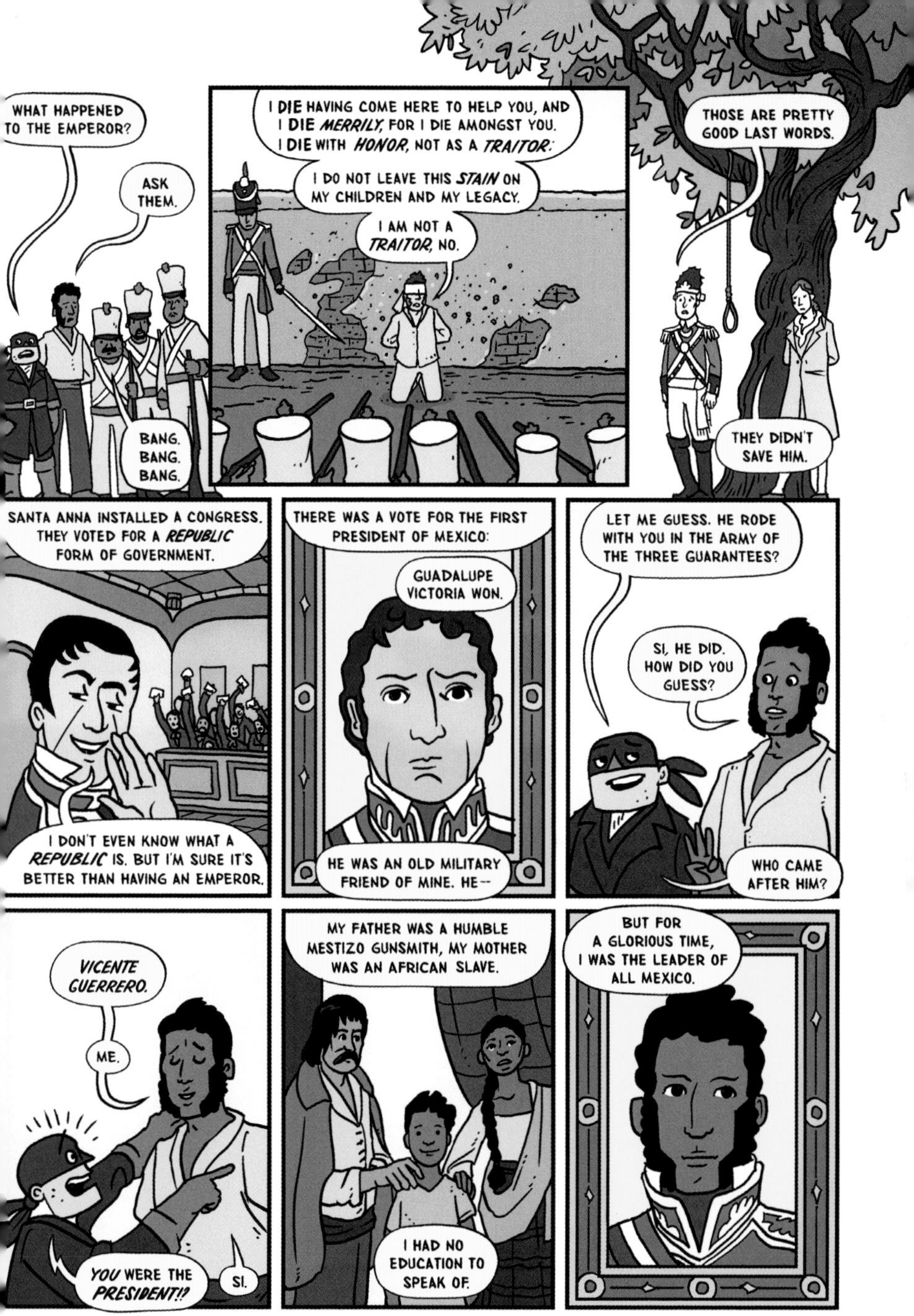
WHAT HAPPENED TO THE EMPEROR?
ASK THEM.
BANG. BANG. BANG.
I DIE HAVING COME HERE TO HELP YOU, AND I DIE MERRILY, FOR I DIE AMONGST YOU. I DIE WITH HONOR, NOT AS A TRAITOR:
I DO NOT LEAVE THIS STAIN ON MY CHILDREN AND MY LEGACY.
I AM NOT A TRAITOR, NO.
THOSE ARE PRETTY GOOD LAST WORDS.
THEY DIDN'T SAVE HIM.
SANTA ANNA INSTALLED A CONGRESS. THEY VOTED FOR A REPUBLIC FORM OF GOVERNMENT.
I DON'T EVEN KNOW WHAT A REPUBLIC IS. BUT I'M SURE IT'S BETTER THAN HAVING AN EMPEROR.
THERE WAS A VOTE FOR THE FIRST PRESIDENT OF MEXICO:
GUADALUPE VICTORIA WON.
HE WAS AN OLD MILITARY FRIEND OF MINE. HE--
LET ME GUESS. HE RODE WITH YOU IN THE ARMY OF THE THREE GUARANTEES?
SI, HE DID. HOW DID YOU GUESS?
WHO CAME AFTER HIM?
VICENTE GUERRERO.
ME.
YOU WERE THE PRESIDENT!?
SI.
MY FATHER WAS A HUMBLE MESTIZO GUNSMITH, MY MOTHER WAS AN AFRICAN SLAVE.
I HAD NO EDUCATION TO SPEAK OF.
BUT FOR A GLORIOUS TIME, I WAS THE LEADER OF ALL MEXICO.

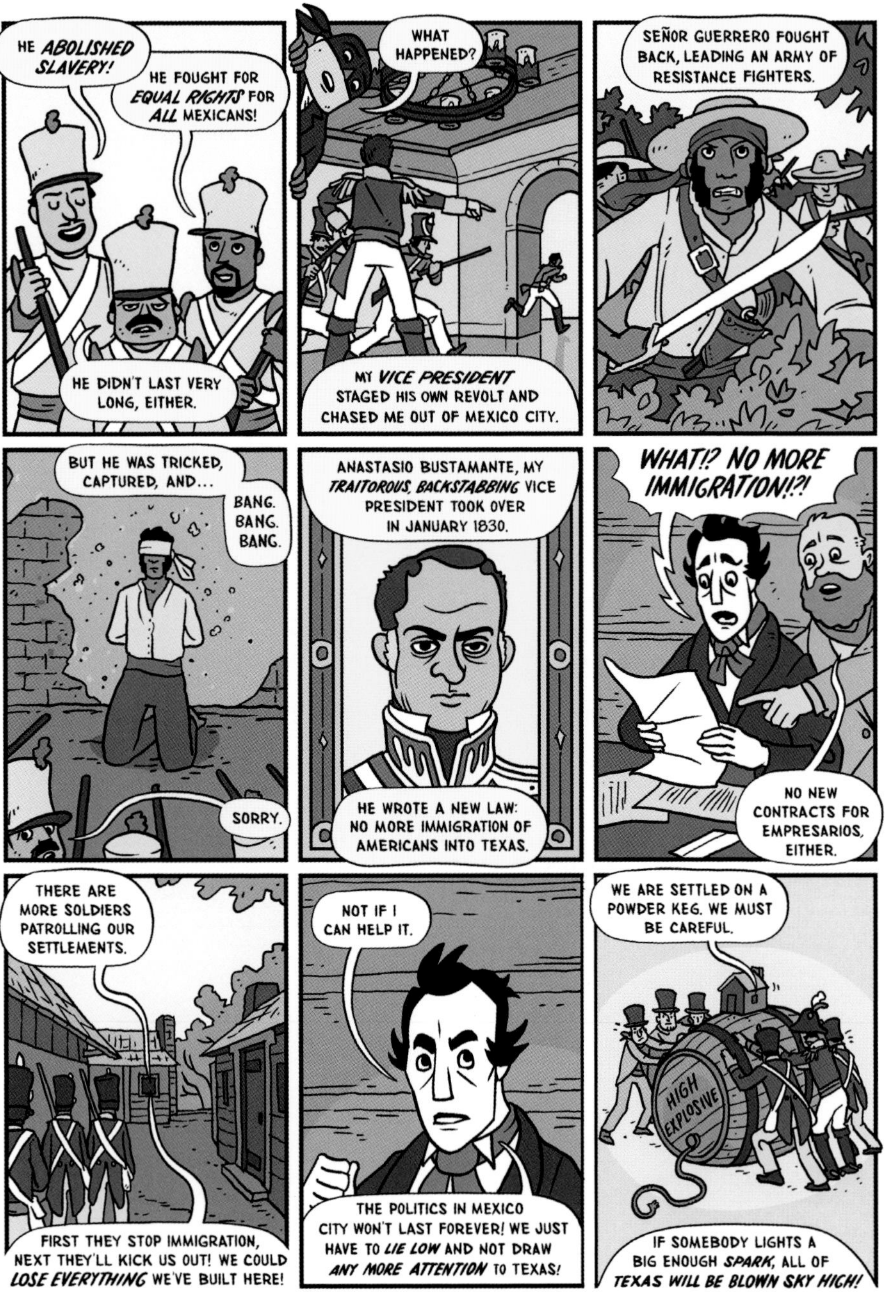
HE *ABOLISHED SLAVERY!*
HE FOUGHT FOR *EQUAL RIGHTS* FOR *ALL* MEXICANS!
HE DIDN'T LAST VERY LONG, EITHER.
WHAT HAPPENED?
MY *VICE PRESIDENT* STAGED HIS OWN REVOLT AND CHASED ME OUT OF MEXICO CITY.
SEÑOR GUERRERO FOUGHT BACK, LEADING AN ARMY OF RESISTANCE FIGHTERS.
BUT HE WAS TRICKED, CAPTURED, AND...
BANG. BANG. BANG.
SORRY.
ANASTASIO BUSTAMANTE, MY *TRAITOROUS, BACKSTABBING* VICE PRESIDENT TOOK OVER IN JANUARY 1830.
HE WROTE A NEW LAW: NO MORE IMMIGRATION OF AMERICANS INTO TEXAS.
WHAT!? NO MORE IMMIGRATION!?!
NO NEW CONTRACTS FOR EMPRESARIOS, EITHER.
THERE ARE MORE SOLDIERS PATROLLING OUR SETTLEMENTS.
FIRST THEY STOP IMMIGRATION, NEXT THEY'LL KICK US OUT! WE COULD *LOSE EVERYTHING* WE'VE BUILT HERE!
NOT IF I CAN HELP IT.
THE POLITICS IN MEXICO CITY WON'T LAST FOREVER! WE JUST HAVE TO *LIE LOW* AND NOT DRAW *ANY MORE ATTENTION* TO TEXAS!
WE ARE SETTLED ON A POWDER KEG. WE MUST BE CAREFUL.
HIGH EXPLOSIVE
IF SOMEBODY LIGHTS A BIG ENOUGH *SPARK*, ALL OF *TEXAS WILL BE BLOWN SKY HIGH!*

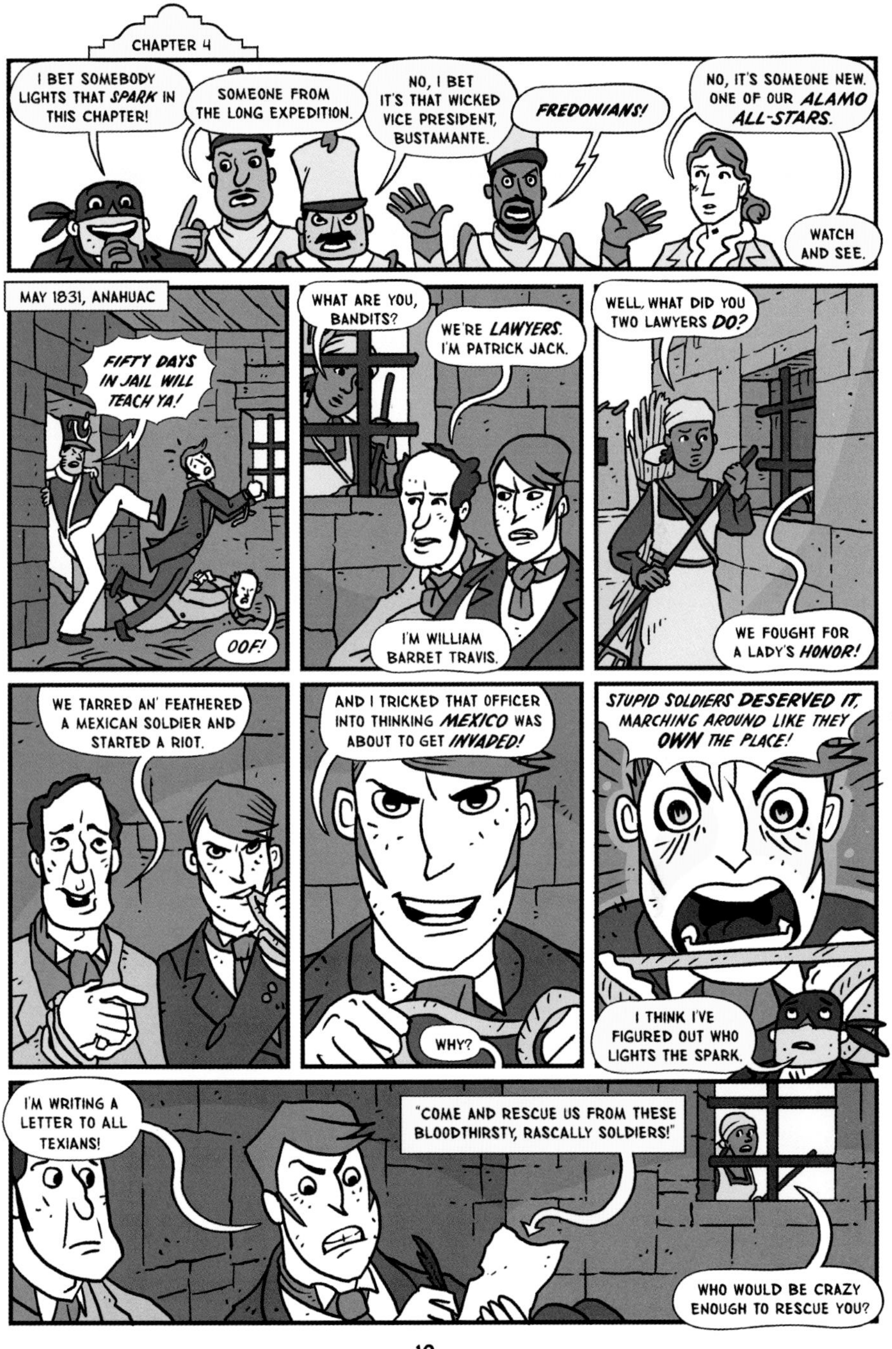
CHAPTER 4
I BET SOMEBODY LIGHTS THAT SPARK IN THIS CHAPTER!
SOMEONE FROM THE LONG EXPEDITION.
NO, I BET IT'S THAT WICKED VICE PRESIDENT, BUSTAMANTE.
FREDONIANS!
NO, IT'S SOMEONE NEW. ONE OF OUR ALAMO ALL-STARS.
WATCH AND SEE.
MAY 1831, ANAHUAC
FIFTY DAYS IN JAIL WILL TEACH YA!
OOF!
WHAT ARE YOU, BANDITS?
WE'RE LAWYERS. I'M PATRICK JACK.
I'M WILLIAM BARRET TRAVIS.
WELL, WHAT DID YOU TWO LAWYERS DO?
WE FOUGHT FOR A LADY'S HONOR!
WE TARRED AN' FEATHERED A MEXICAN SOLDIER AND STARTED A RIOT.
AND I TRICKED THAT OFFICER INTO THINKING MEXICO WAS ABOUT TO GET INVADED!
WHY?
STUPID SOLDIERS DESERVED IT, MARCHING AROUND LIKE THEY OWN THE PLACE!
I THINK I'VE FIGURED OUT WHO LIGHTS THE SPARK.
I'M WRITING A LETTER TO ALL TEXIANS!
"COME AND RESCUE US FROM THESE BLOODTHIRSTY, RASCALLY SOLDIERS!"
WHO WOULD BE CRAZY ENOUGH TO RESCUE YOU?

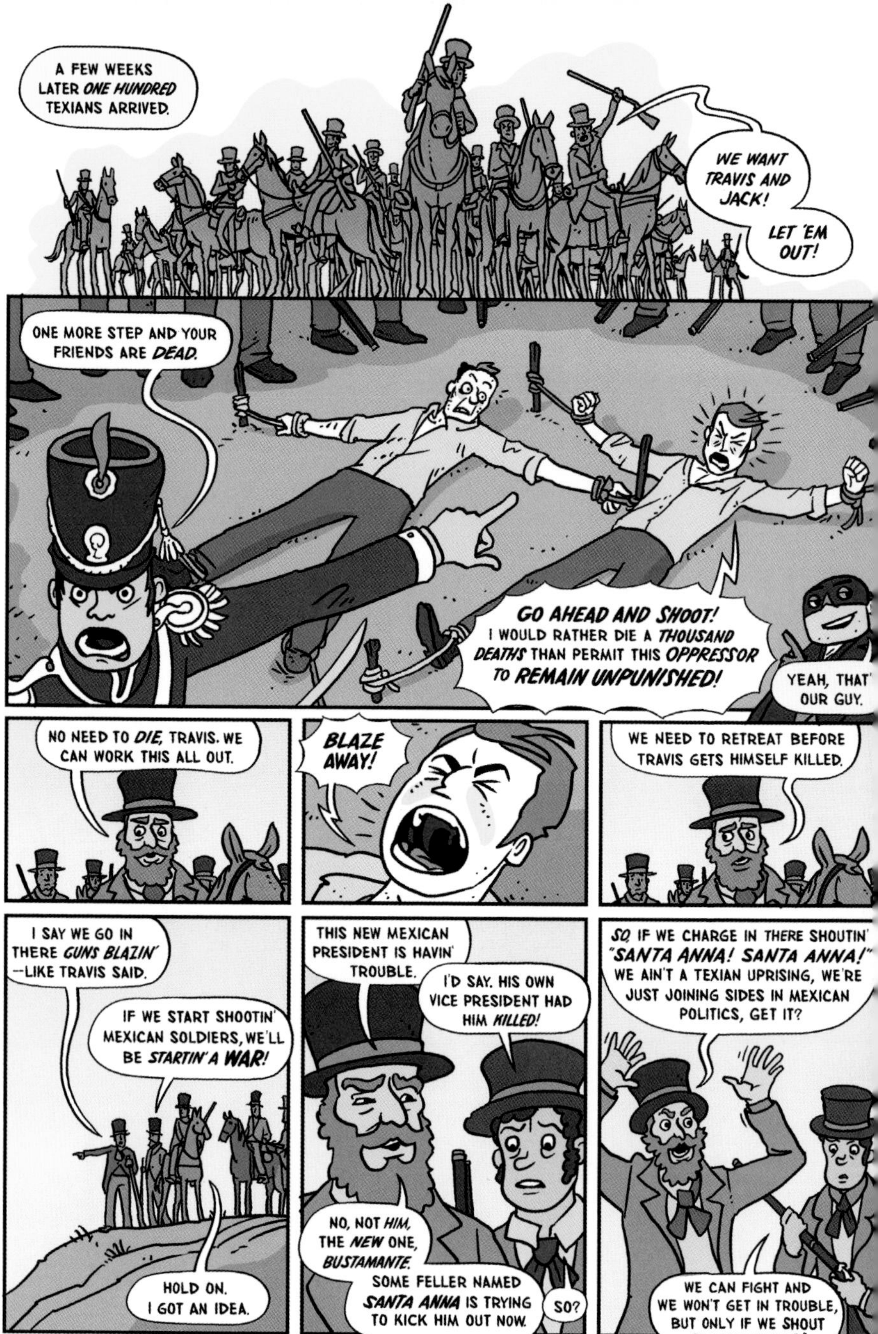
A FEW WEEKS LATER ONE HUNDRED TEXIANS ARRIVED.
WE WANT TRAVIS AND JACK!
LET 'EM OUT!
ONE MORE STEP AND YOUR FRIENDS ARE DEAD.
GO AHEAD AND SHOOT! I WOULD RATHER DIE A THOUSAND DEATHS THAN PERMIT THIS OPPRESSOR TO REMAIN UNPUNISHED!
YEAH, THAT' OUR GUY.
NO NEED TO DIE, TRAVIS. WE CAN WORK THIS ALL OUT.
BLAZE AWAY!
WE NEED TO RETREAT BEFORE TRAVIS GETS HIMSELF KILLED.
I SAY WE GO IN THERE GUNS BLAZIN' --LIKE TRAVIS SAID.
IF WE START SHOOTIN' MEXICAN SOLDIERS, WE'LL BE STARTIN' A WAR!
HOLD ON. I GOT AN IDEA.
THIS NEW MEXICAN PRESIDENT IS HAVIN' TROUBLE.
I'D SAY. HIS OWN VICE PRESIDENT HAD HIM KILLED!
NO, NOT HIM, THE NEW ONE, BUSTAMANTE.
SOME FELLER NAMED SANTA ANNA IS TRYING TO KICK HIM OUT NOW.
SO?
SO, IF WE CHARGE IN THERE SHOUTIN' "SANTA ANNA! SANTA ANNA!" WE AIN'T A TEXIAN UPRISING, WE'RE JUST JOINING SIDES IN MEXICAN POLITICS, GET IT?
WE CAN FIGHT AND WE WON'T GET IN TROUBLE, BUT ONLY IF WE SHOUT "SANTY ANNY?"

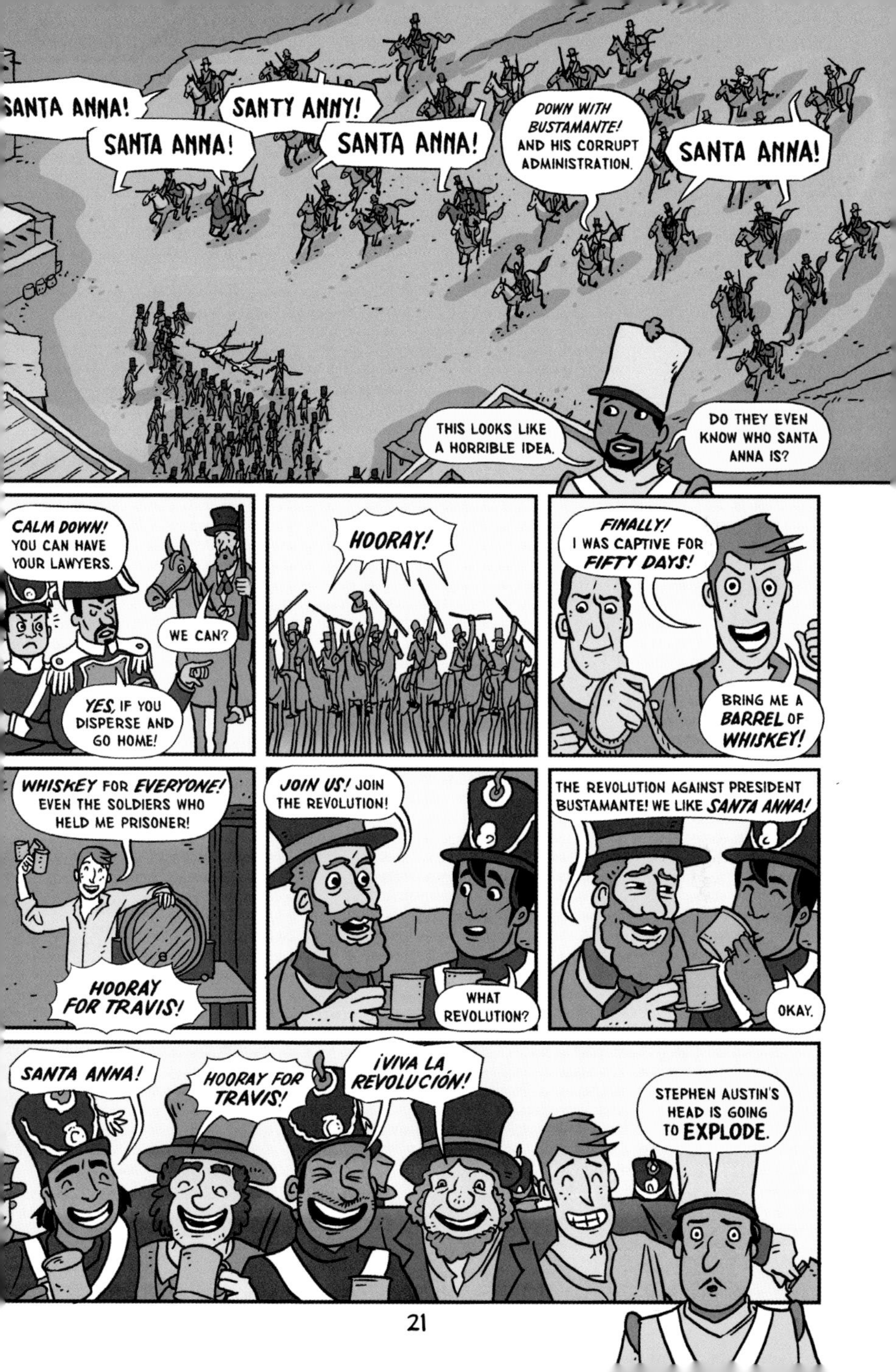
SANTA ANNA!
SANTY ANNY!
SANTA ANNA!
SANTA ANNA!
DOWN WITH BUSTAMANTE! AND HIS CORRUPT ADMINISTRATION.
SANTA ANNA!
THIS LOOKS LIKE A HORRIBLE IDEA.
DO THEY EVEN KNOW WHO SANTA ANNA IS?
CALM DOWN! YOU CAN HAVE YOUR LAWYERS.
WE CAN?
YES, IF YOU DISPERSE AND GO HOME!
HOORAY!
FINALLY! I WAS CAPTIVE FOR FIFTY DAYS!
BRING ME A BARREL OF WHISKEY!
WHISKEY FOR EVERYONE! EVEN THE SOLDIERS WHO HELD ME PRISONER!
HOORAY FOR TRAVIS!
JOIN US! JOIN THE REVOLUTION!
WHAT REVOLUTION?
THE REVOLUTION AGAINST PRESIDENT BUSTAMANTE! WE LIKE SANTA ANNA!
OKAY.
SANTA ANNA!
HOORAY FOR TRAVIS!
¡VIVA LA REVOLUCIÓN!
STEPHEN AUSTIN'S HEAD IS GOING TO EXPLODE.

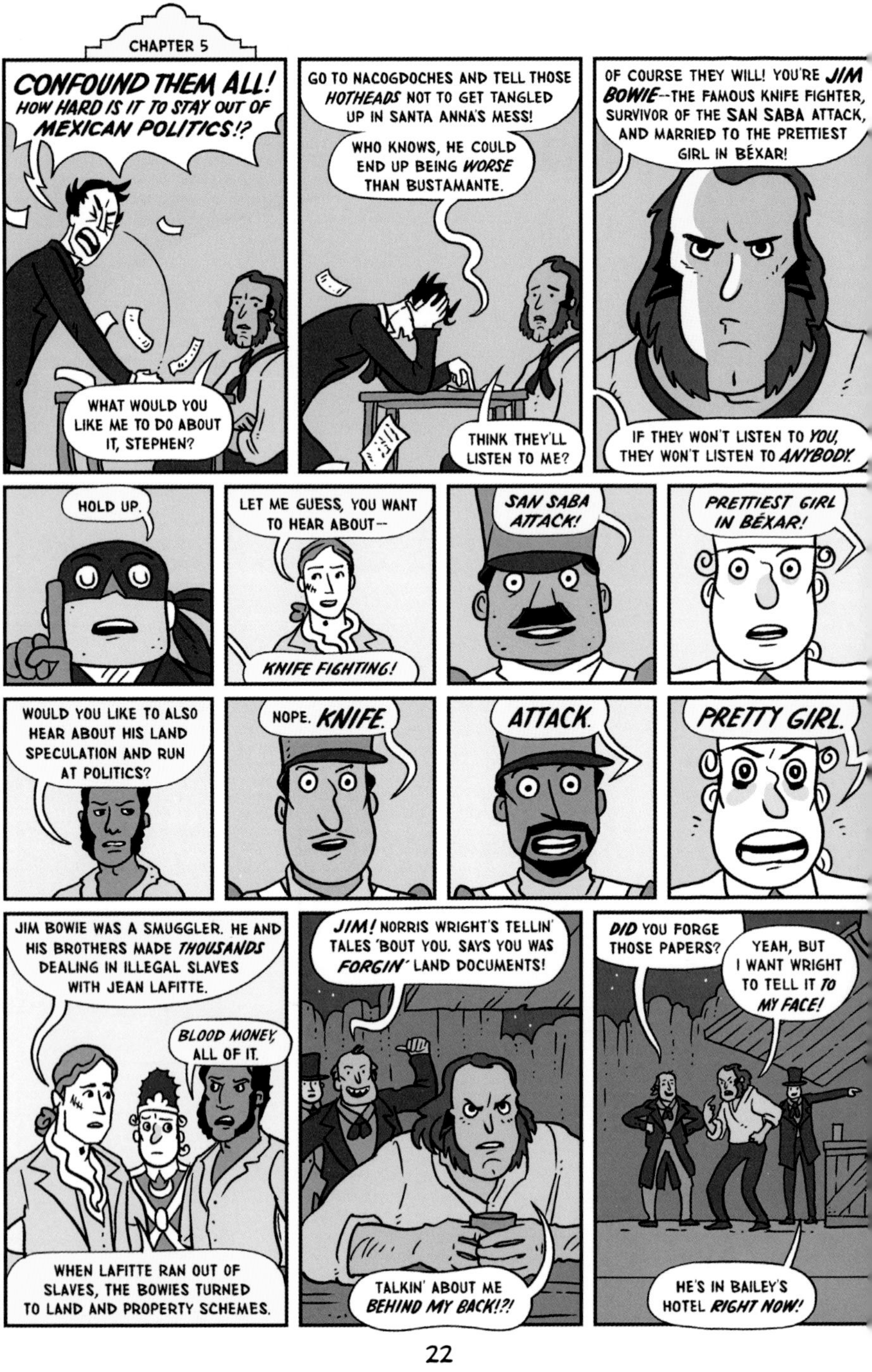
CHAPTER 5
CONFOUND THEM ALL! HOW HARD IS IT TO STAY OUT OF MEXICAN POLITICS!?
WHAT WOULD YOU LIKE ME TO DO ABOUT IT, STEPHEN?
GO TO NACOGDOCHES AND TELL THOSE HOTHEADS NOT TO GET TANGLED UP IN SANTA ANNA'S MESS!
WHO KNOWS, HE COULD END UP BEING WORSE THAN BUSTAMANTE.
THINK THEY'LL LISTEN TO ME?
OF COURSE THEY WILL! YOU'RE JIM BOWIE--THE FAMOUS KNIFE FIGHTER, SURVIVOR OF THE SAN SABA ATTACK, AND MARRIED TO THE PRETTIEST GIRL IN BÉXAR!
IF THEY WON'T LISTEN TO YOU, THEY WON'T LISTEN TO ANYBODY.
HOLD UP.
LET ME GUESS, YOU WANT TO HEAR ABOUT--
KNIFE FIGHTING!
SAN SABA ATTACK!
PRETTIEST GIRL IN BÉXAR!
WOULD YOU LIKE TO ALSO HEAR ABOUT HIS LAND SPECULATION AND RUN AT POLITICS?
NOPE. KNIFE.
ATTACK.
PRETTY GIRL.
JIM BOWIE WAS A SMUGGLER. HE AND HIS BROTHERS MADE THOUSANDS DEALING IN ILLEGAL SLAVES WITH JEAN LAFITTE.
BLOOD MONEY, ALL OF IT.
WHEN LAFITTE RAN OUT OF SLAVES, THE BOWIES TURNED TO LAND AND PROPERTY SCHEMES.
JIM! NORRIS WRIGHT'S TELLIN' TALES 'BOUT YOU. SAYS YOU WAS FORGIN' LAND DOCUMENTS!
TALKIN' ABOUT ME BEHIND MY BACK!?!
DID YOU FORGE THOSE PAPERS?
YEAH, BUT I WANT WRIGHT TO TELL IT TO MY FACE!
HE'S IN BAILEY'S HOTEL RIGHT NOW!

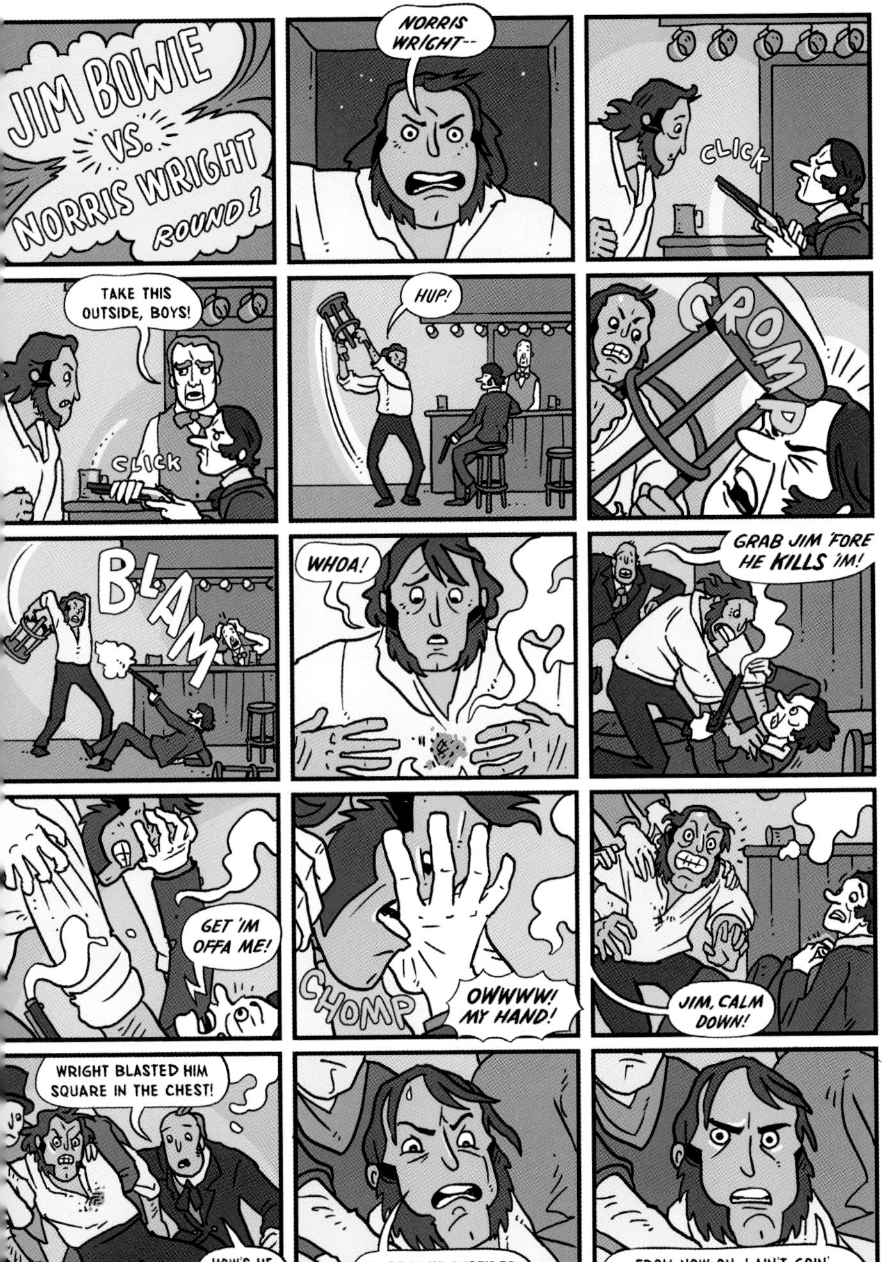
JIM BOWIE VS. NORRIS WRIGHT
ROUND 1
NORRIS WRIGHT--
CLICK
TAKE THIS OUTSIDE, BOYS!
CLICK
HUP!
CROMP
BLAM
WHOA!
GRAB JIM 'FORE HE KILLS 'IM!
GET 'IM OFFA ME!
CHOMP
OWWWW! MY HAND!
JIM, CALM DOWN!
WRIGHT BLASTED HIM SQUARE IN THE CHEST!
HOW'S HE STILL ALIVE?
MUST HAVE MISFIRED. CAN'T TRUST A PISTOL.
FROM NOW ON, I AIN'T GOIN' NOWHERE WITHOUT A BIG KNIFE.

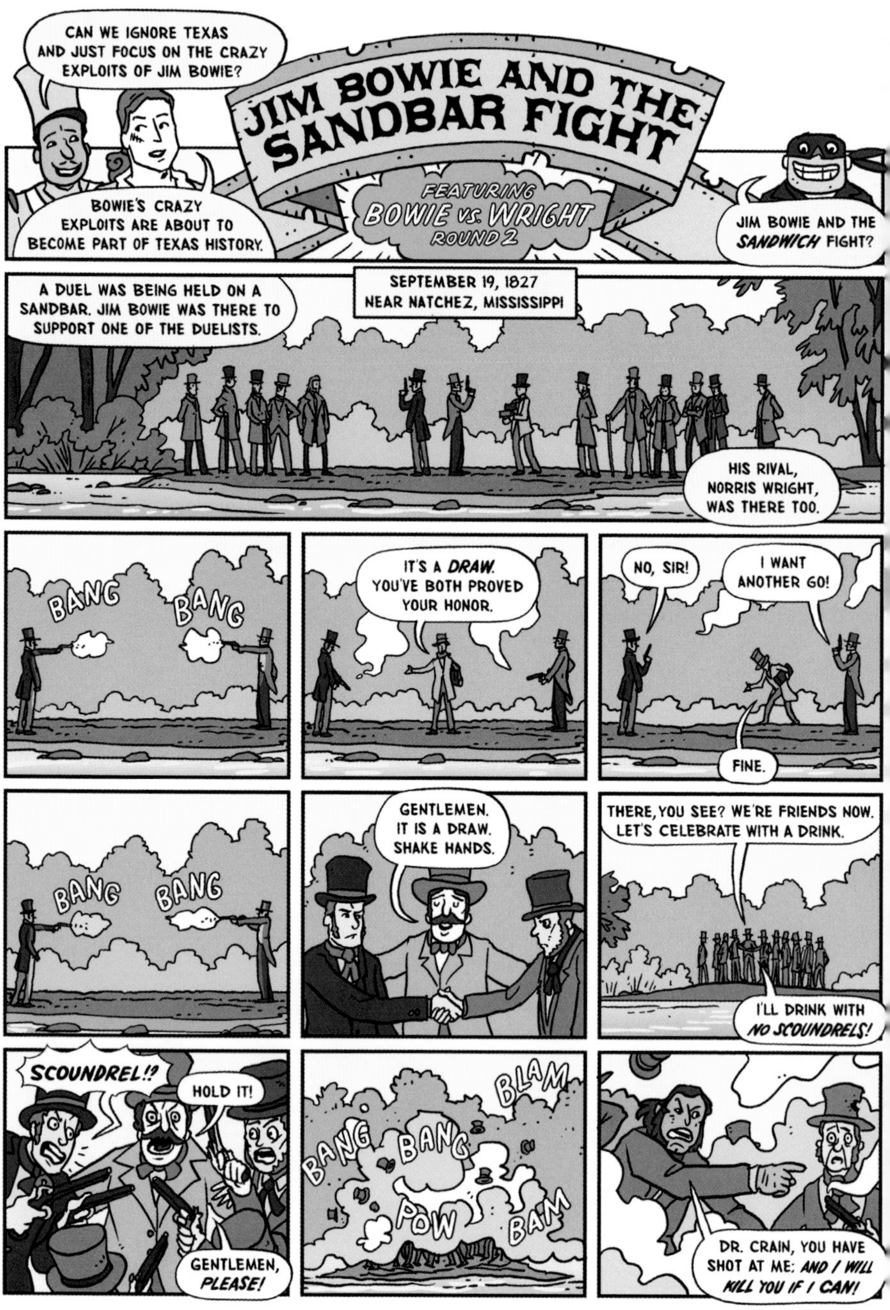
CAN WE IGNORE TEXAS AND JUST FOCUS ON THE CRAZY EXPLOITS OF JIM BOWIE?
JIM BOWIE AND THE SANDBAR FIGHT
BOWIE'S CRAZY EXPLOITS ARE ABOUT TO BECOME PART OF TEXAS HISTORY.
FEATURING BOWIE vs. WRIGHT ROUND 2
JIM BOWIE AND THE *SANDWICH* FIGHT?
A DUEL WAS BEING HELD ON A SANDBAR. JIM BOWIE WAS THERE TO SUPPORT ONE OF THE DUELISTS.
SEPTEMBER 19, 1827
NEAR NATCHEZ, MISSISSIPPI
HIS RIVAL, NORRIS WRIGHT, WAS THERE TOO.
BANG
BANG
IT'S A *DRAW*. YOU'VE BOTH PROVED YOUR HONOR.
NO, SIR!
I WANT ANOTHER GO!
FINE.
BANG
BANG
GENTLEMEN. IT IS A DRAW. SHAKE HANDS.
THERE, YOU SEE? WE'RE FRIENDS NOW. LET'S CELEBRATE WITH A DRINK.
I'LL DRINK WITH *NO SCOUNDRELS!*
SCOUNDREL!?
HOLD IT!
GENTLEMEN, *PLEASE!*
BLAM
BANG
BANG
POW
BAM
DR. CRAIN, YOU HAVE SHOT AT ME; *AND I WILL KILL YOU IF I CAN!*

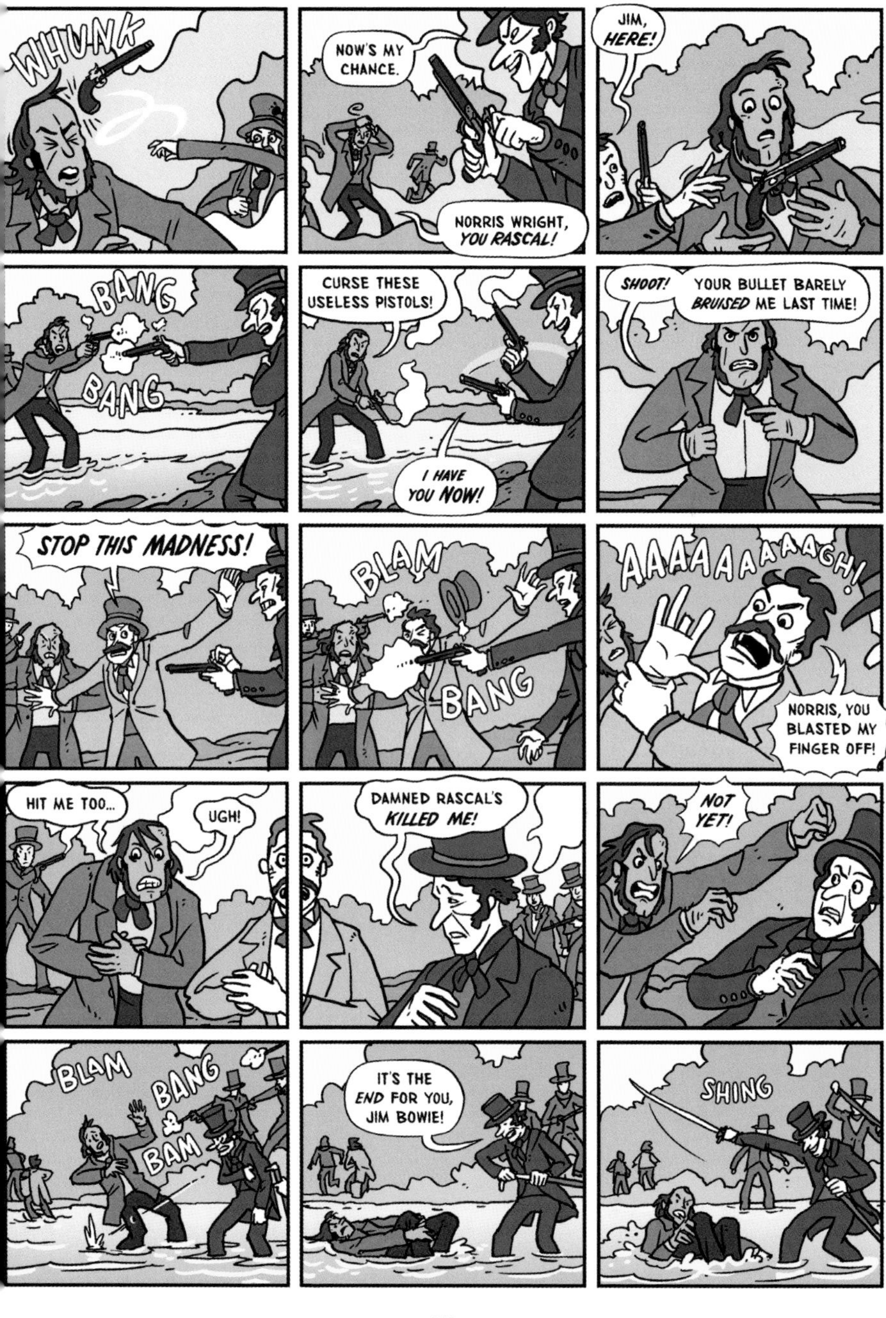
WHUNK
NOW'S MY CHANCE.
NORRIS WRIGHT, YOU RASCAL!
JIM, HERE!
BANG
BANG
CURSE THESE USELESS PISTOLS!
I HAVE YOU NOW!
SHOOT!
YOUR BULLET BARELY BRUISED ME LAST TIME!
STOP THIS MADNESS!
BLAM
BANG
AAAAAAAAAAGH!
NORRIS, YOU BLASTED MY FINGER OFF!
HIT ME TOO...
UGH!
DAMNED RASCAL'S KILLED ME!
NOT YET!
BLAM
BANG
BAM
IT'S THE END FOR YOU, JIM BOWIE!
SHING

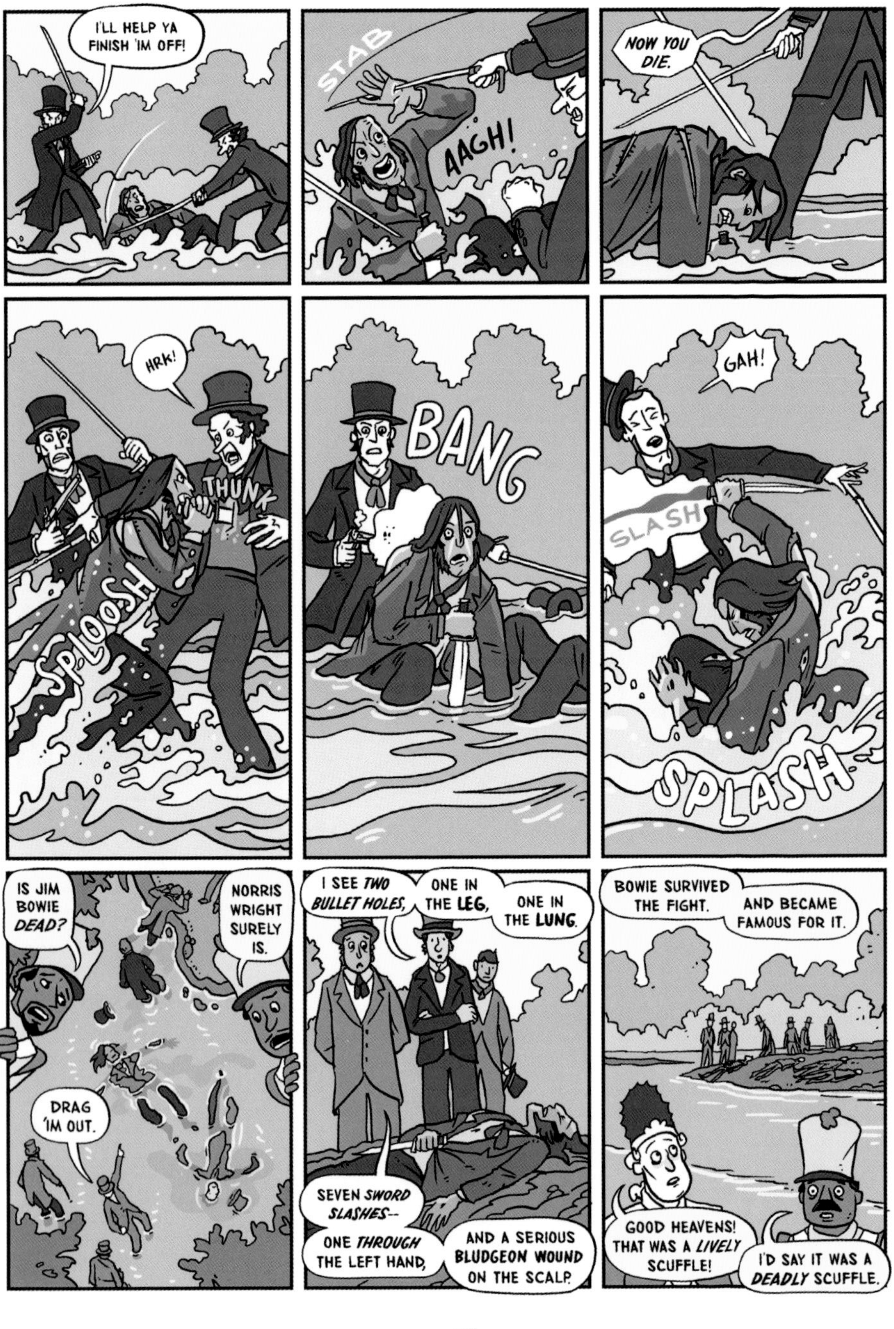
I'LL HELP YA FINISH 'IM OFF!
STAB
AAGH!
NOW YOU DIE.
HRK!
THUNK
SPLOOSH
BANG
GAH!
SLASH
SPLASH
IS JIM BOWIE DEAD?
NORRIS WRIGHT SURELY IS.
DRAG 'IM OUT.
I SEE TWO BULLET HOLES,
ONE IN THE LEG,
ONE IN THE LUNG.
SEVEN SWORD SLASHES--
ONE THROUGH THE LEFT HAND,
AND A SERIOUS BLUDGEON WOUND ON THE SCALP.
BOWIE SURVIVED THE FIGHT.
AND BECAME FAMOUS FOR IT.
GOOD HEAVENS! THAT WAS A LIVELY SCUFFLE!
I'D SAY IT WAS A DEADLY SCUFFLE.

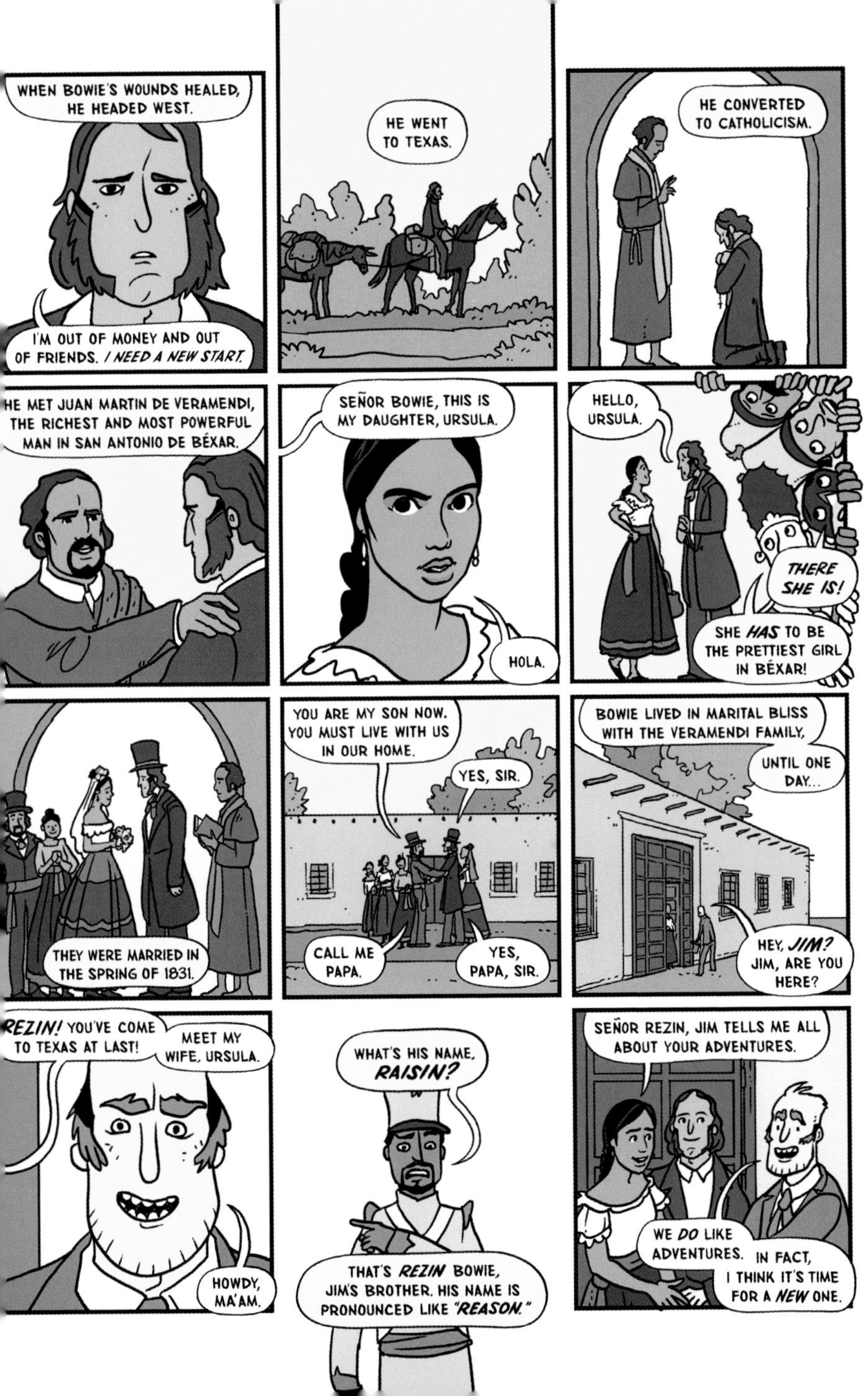
WHEN BOWIE'S WOUNDS HEALED, HE HEADED WEST.
I'M OUT OF MONEY AND OUT OF FRIENDS. I NEED A NEW START.
HE WENT TO TEXAS.
HE CONVERTED TO CATHOLICISM.
HE MET JUAN MARTIN DE VERAMENDI, THE RICHEST AND MOST POWERFUL MAN IN SAN ANTONIO DE BÉXAR.
SEÑOR BOWIE, THIS IS MY DAUGHTER, URSULA.
HOLA.
HELLO, URSULA.
THERE SHE IS!
SHE HAS TO BE THE PRETTIEST GIRL IN BÉXAR!
THEY WERE MARRIED IN THE SPRING OF 1831.
YOU ARE MY SON NOW. YOU MUST LIVE WITH US IN OUR HOME.
YES, SIR.
CALL ME PAPA.
YES, PAPA, SIR.
BOWIE LIVED IN MARITAL BLISS WITH THE VERAMENDI FAMILY,
UNTIL ONE DAY...
HEY, JIM? JIM, ARE YOU HERE?
REZIN! YOU'VE COME TO TEXAS AT LAST!
MEET MY WIFE, URSULA.
HOWDY, MA'AM.
WHAT'S HIS NAME, RAISIN?
THAT'S REZIN BOWIE, JIM'S BROTHER. HIS NAME IS PRONOUNCED LIKE "REASON."
SEÑOR REZIN, JIM TELLS ME ALL ABOUT YOUR ADVENTURES.
WE DO LIKE ADVENTURES.
IN FACT, I THINK IT'S TIME FOR A NEW ONE.

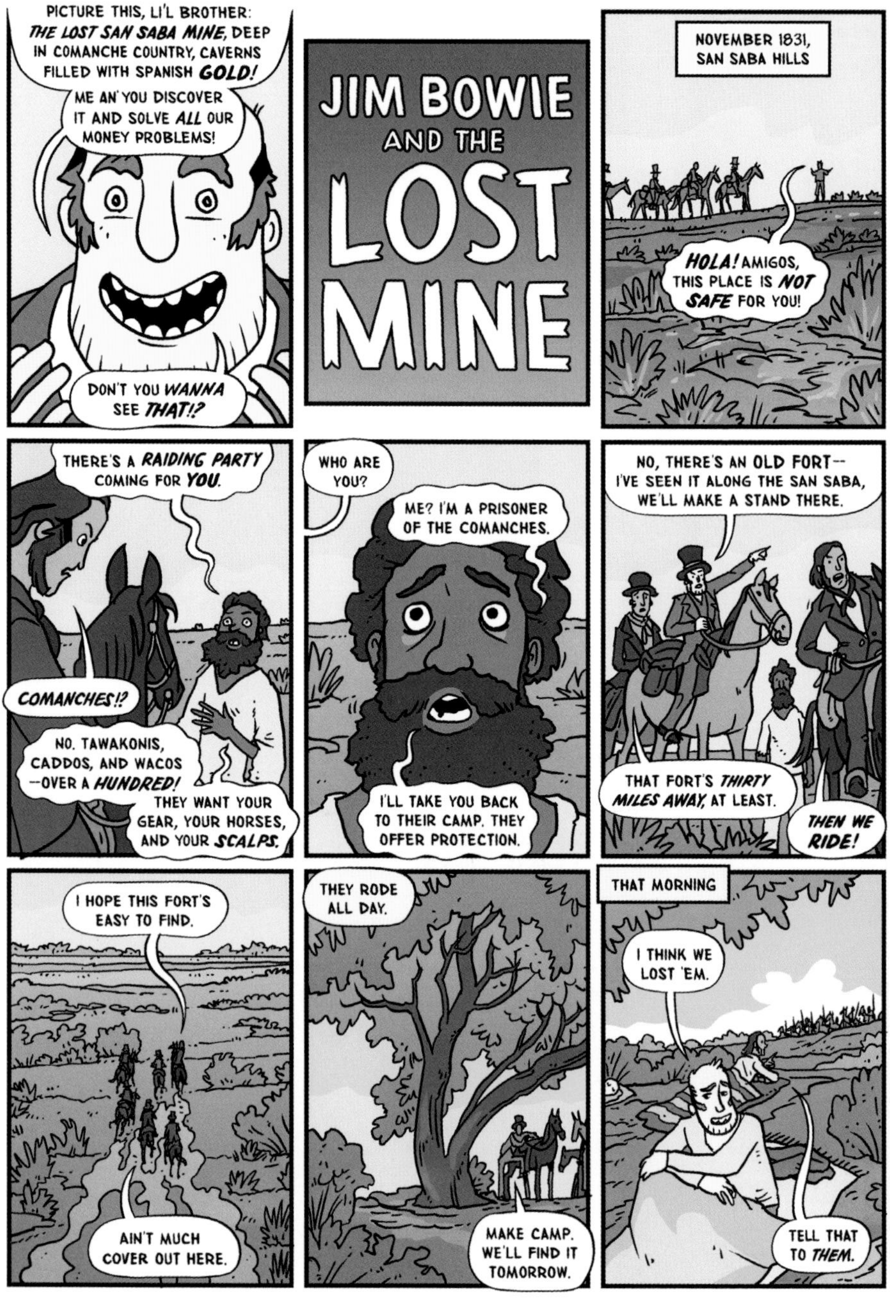
PICTURE THIS, LI'L BROTHER: THE LOST SAN SABA MINE, DEEP IN COMANCHE COUNTRY, CAVERNS FILLED WITH SPANISH GOLD!
ME AN' YOU DISCOVER IT AND SOLVE ALL OUR MONEY PROBLEMS!
DON'T YOU WANNA SEE THAT!?
JIM BOWIE AND THE LOST MINE
NOVEMBER 1831, SAN SABA HILLS
HOLA! AMIGOS, THIS PLACE IS NOT SAFE FOR YOU!
THERE'S A RAIDING PARTY COMING FOR YOU.
COMANCHES!?
NO. TAWAKONIS, CADDOS, AND WACOS --OVER A HUNDRED!
THEY WANT YOUR GEAR, YOUR HORSES, AND YOUR SCALPS.
WHO ARE YOU?
ME? I'M A PRISONER OF THE COMANCHES.
I'LL TAKE YOU BACK TO THEIR CAMP. THEY OFFER PROTECTION.
NO, THERE'S AN OLD FORT-- I'VE SEEN IT ALONG THE SAN SABA, WE'LL MAKE A STAND THERE.
THAT FORT'S THIRTY MILES AWAY, AT LEAST.
THEN WE RIDE!
I HOPE THIS FORT'S EASY TO FIND.
AIN'T MUCH COVER OUT HERE.
THEY RODE ALL DAY.
MAKE CAMP. WE'LL FIND IT TOMORROW.
THAT MORNING
I THINK WE LOST 'EM.
TELL THAT TO THEM.

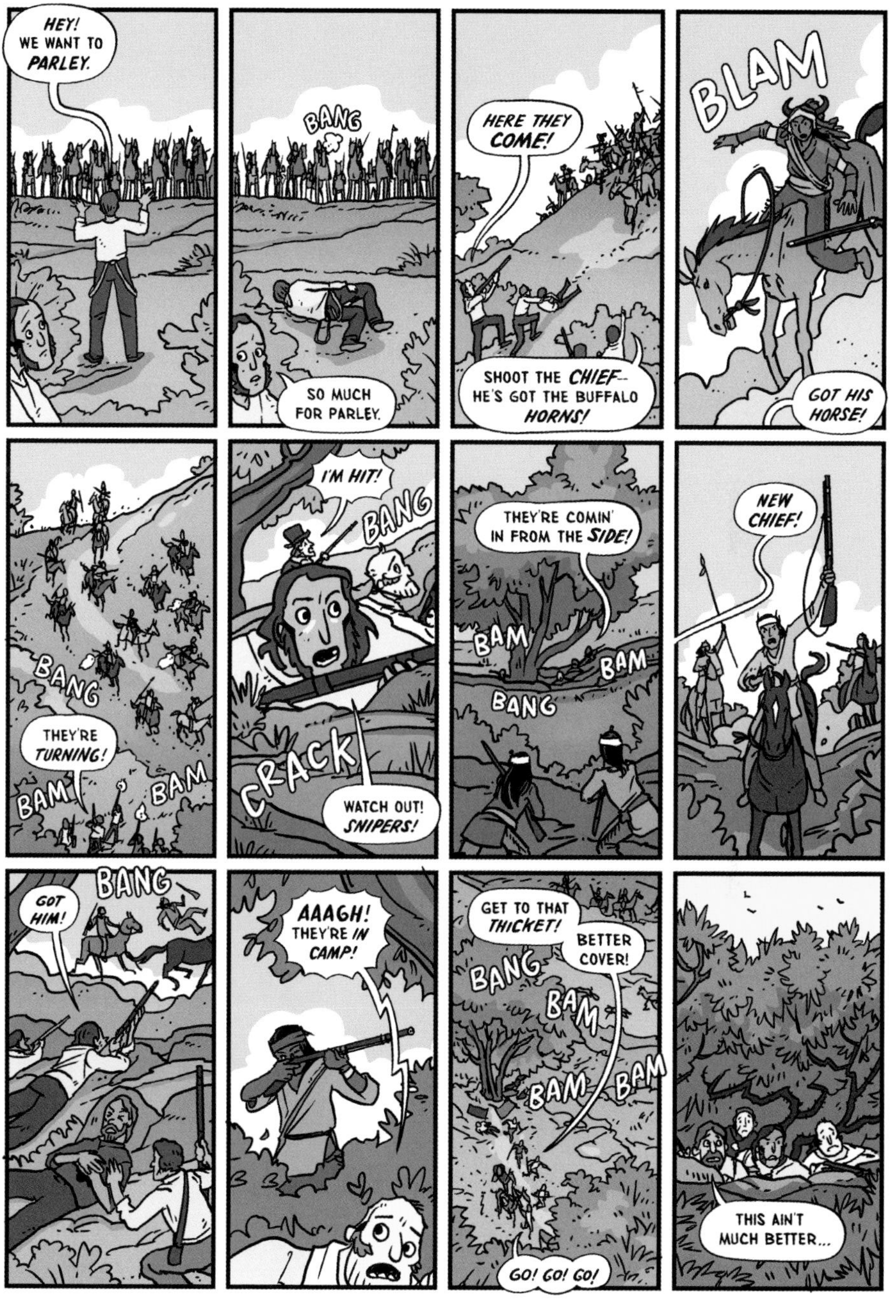
HEY! WE WANT TO PARLEY.
BANG
SO MUCH FOR PARLEY.
HERE THEY COME!
SHOOT THE CHIEF-- HE'S GOT THE BUFFALO HORNS!
BLAM
GOT HIS HORSE!
BANG
THEY'RE TURNING!
BAM
BAM
I'M HIT!
BANG
CRACK
WATCH OUT! SNIPERS!
THEY'RE COMIN' IN FROM THE SIDE!
BAM
BAM
BANG
NEW CHIEF!
BANG
GOT HIM!
AAAGH! THEY'RE IN CAMP!
GET TO THAT THICKET!
BETTER COVER!
BANG
BAM
BAM
BAM
GO! GO! GO!
THIS AIN'T MUCH BETTER...

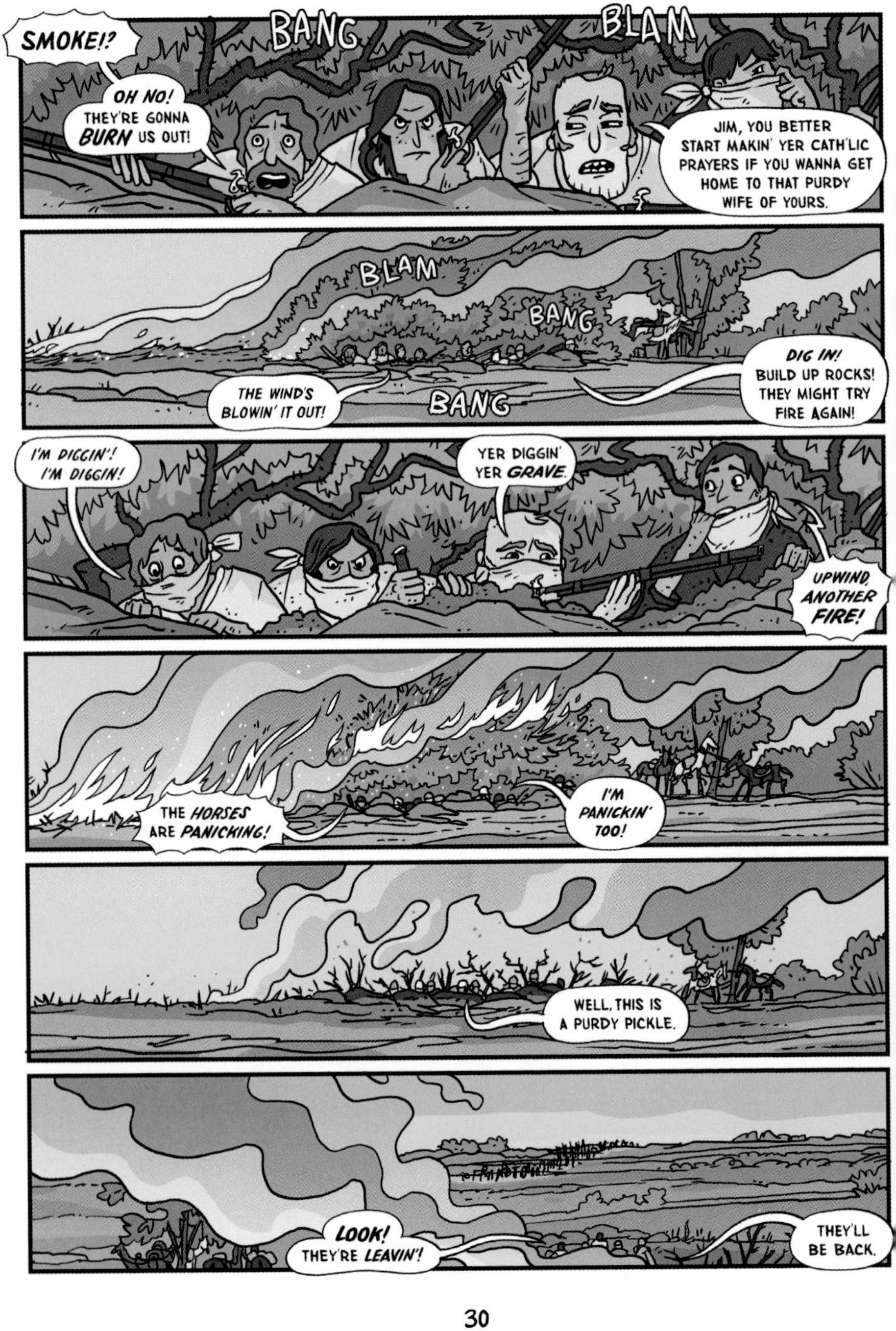
SMOKE!?
BANG
BLAM
OH NO! THEY'RE GONNA BURN US OUT!
JIM, YOU BETTER START MAKIN' YER CATH'LIC PRAYERS IF YOU WANNA GET HOME TO THAT PURDY WIFE OF YOURS.
BLAM
BANG
THE WIND'S BLOWIN' IT OUT!
BANG
DIG IN! BUILD UP ROCKS! THEY MIGHT TRY FIRE AGAIN!
I'M DIGGIN'! I'M DIGGIN!
YER DIGGIN' YER GRAVE.
UPWIND, ANOTHER FIRE!
THE HORSES ARE PANICKING!
I'M PANICKIN' TOO!
WELL, THIS IS A PURDY PICKLE.
LOOK! THEY'RE LEAVIN'!
THEY'LL BE BACK.

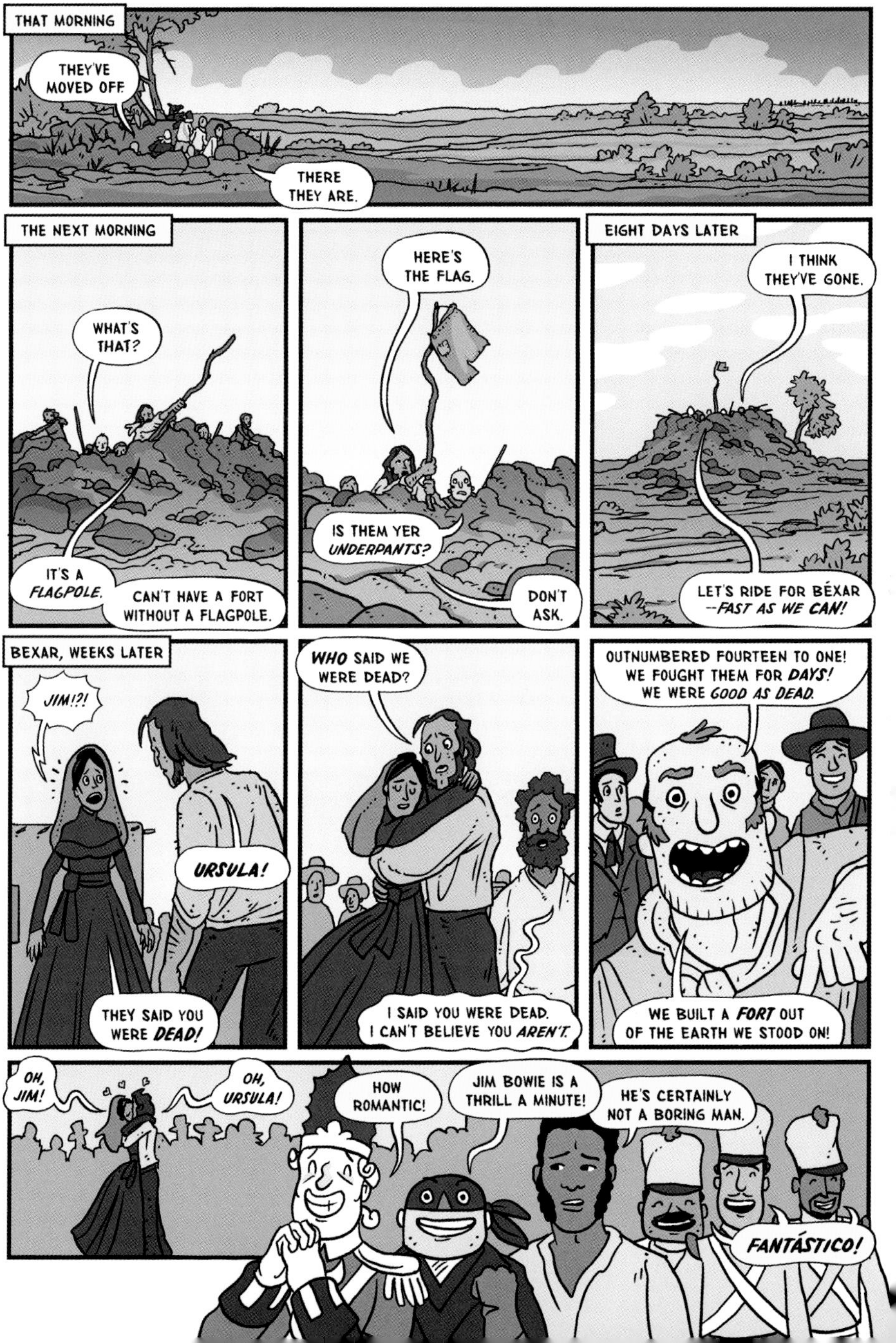
THAT MORNING
THEY'VE MOVED OFF.
THERE THEY ARE.
THE NEXT MORNING
WHAT'S THAT?
IT'S A FLAGPOLE.
CAN'T HAVE A FORT WITHOUT A FLAGPOLE.
HERE'S THE FLAG.
IS THEM YER UNDERPANTS?
DON'T ASK.
EIGHT DAYS LATER
I THINK THEY'VE GONE.
LET'S RIDE FOR BÉXAR --FAST AS WE CAN!
BEXAR, WEEKS LATER
JIM!?!
URSULA!
THEY SAID YOU WERE DEAD!
WHO SAID WE WERE DEAD?
I SAID YOU WERE DEAD. I CAN'T BELIEVE YOU AREN'T.
OUTNUMBERED FOURTEEN TO ONE! WE FOUGHT THEM FOR DAYS! WE WERE GOOD AS DEAD.
WE BUILT A FORT OUT OF THE EARTH WE STOOD ON!
OH, JIM!
OH, URSULA!
HOW ROMANTIC!
JIM BOWIE IS A THRILL A MINUTE!
HE'S CERTAINLY NOT A BORING MAN.
FANTÁSTICO!

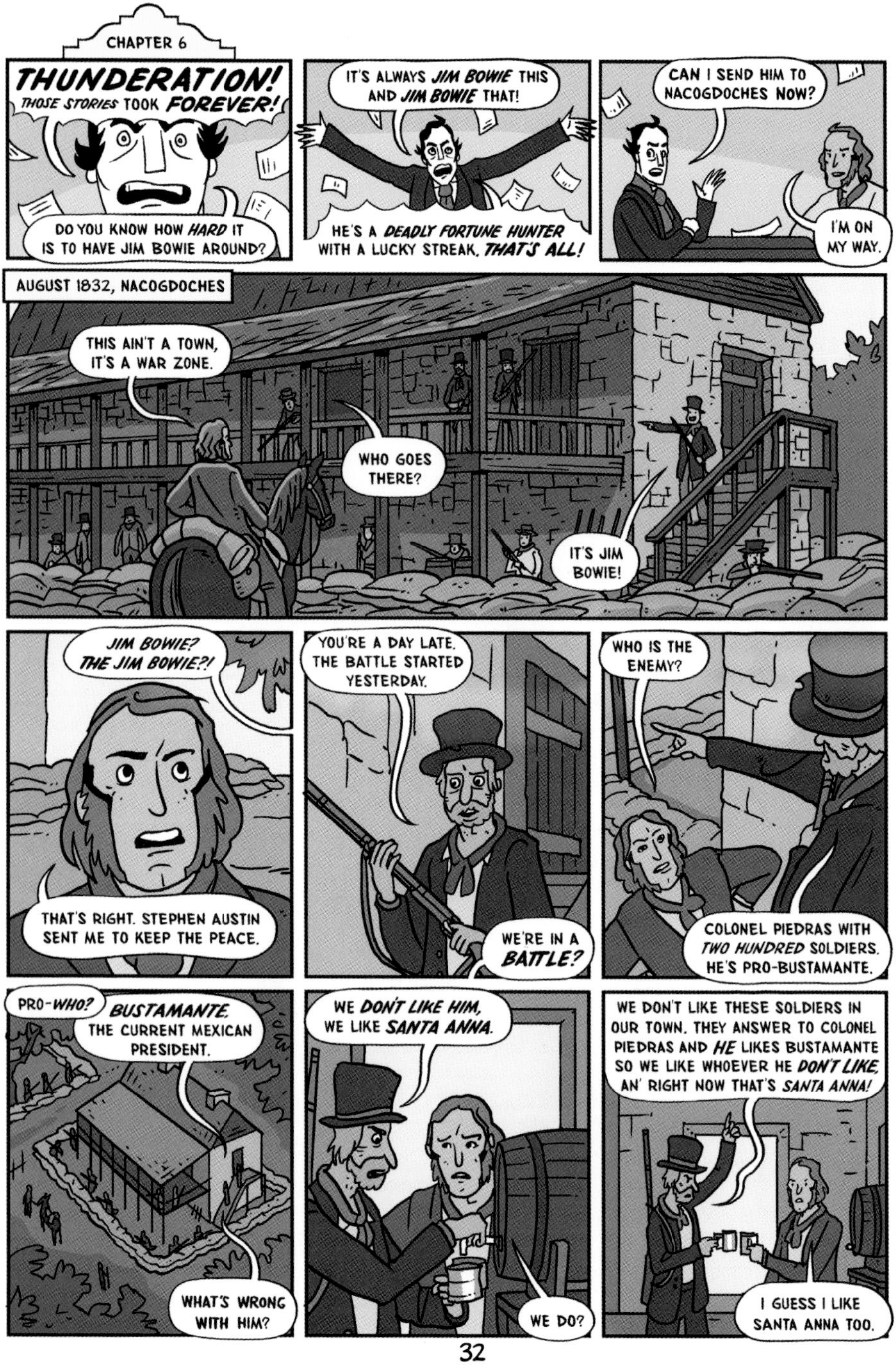
CHAPTER 6
THUNDERATION! THOSE STORIES TOOK FOREVER!
DO YOU KNOW HOW HARD IT IS TO HAVE JIM BOWIE AROUND?
IT'S ALWAYS JIM BOWIE THIS AND JIM BOWIE THAT!
HE'S A DEADLY FORTUNE HUNTER WITH A LUCKY STREAK, THAT'S ALL!
CAN I SEND HIM TO NACOGDOCHES NOW?
I'M ON MY WAY.
AUGUST 1832, NACOGDOCHES
THIS AIN'T A TOWN, IT'S A WAR ZONE.
WHO GOES THERE?
IT'S JIM BOWIE!
JIM BOWIE? THE JIM BOWIE?!
THAT'S RIGHT. STEPHEN AUSTIN SENT ME TO KEEP THE PEACE.
YOU'RE A DAY LATE. THE BATTLE STARTED YESTERDAY.
WE'RE IN A BATTLE?
WHO IS THE ENEMY?
COLONEL PIEDRAS WITH TWO HUNDRED SOLDIERS. HE'S PRO-BUSTAMANTE.
PRO-WHO?
BUSTAMANTE. THE CURRENT MEXICAN PRESIDENT.
WHAT'S WRONG WITH HIM?
WE DON'T LIKE HIM, WE LIKE SANTA ANNA.
WE DO?
WE DON'T LIKE THESE SOLDIERS IN OUR TOWN. THEY ANSWER TO COLONEL PIEDRAS AND HE LIKES BUSTAMANTE SO WE LIKE WHOEVER HE DON'T LIKE, AN' RIGHT NOW THAT'S SANTA ANNA!
I GUESS I LIKE SANTA ANNA TOO.

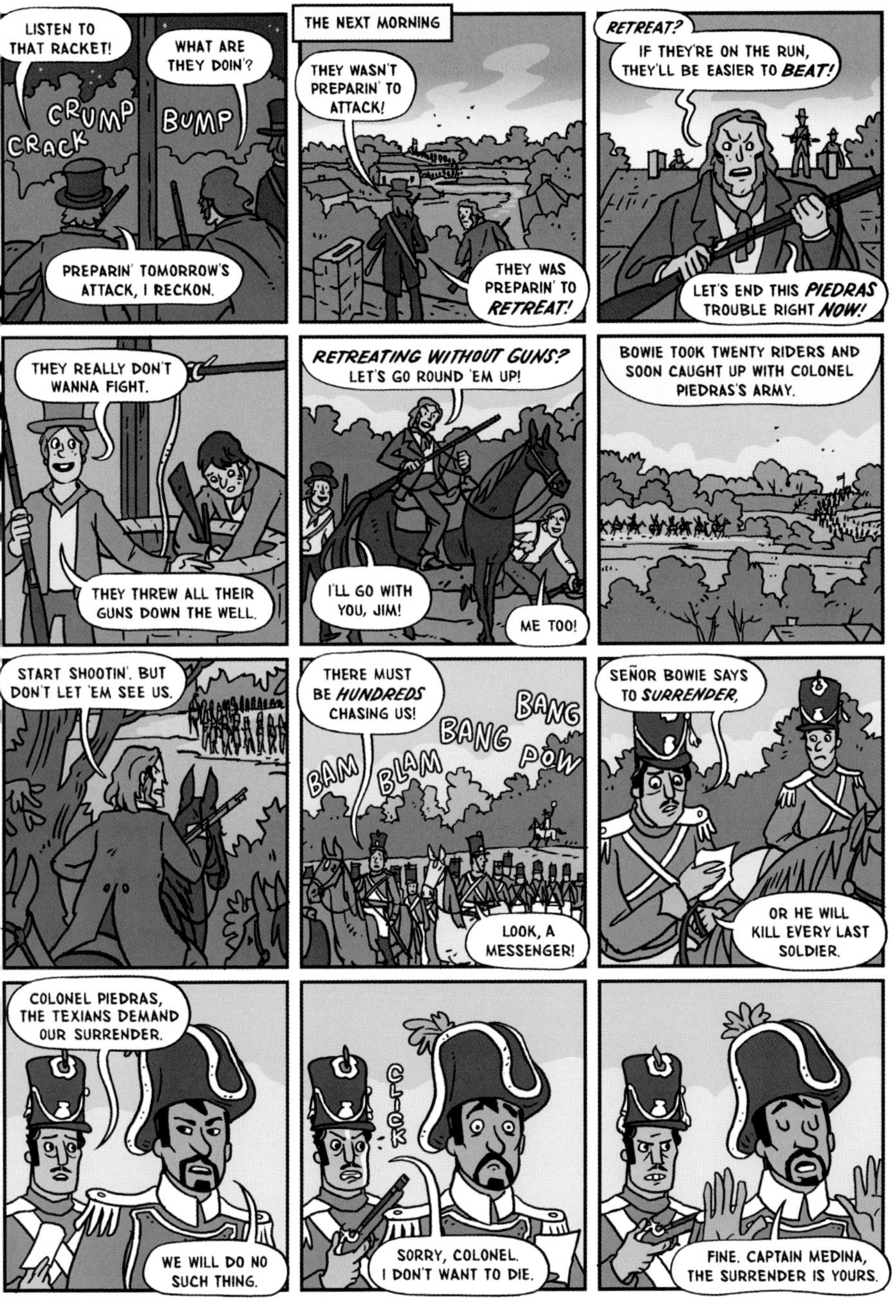
LISTEN TO THAT RACKET!
WHAT ARE THEY DOIN'?
CRUMP
CRACK
BUMP
PREPARIN' TOMORROW'S ATTACK, I RECKON.
THE NEXT MORNING
THEY WASN'T PREPARIN' TO ATTACK!
THEY WAS PREPARIN' TO RETREAT!
RETREAT?
IF THEY'RE ON THE RUN, THEY'LL BE EASIER TO BEAT!
LET'S END THIS PIEDRAS TROUBLE RIGHT NOW!
THEY REALLY DON'T WANNA FIGHT.
THEY THREW ALL THEIR GUNS DOWN THE WELL.
RETREATING WITHOUT GUNS? LET'S GO ROUND 'EM UP!
I'LL GO WITH YOU, JIM!
ME TOO!
BOWIE TOOK TWENTY RIDERS AND SOON CAUGHT UP WITH COLONEL PIEDRAS'S ARMY.
START SHOOTIN'. BUT DON'T LET 'EM SEE US.
THERE MUST BE HUNDREDS CHASING US!
BAM
BLAM
BANG
BANG
POW
LOOK, A MESSENGER!
SEÑOR BOWIE SAYS TO SURRENDER,
OR HE WILL KILL EVERY LAST SOLDIER.
COLONEL PIEDRAS, THE TEXIANS DEMAND OUR SURRENDER.
WE WILL DO NO SUCH THING.
CLICK
SORRY, COLONEL. I DON'T WANT TO DIE.
FINE. CAPTAIN MEDINA, THE SURRENDER IS YOURS.

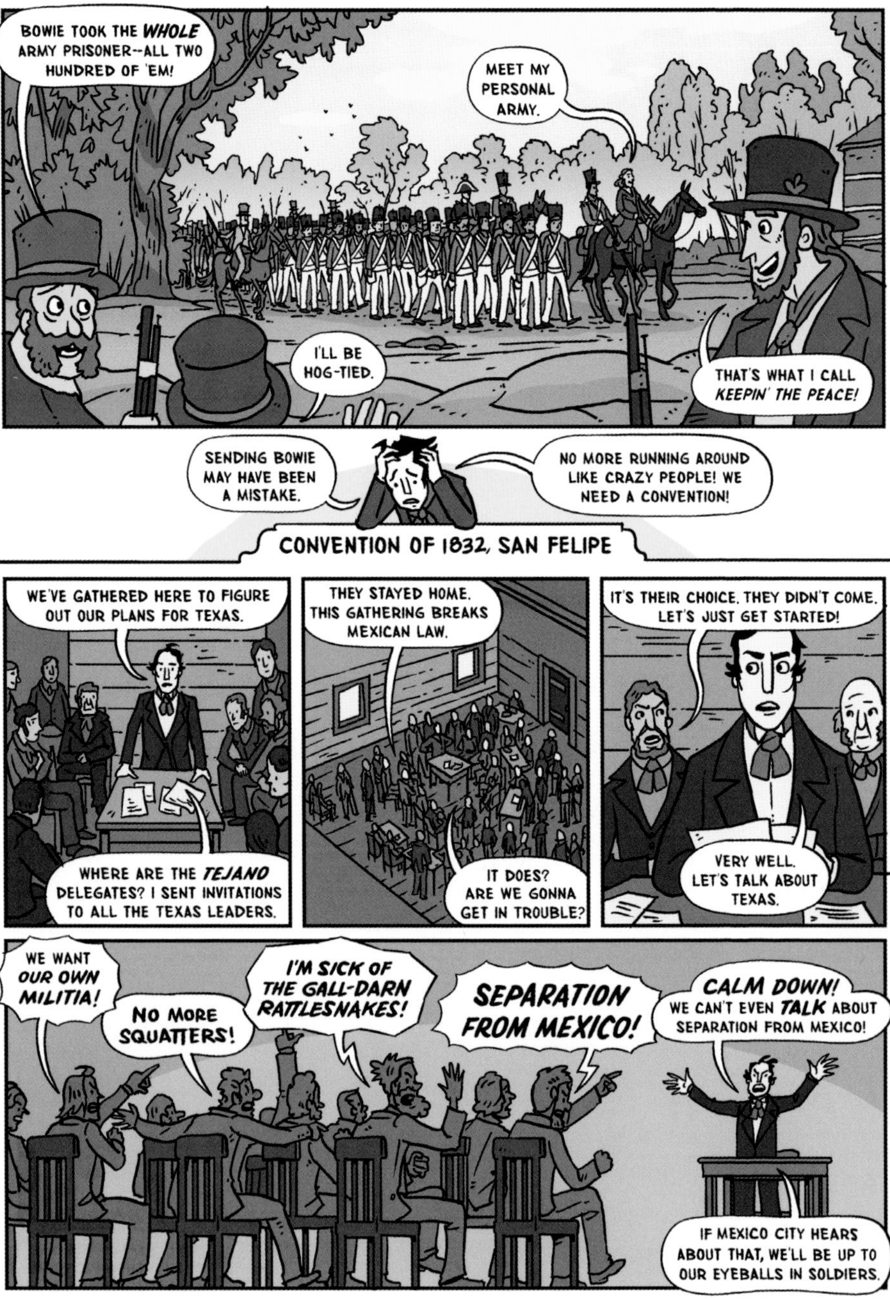

BOWIE TOOK THE *WHOLE* ARMY PRISONER--ALL TWO HUNDRED OF 'EM!
MEET MY PERSONAL ARMY.
I'LL BE HOG-TIED.
THAT'S WHAT I CALL *KEEPIN' THE PEACE!*
SENDING BOWIE MAY HAVE BEEN A MISTAKE.
NO MORE RUNNING AROUND LIKE CRAZY PEOPLE! WE NEED A CONVENTION!
CONVENTION OF 1832, SAN FELIPE
WE'VE GATHERED HERE TO FIGURE OUT OUR PLANS FOR TEXAS.
WHERE ARE THE *TEJANO* DELEGATES? I SENT INVITATIONS TO ALL THE TEXAS LEADERS.
THEY STAYED HOME. THIS GATHERING BREAKS MEXICAN LAW.
IT DOES? ARE WE GONNA GET IN TROUBLE?
IT'S THEIR CHOICE. THEY DIDN'T COME. LET'S JUST GET STARTED!
VERY WELL. LET'S TALK ABOUT TEXAS.
WE WANT *OUR OWN MILITIA!*
NO MORE SQUATTERS!
I'M SICK OF THE GALL-DARN RATTLESNAKES!
SEPARATION FROM MEXICO!
CALM DOWN! WE CAN'T EVEN *TALK* ABOUT SEPARATION FROM MEXICO!
IF MEXICO CITY HEARS ABOUT THAT, WE'LL BE UP TO OUR EYEBALLS IN SOLDIERS.

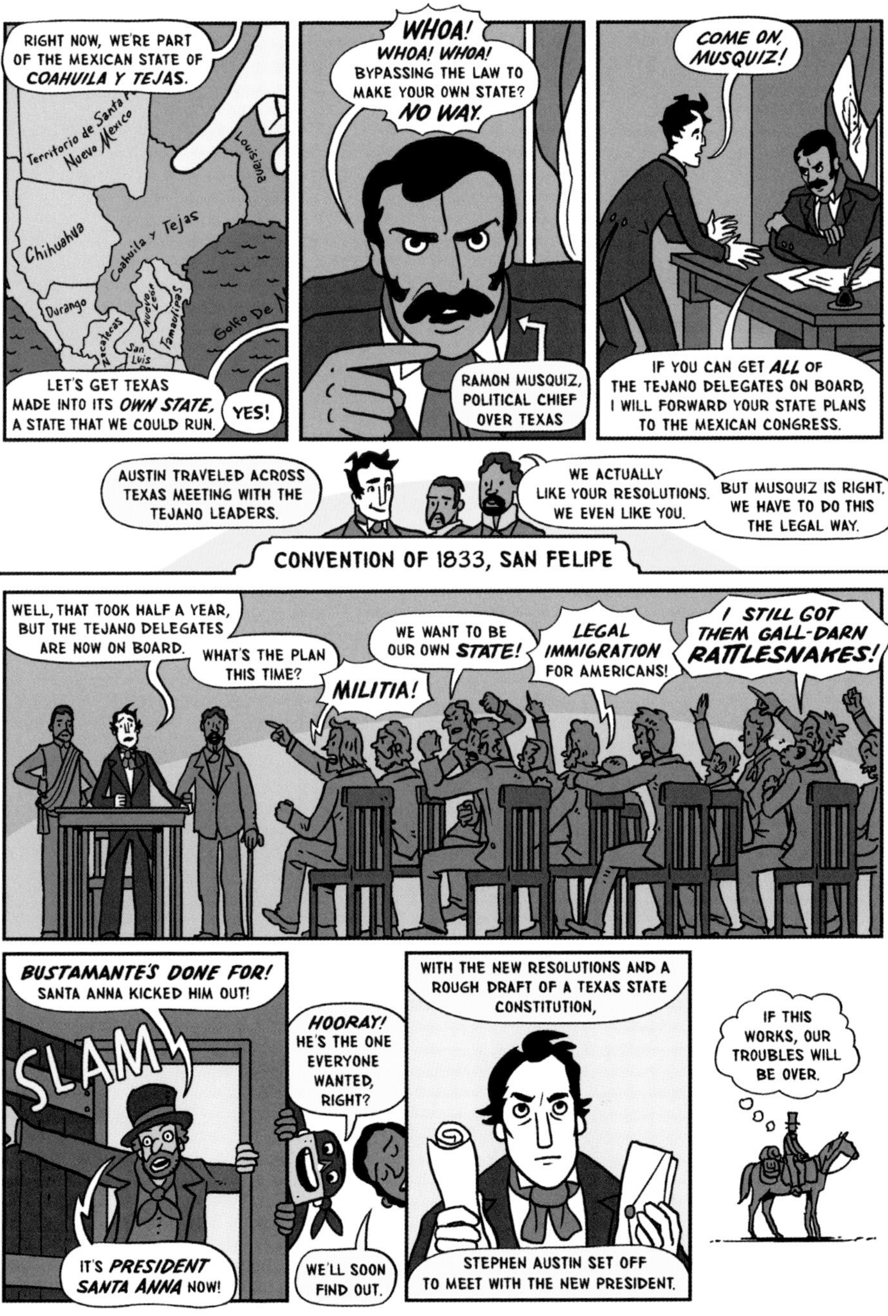

RIGHT NOW, WE'RE PART OF THE MEXICAN STATE OF *COAHUILA Y TEJAS.*
Nuevo Mexico
Louisiana
Chihuahua
Coahuila y Tejas
Durango
Nuevo Leon
Tamaulipas
Zacatecas
San Luis
Golfo De
LET'S GET TEXAS MADE INTO ITS *OWN STATE,* A STATE THAT WE COULD RUN.
YES!
WHOA! *WHOA! WHOA!* BYPASSING THE LAW TO MAKE YOUR OWN STATE? *NO WAY.*
RAMON MUSQUIZ, POLITICAL CHIEF OVER TEXAS
COME ON, MUSQUIZ!
IF YOU CAN GET *ALL* OF THE TEJANO DELEGATES ON BOARD, I WILL FORWARD YOUR STATE PLANS TO THE MEXICAN CONGRESS.
AUSTIN TRAVELED ACROSS TEXAS MEETING WITH THE TEJANO LEADERS.
WE ACTUALLY LIKE YOUR RESOLUTIONS. WE EVEN LIKE YOU.
BUT MUSQUIZ IS RIGHT. WE HAVE TO DO THIS THE LEGAL WAY.
CONVENTION OF 1833, SAN FELIPE
WELL, THAT TOOK HALF A YEAR, BUT THE TEJANO DELEGATES ARE NOW ON BOARD.
WHAT'S THE PLAN THIS TIME?
MILITIA!
WE WANT TO BE OUR OWN *STATE!*
LEGAL IMMIGRATION FOR AMERICANS!
I STILL GOT THEM GALL-DARN RATTLESNAKES!
BUSTAMANTE'S DONE FOR! SANTA ANNA KICKED HIM OUT!
SLAM
IT'S *PRESIDENT SANTA ANNA* NOW!
HOORAY! HE'S THE ONE EVERYONE WANTED, RIGHT?
WE'LL SOON FIND OUT.
WITH THE NEW RESOLUTIONS AND A ROUGH DRAFT OF A TEXAS STATE CONSTITUTION,
STEPHEN AUSTIN SET OFF TO MEET WITH THE NEW PRESIDENT.
IF THIS WORKS, OUR TROUBLES WILL BE OVER.

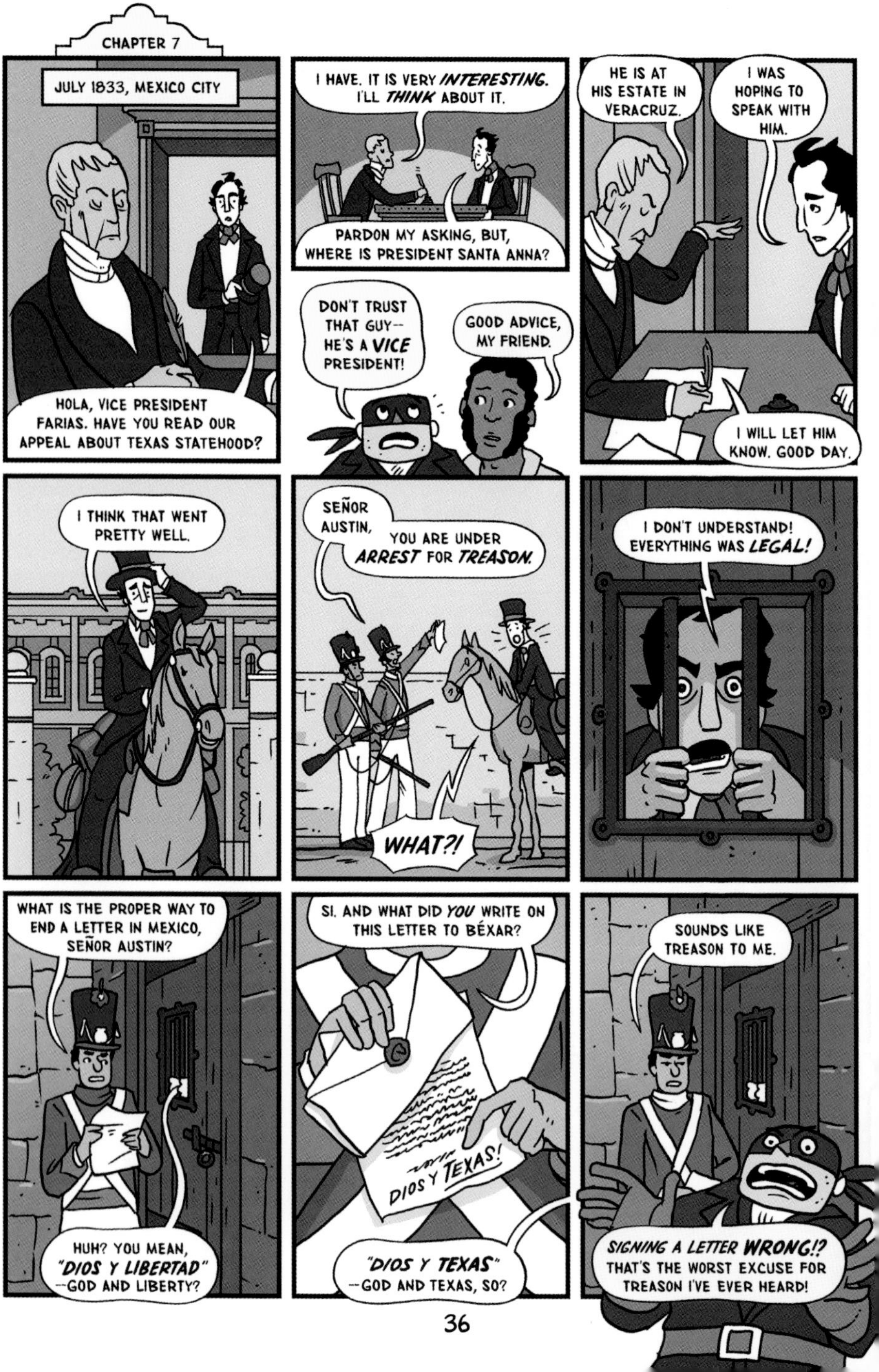
JULY 1833, MEXICO CITY
HOLA, VICE PRESIDENT FARIAS. HAVE YOU READ OUR APPEAL ABOUT TEXAS STATEHOOD?
I HAVE. IT IS VERY *INTERESTING.* I'LL *THINK* ABOUT IT.
PARDON MY ASKING, BUT, WHERE IS PRESIDENT SANTA ANNA?
DON'T TRUST THAT GUY-- HE'S A *VICE* PRESIDENT!
GOOD ADVICE, MY FRIEND.
HE IS AT HIS ESTATE IN VERACRUZ.
I WAS HOPING TO SPEAK WITH HIM.
I WILL LET HIM KNOW. GOOD DAY.
I THINK THAT WENT PRETTY WELL.
SEÑOR AUSTIN,
YOU ARE UNDER *ARREST* FOR *TREASON.*
WHAT?!
I DON'T UNDERSTAND! EVERYTHING WAS *LEGAL!*
WHAT IS THE PROPER WAY TO END A LETTER IN MEXICO, SEÑOR AUSTIN?
HUH? YOU MEAN, *"DIOS Y LIBERTAD"* --GOD AND LIBERTY?
SI. AND WHAT DID *YOU* WRITE ON THIS LETTER TO BÉXAR?
DIOS Y TEXAS!
"DIOS Y TEXAS" --GOD AND TEXAS, SO?
SOUNDS LIKE TREASON TO ME.
SIGNING A LETTER WRONG!? THAT'S THE WORST EXCUSE FOR TREASON I'VE EVER HEARD!

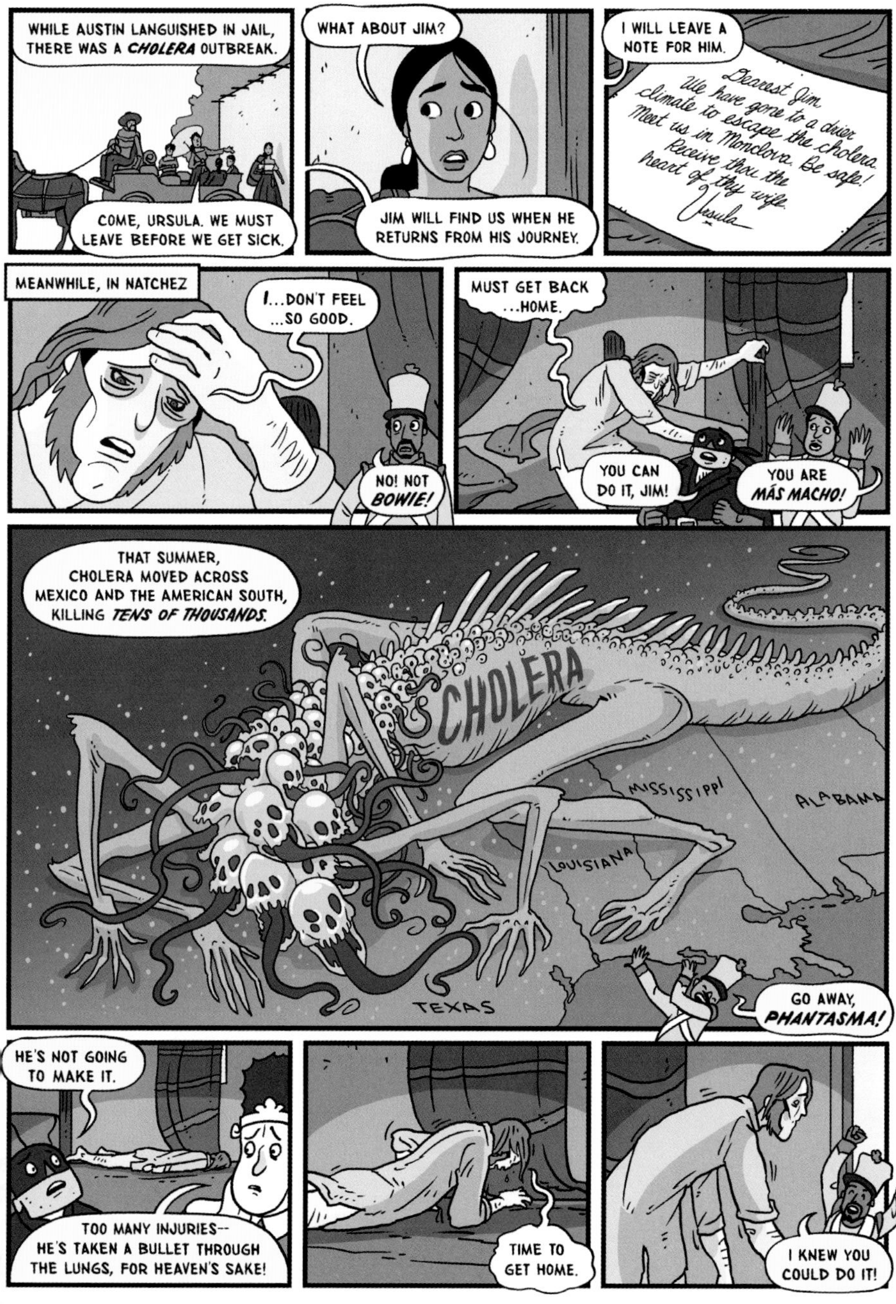
WHILE AUSTIN LANGUISHED IN JAIL, THERE WAS A *CHOLERA* OUTBREAK.
COME, URSULA. WE MUST LEAVE BEFORE WE GET SICK.
WHAT ABOUT JIM?
JIM WILL FIND US WHEN HE RETURNS FROM HIS JOURNEY.
I WILL LEAVE A NOTE FOR HIM.
Dearest Jim
We have gone to a drier climate to escape the cholera.
Meet us in Monclova. Be safe!
Receive thou the heart of thy wife.
Ursula
MEANWHILE, IN NATCHEZ
I...DON'T FEEL ...SO GOOD.
NO! NOT *BOWIE!*
MUST GET BACK ...HOME.
YOU CAN DO IT, JIM!
YOU ARE *MÁS MACHO!*
THAT SUMMER, CHOLERA MOVED ACROSS MEXICO AND THE AMERICAN SOUTH, KILLING *TENS OF THOUSANDS.*
CHOLERA
MISSISSIPPI
ALABAMA
LOUISIANA
TEXAS
GO AWAY, *PHANTASMA!*
HE'S NOT GOING TO MAKE IT.
TOO MANY INJURIES-- HE'S TAKEN A BULLET THROUGH THE LUNGS, FOR HEAVEN'S SAKE!
TIME TO GET HOME.
I KNEW YOU COULD DO IT!

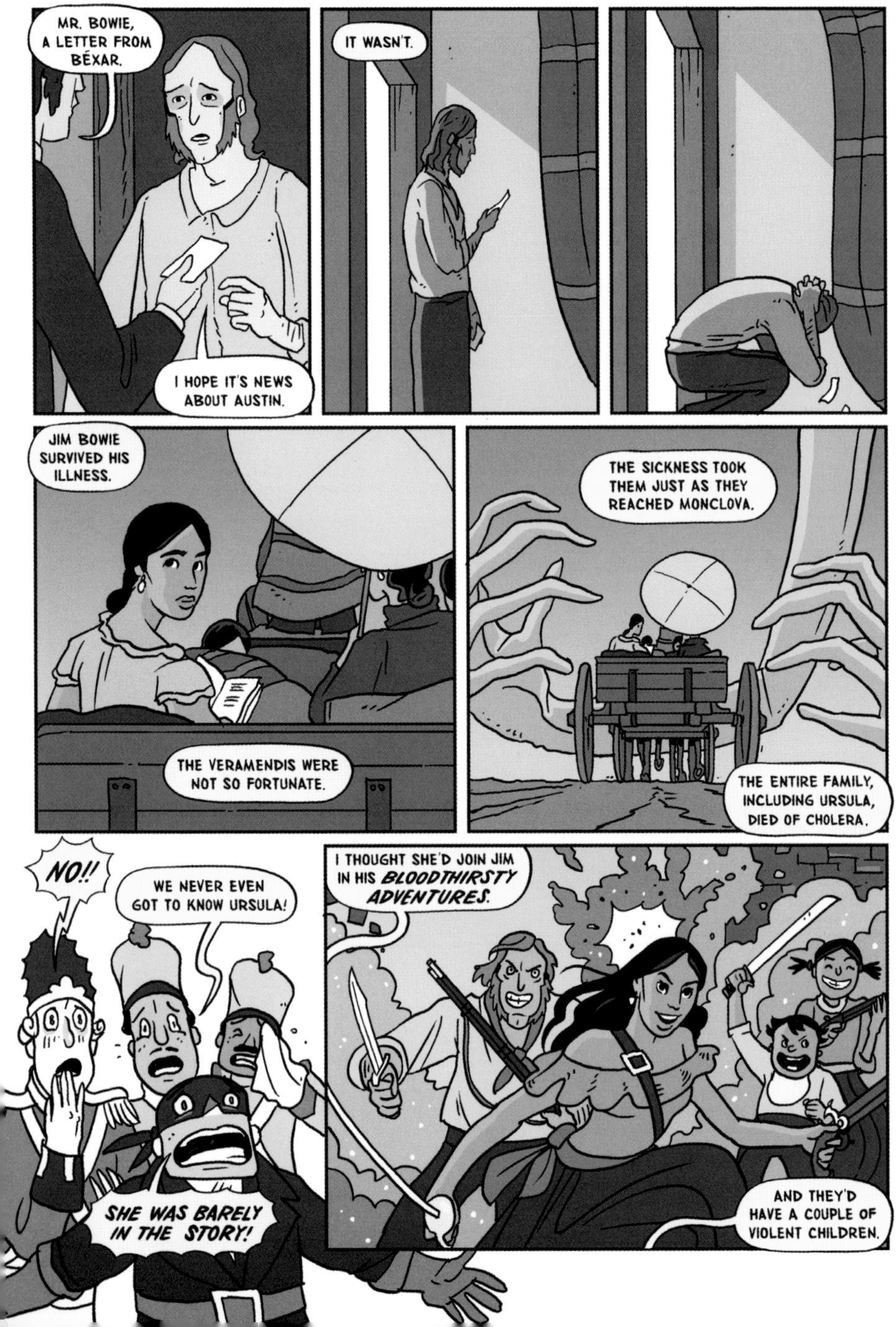
MR. BOWIE, A LETTER FROM BÉXAR.
I HOPE IT'S NEWS ABOUT AUSTIN.
IT WASN'T.
JIM BOWIE SURVIVED HIS ILLNESS.
THE VERAMENDIS WERE NOT SO FORTUNATE.
THE SICKNESS TOOK THEM JUST AS THEY REACHED MONCLOVA.
THE ENTIRE FAMILY, INCLUDING URSULA, DIED OF CHOLERA.
NO!!
WE NEVER EVEN GOT TO KNOW URSULA!
SHE WAS BARELY IN THE STORY!
I THOUGHT SHE'D JOIN JIM IN HIS BLOODTHIRSTY ADVENTURES.
AND THEY'D HAVE A COUPLE OF VIOLENT CHILDREN.

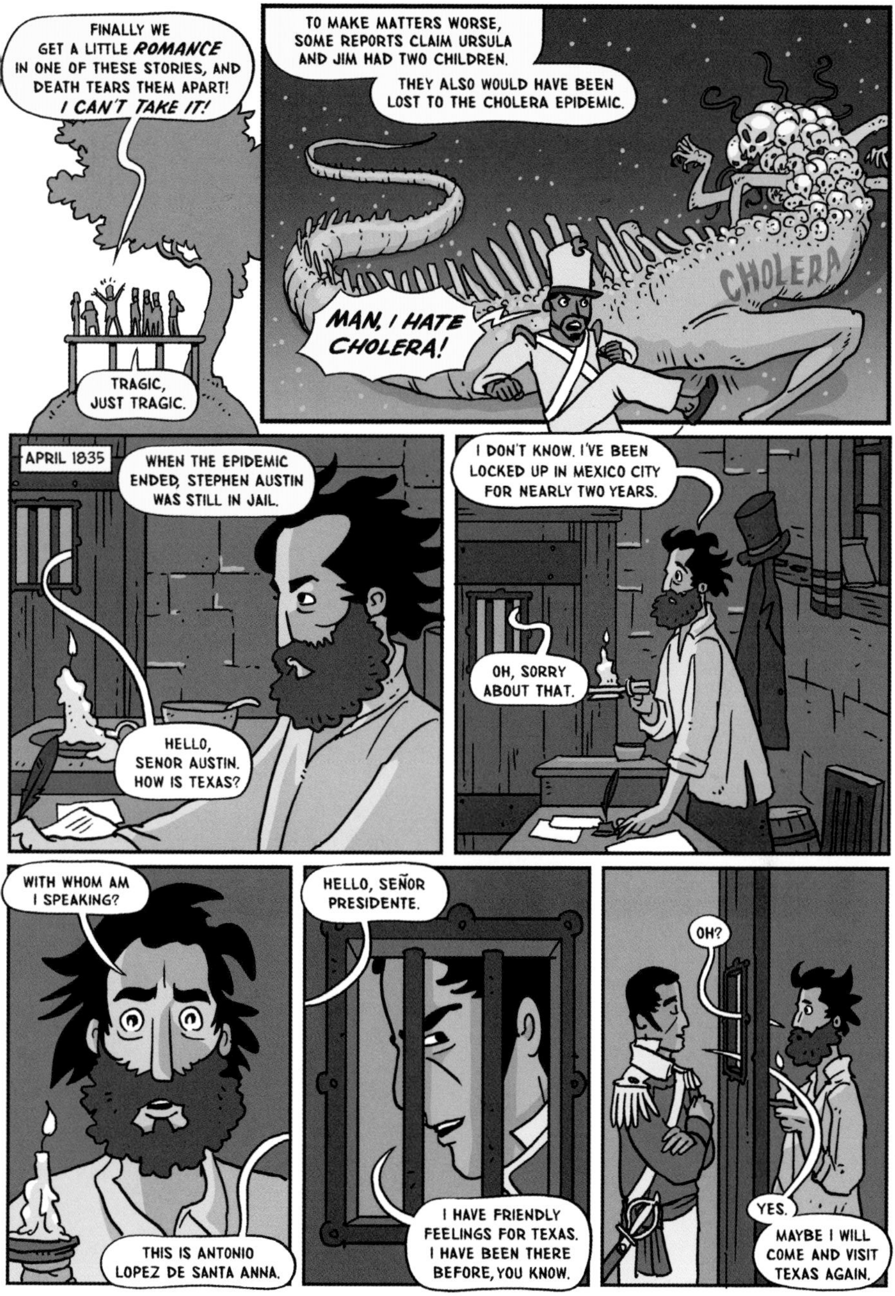
FINALLY WE GET A LITTLE ROMANCE IN ONE OF THESE STORIES, AND DEATH TEARS THEM APART! I CAN'T TAKE IT!
TRAGIC, JUST TRAGIC.
TO MAKE MATTERS WORSE, SOME REPORTS CLAIM URSULA AND JIM HAD TWO CHILDREN.
THEY ALSO WOULD HAVE BEEN LOST TO THE CHOLERA EPIDEMIC.
CHOLERA
MAN, I HATE CHOLERA!
APRIL 1835
WHEN THE EPIDEMIC ENDED, STEPHEN AUSTIN WAS STILL IN JAIL.
HELLO, SENOR AUSTIN. HOW IS TEXAS?
I DON'T KNOW. I'VE BEEN LOCKED UP IN MEXICO CITY FOR NEARLY TWO YEARS.
OH, SORRY ABOUT THAT.
WITH WHOM AM I SPEAKING?
THIS IS ANTONIO LOPEZ DE SANTA ANNA.
HELLO, SEÑOR PRESIDENTE.
I HAVE FRIENDLY FEELINGS FOR TEXAS. I HAVE BEEN THERE BEFORE, YOU KNOW.
OH?
YES.
MAYBE I WILL COME AND VISIT TEXAS AGAIN.

CHAPTER 8

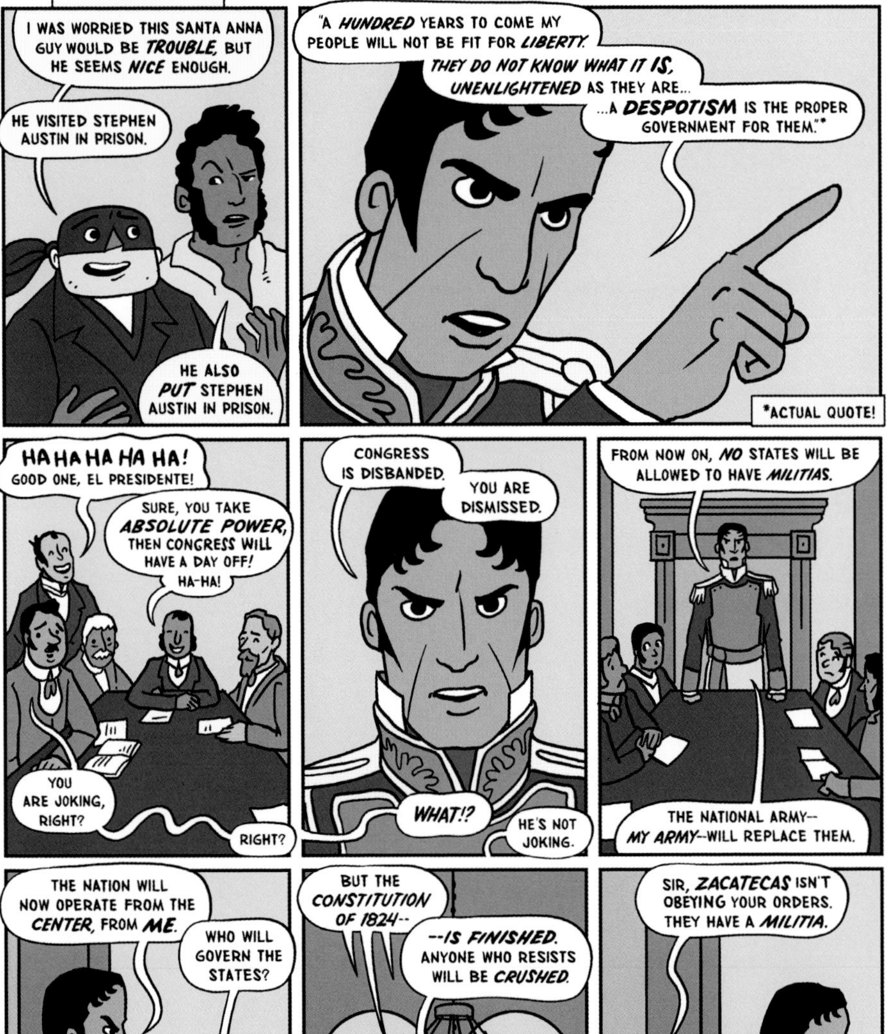
I WAS WORRIED THIS SANTA ANNA GUY WOULD BE TROUBLE, BUT HE SEEMS NICE ENOUGH.
HE VISITED STEPHEN AUSTIN IN PRISON.
HE ALSO PUT STEPHEN AUSTIN IN PRISON.
"A HUNDRED YEARS TO COME MY PEOPLE WILL NOT BE FIT FOR LIBERTY.
THEY DO NOT KNOW WHAT IT IS, UNENLIGHTENED AS THEY ARE...
...A DESPOTISM IS THE PROPER GOVERNMENT FOR THEM."*
*ACTUAL QUOTE!
HA HA HA HA HA HA! GOOD ONE, EL PRESIDENTE!
SURE, YOU TAKE ABSOLUTE POWER, THEN CONGRESS WILL HAVE A DAY OFF! HA-HA!
YOU ARE JOKING, RIGHT?
RIGHT?
CONGRESS IS DISBANDED.
YOU ARE DISMISSED.
WHAT!?
HE'S NOT JOKING.
FROM NOW ON, NO STATES WILL BE ALLOWED TO HAVE MILITIAS.
THE NATIONAL ARMY-- MY ARMY--WILL REPLACE THEM.
THE NATION WILL NOW OPERATE FROM THE CENTER, FROM ME.
WHO WILL GOVERN THE STATES?
I WILL.
BUT THE CONSTITUTION OF 1824--
--IS FINISHED. ANYONE WHO RESISTS WILL BE CRUSHED.
SIR, ZACATECAS ISN'T OBEYING YOUR ORDERS. THEY HAVE A MILITIA.
GET MY HORSE-- MY WAR HORSE.

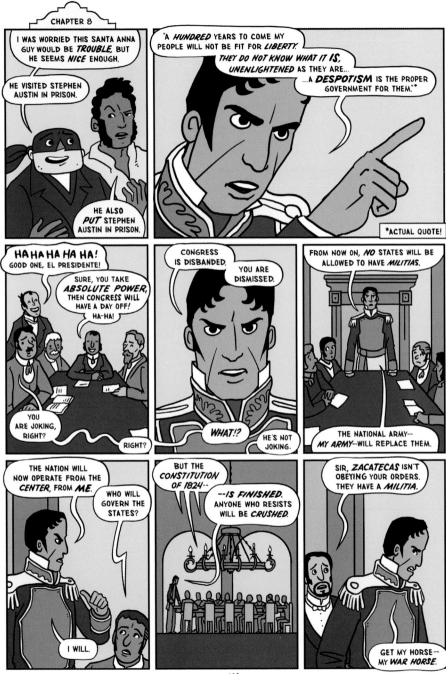

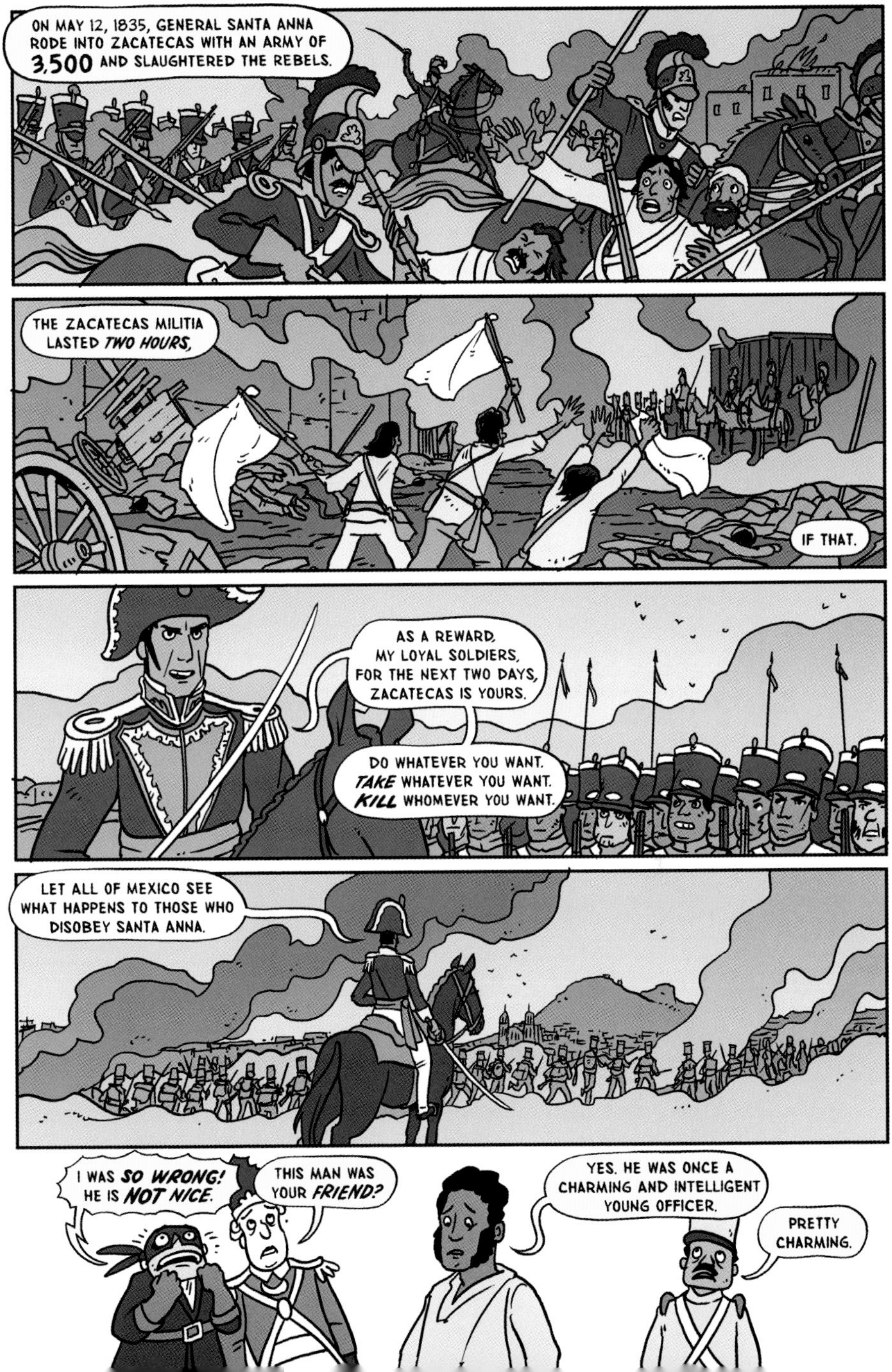
ON MAY 12, 1835, GENERAL SANTA ANNA RODE INTO ZACATECAS WITH AN ARMY OF 3,500 AND SLAUGHTERED THE REBELS.
THE ZACATECAS MILITIA LASTED *TWO HOURS,*
IF THAT.
AS A REWARD, MY LOYAL SOLDIERS, FOR THE NEXT TWO DAYS, ZACATECAS IS YOURS.
DO WHATEVER YOU WANT. *TAKE* WHATEVER YOU WANT. *KILL* WHOMEVER YOU WANT.
LET ALL OF MEXICO SEE WHAT HAPPENS TO THOSE WHO DISOBEY SANTA ANNA.
I WAS *SO WRONG!* HE IS *NOT NICE.*
THIS MAN WAS YOUR *FRIEND?*
YES. HE WAS ONCE A CHARMING AND INTELLIGENT YOUNG OFFICER.
PRETTY CHARMING.

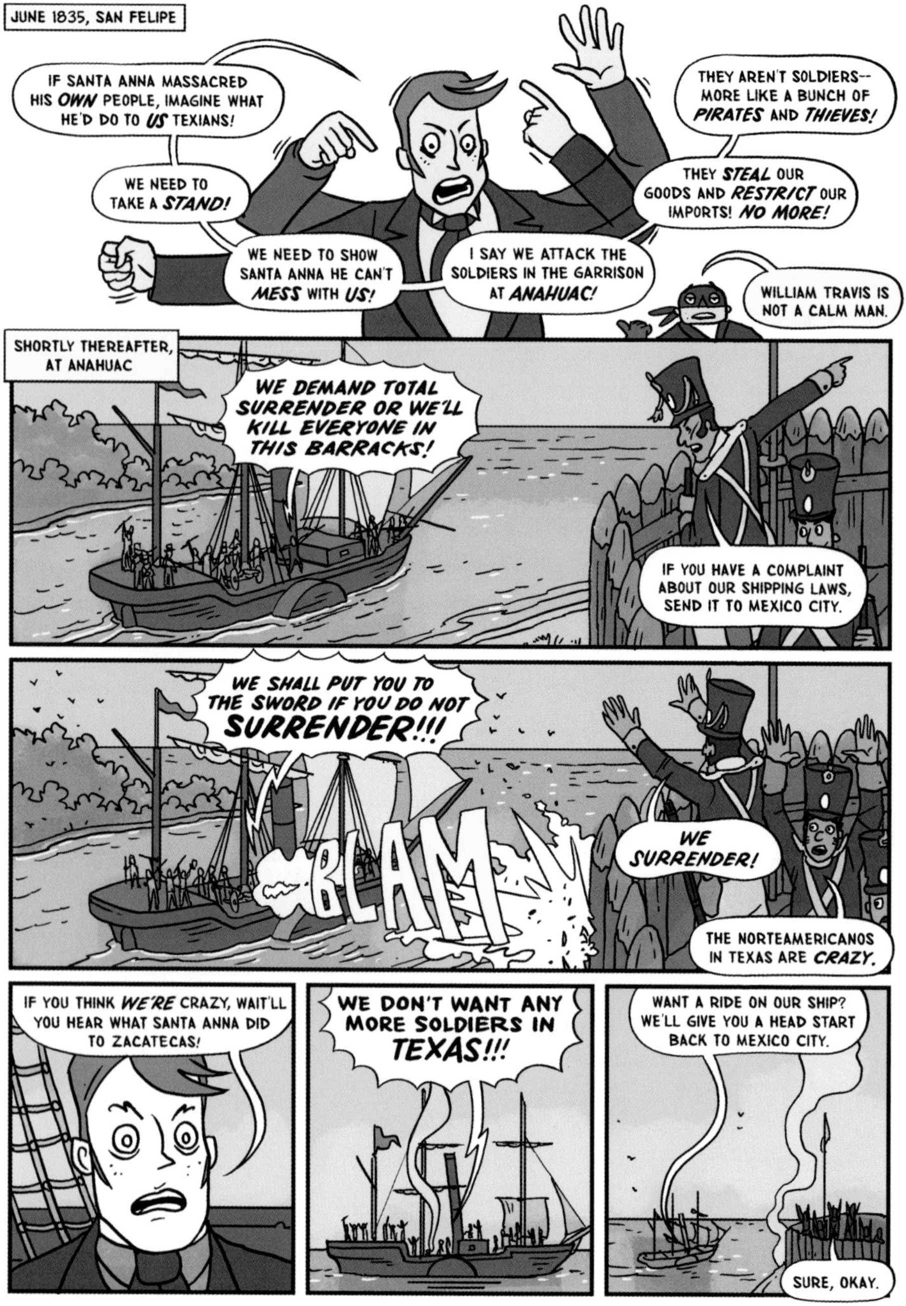
JUNE 1835, SAN FELIPE
IF SANTA ANNA MASSACRED HIS OWN PEOPLE, IMAGINE WHAT HE'D DO TO US TEXIANS!
WE NEED TO TAKE A STAND!
WE NEED TO SHOW SANTA ANNA HE CAN'T MESS WITH US!
I SAY WE ATTACK THE SOLDIERS IN THE GARRISON AT ANAHUAC!
THEY AREN'T SOLDIERS-- MORE LIKE A BUNCH OF PIRATES AND THIEVES!
THEY STEAL OUR GOODS AND RESTRICT OUR IMPORTS! NO MORE!
WILLIAM TRAVIS IS NOT A CALM MAN.
SHORTLY THEREAFTER, AT ANAHUAC
WE DEMAND TOTAL SURRENDER OR WE'LL KILL EVERYONE IN THIS BARRACKS!
IF YOU HAVE A COMPLAINT ABOUT OUR SHIPPING LAWS, SEND IT TO MEXICO CITY.
WE SHALL PUT YOU TO THE SWORD IF YOU DO NOT SURRENDER!!!
BLAM
WE SURRENDER!
THE NORTEAMERICANOS IN TEXAS ARE CRAZY.
IF YOU THINK WE'RE CRAZY, WAIT'LL YOU HEAR WHAT SANTA ANNA DID TO ZACATECAS!
WE DON'T WANT ANY MORE SOLDIERS IN TEXAS!!!
WANT A RIDE ON OUR SHIP? WE'LL GIVE YOU A HEAD START BACK TO MEXICO CITY.
SURE, OKAY.

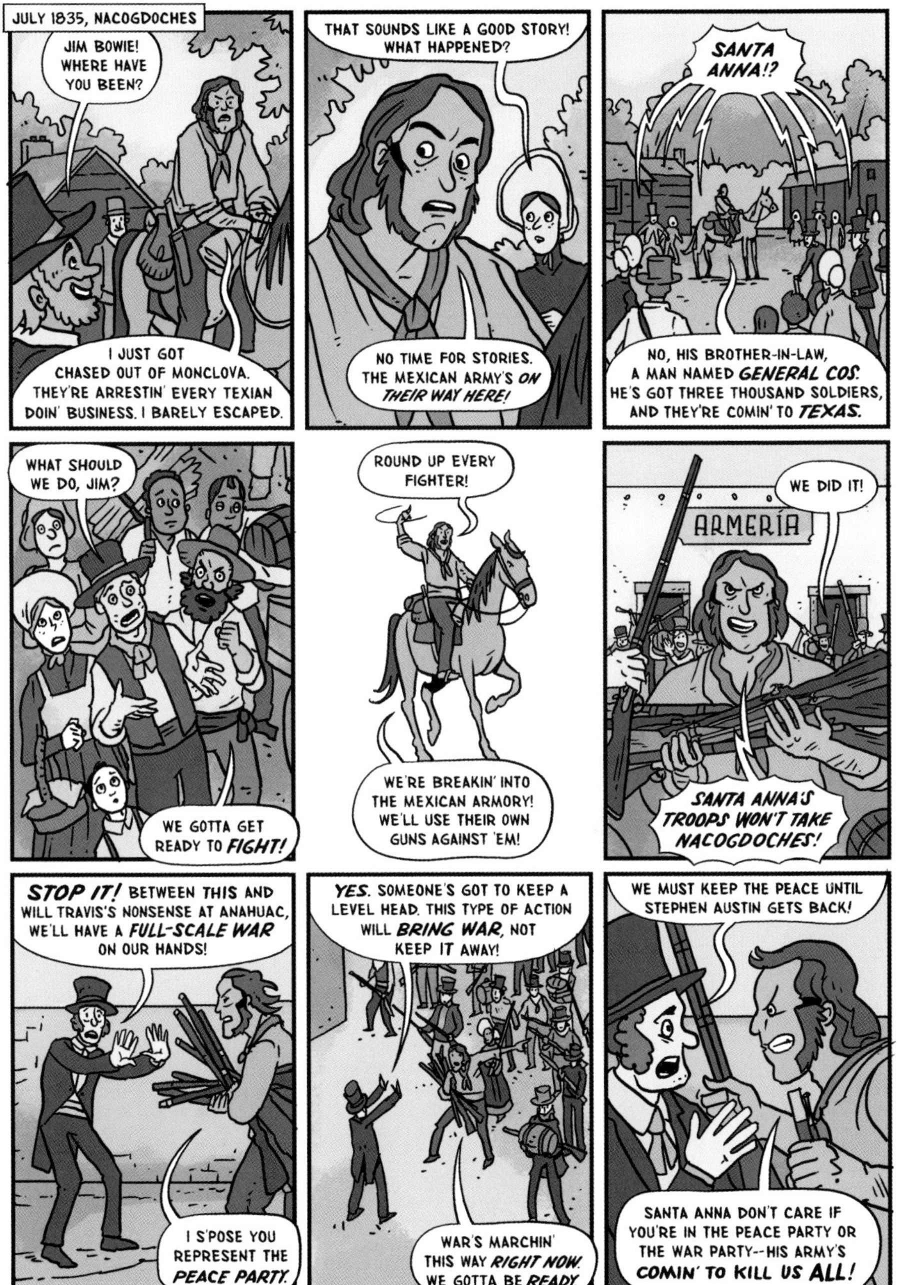
JULY 1835, NACOGDOCHES
JIM BOWIE! WHERE HAVE YOU BEEN?
I JUST GOT CHASED OUT OF MONCLOVA. THEY'RE ARRESTIN' EVERY TEXIAN DOIN' BUSINESS. I BARELY ESCAPED.
THAT SOUNDS LIKE A GOOD STORY! WHAT HAPPENED?
NO TIME FOR STORIES. THE MEXICAN ARMY'S ON THEIR WAY HERE!
SANTA ANNA!?
NO, HIS BROTHER-IN-LAW, A MAN NAMED GENERAL COS. HE'S GOT THREE THOUSAND SOLDIERS, AND THEY'RE COMIN' TO TEXAS.
WHAT SHOULD WE DO, JIM?
WE GOTTA GET READY TO FIGHT!
ROUND UP EVERY FIGHTER!
WE'RE BREAKIN' INTO THE MEXICAN ARMORY! WE'LL USE THEIR OWN GUNS AGAINST 'EM!
ARMERIA
WE DID IT!
SANTA ANNA'S TROOPS WON'T TAKE NACOGDOCHES!
STOP IT! BETWEEN THIS AND WILL TRAVIS'S NONSENSE AT ANAHUAC, WE'LL HAVE A FULL-SCALE WAR ON OUR HANDS!
I S'POSE YOU REPRESENT THE PEACE PARTY.
YES. SOMEONE'S GOT TO KEEP A LEVEL HEAD. THIS TYPE OF ACTION WILL BRING WAR, NOT KEEP IT AWAY!
WAR'S MARCHIN' THIS WAY RIGHT NOW. WE GOTTA BE READY.
WE MUST KEEP THE PEACE UNTIL STEPHEN AUSTIN GETS BACK!
SANTA ANNA DON'T CARE IF YOU'RE IN THE PEACE PARTY OR THE WAR PARTY--HIS ARMY'S COMIN' TO KILL US ALL!

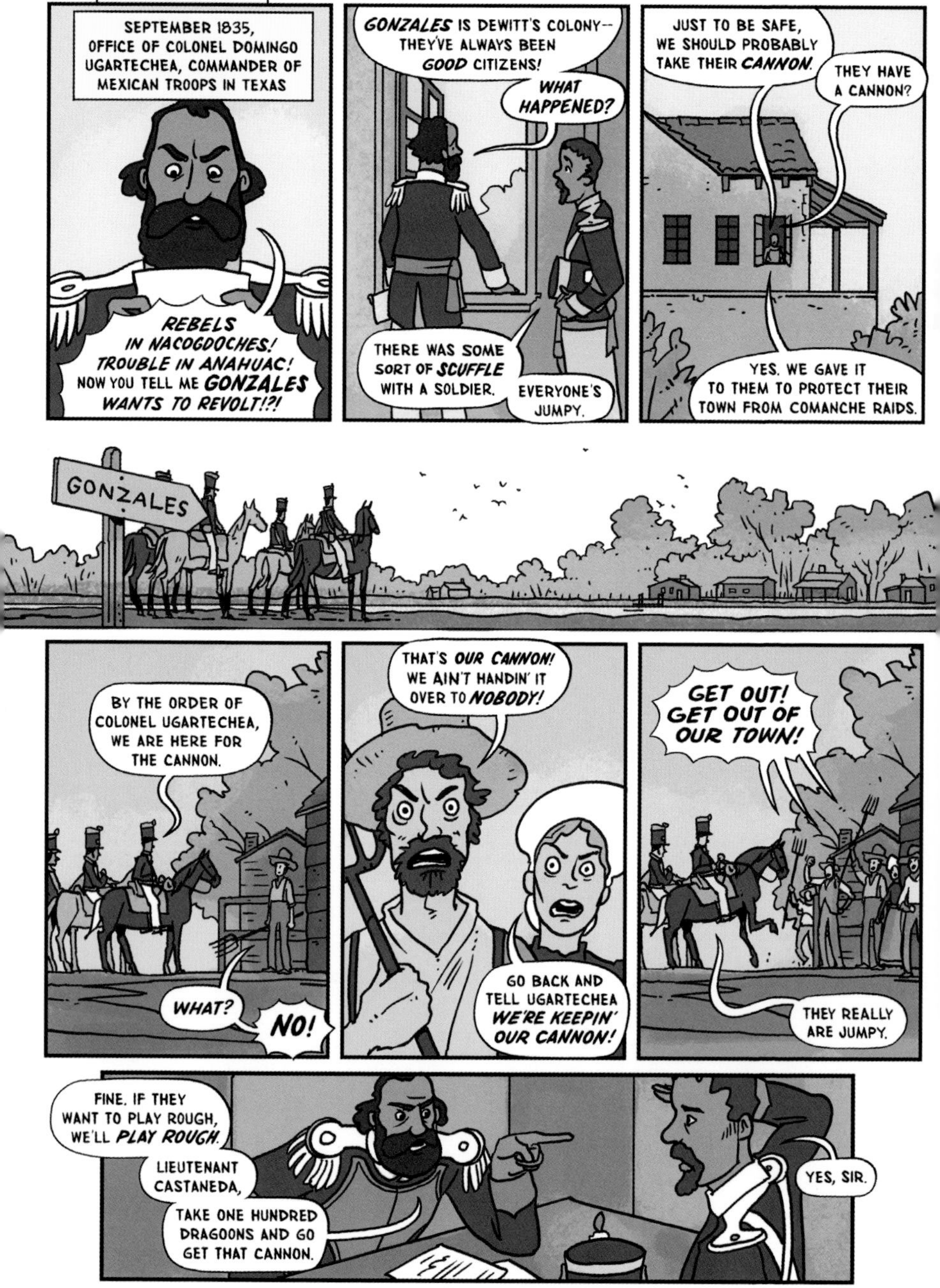

SEPTEMBER 1835, OFFICE OF COLONEL DOMINGO UGARTECHEA, COMMANDER OF MEXICAN TROOPS IN TEXAS
REBELS IN NACOGDOCHES! TROUBLE IN ANAHUAC! NOW YOU TELL ME GONZALES WANTS TO REVOLT!?!
GONZALES IS DEWITT'S COLONY-- THEY'VE ALWAYS BEEN GOOD CITIZENS!
WHAT HAPPENED?
THERE WAS SOME SORT OF SCUFFLE WITH A SOLDIER.
EVERYONE'S JUMPY.
JUST TO BE SAFE, WE SHOULD PROBABLY TAKE THEIR CANNON.
THEY HAVE A CANNON?
YES. WE GAVE IT TO THEM TO PROTECT THEIR TOWN FROM COMANCHE RAIDS.
GONZALES
BY THE ORDER OF COLONEL UGARTECHEA, WE ARE HERE FOR THE CANNON.
WHAT?
NO!
THAT'S OUR CANNON! WE AIN'T HANDIN' IT OVER TO NOBODY!
GO BACK AND TELL UGARTECHEA WE'RE KEEPIN' OUR CANNON!
GET OUT! GET OUT OF OUR TOWN!
THEY REALLY ARE JUMPY.
FINE. IF THEY WANT TO PLAY ROUGH, WE'LL PLAY ROUGH.
LIEUTENANT CASTANEDA,
TAKE ONE HUNDRED DRAGOONS AND GO GET THAT CANNON.
YES, SIR.

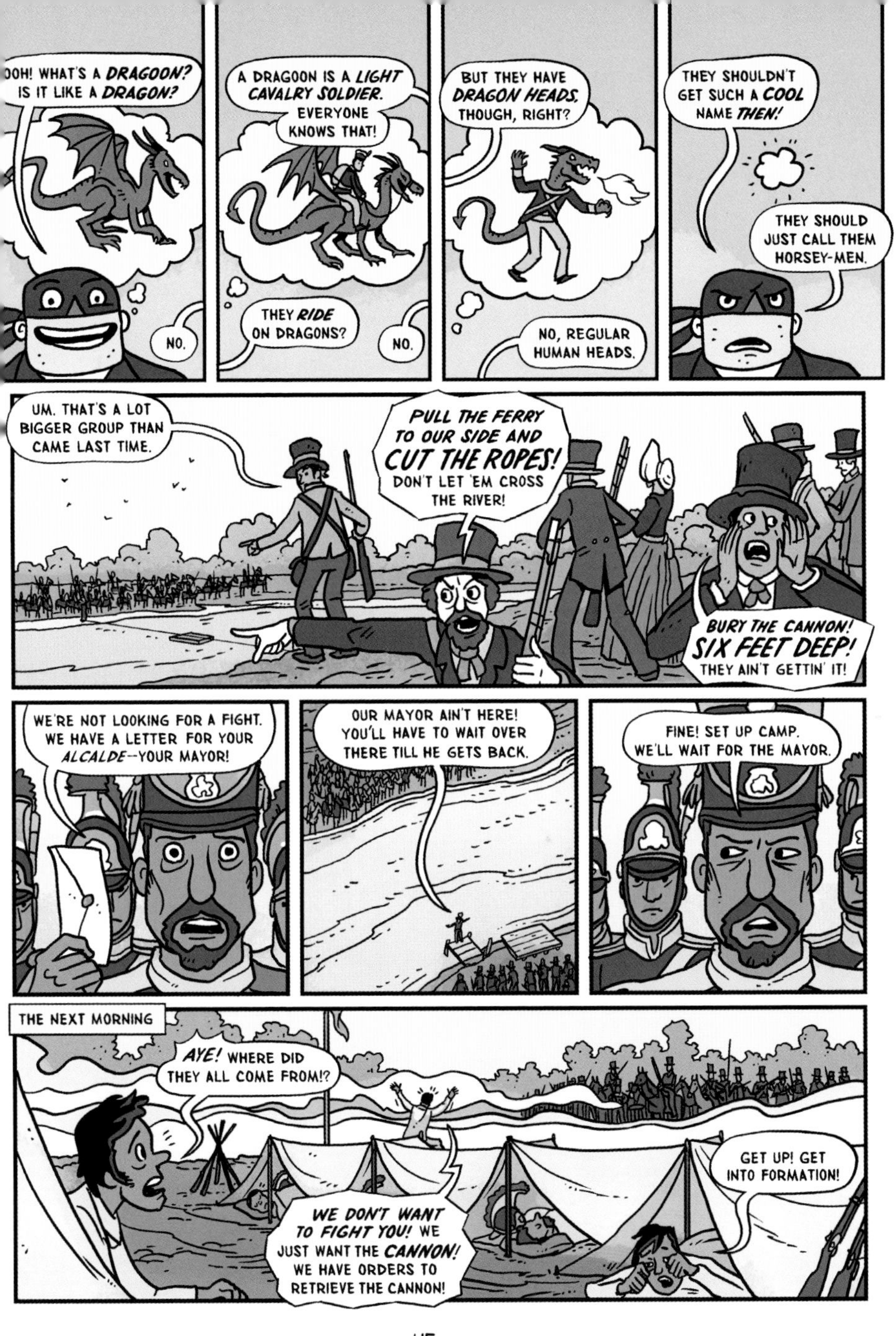
OOH! WHAT'S A DRAGOON? IS IT LIKE A DRAGON?
NO.
A DRAGOON IS A LIGHT CAVALRY SOLDIER.
EVERYONE KNOWS THAT!
THEY RIDE ON DRAGONS?
NO.
BUT THEY HAVE DRAGON HEADS, THOUGH, RIGHT?
NO, REGULAR HUMAN HEADS.
THEY SHOULDN'T GET SUCH A COOL NAME THEN!
THEY SHOULD JUST CALL THEM HORSEY-MEN.
UM. THAT'S A LOT BIGGER GROUP THAN CAME LAST TIME.
PULL THE FERRY TO OUR SIDE AND CUT THE ROPES!
DON'T LET 'EM CROSS THE RIVER!
BURY THE CANNON! SIX FEET DEEP!
THEY AIN'T GETTIN' IT!
WE'RE NOT LOOKING FOR A FIGHT. WE HAVE A LETTER FOR YOUR ALCALDE--YOUR MAYOR!
OUR MAYOR AIN'T HERE! YOU'LL HAVE TO WAIT OVER THERE TILL HE GETS BACK.
FINE! SET UP CAMP. WE'LL WAIT FOR THE MAYOR.
THE NEXT MORNING
AYE! WHERE DID THEY ALL COME FROM!?
WE DON'T WANT TO FIGHT YOU! WE JUST WANT THE CANNON! WE HAVE ORDERS TO RETRIEVE THE CANNON!
GET UP! GET INTO FORMATION!

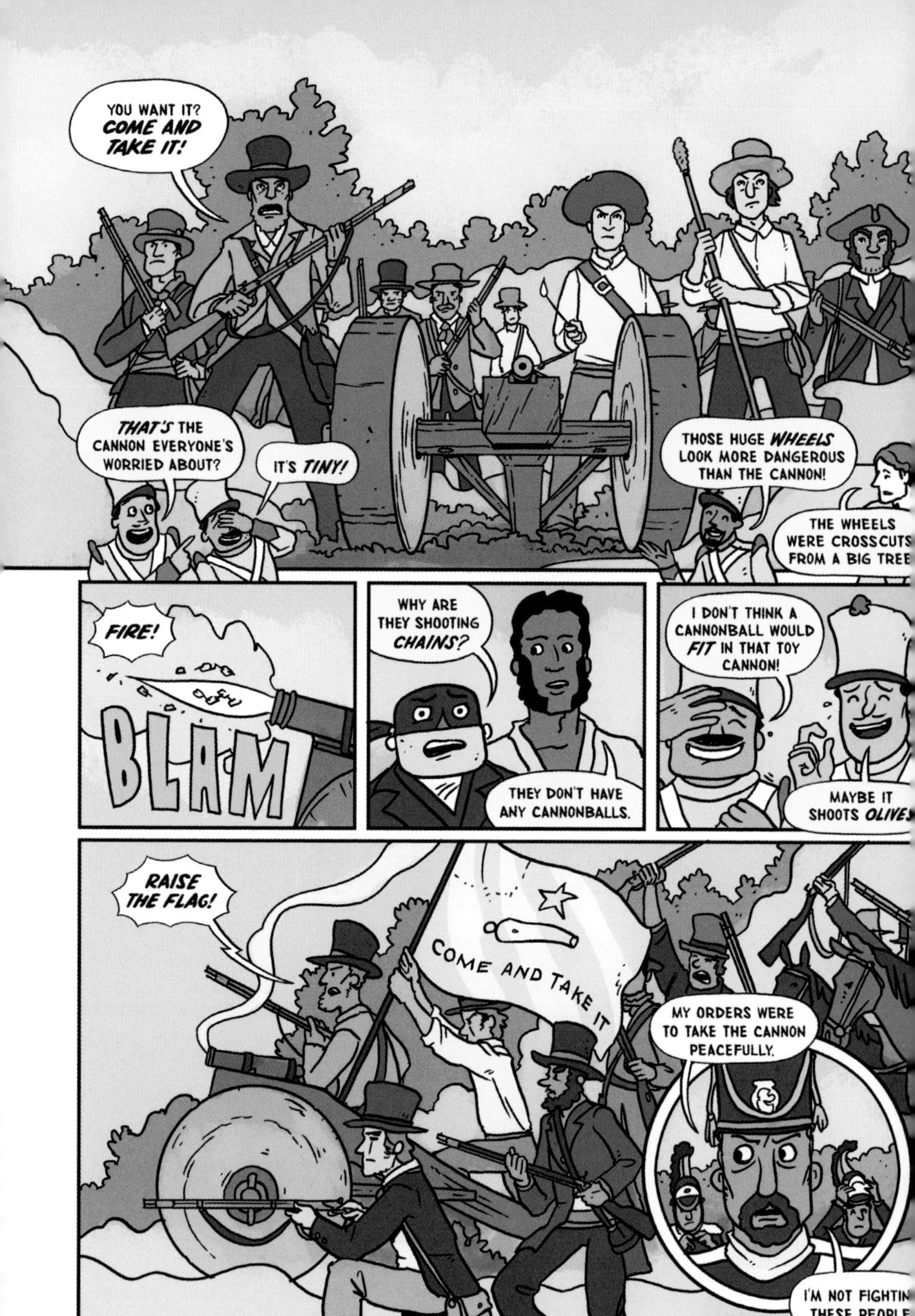
YOU WANT IT? COME AND TAKE IT!
THAT'S THE CANNON EVERYONE'S WORRIED ABOUT?
IT'S TINY!
THOSE HUGE WHEELS LOOK MORE DANGEROUS THAN THE CANNON!
THE WHEELS WERE CROSSCUTS FROM A BIG TREE
FIRE!
BLAM
WHY ARE THEY SHOOTING CHAINS?
THEY DON'T HAVE ANY CANNONBALLS.
I DON'T THINK A CANNONBALL WOULD FIT IN THAT TOY CANNON!
MAYBE IT SHOOTS OLIVES
RAISE THE FLAG!
COME AND TAKE IT
MY ORDERS WERE TO TAKE THE CANNON PEACEFULLY.
I'M NOT FIGHTIN THESE PEOPLE

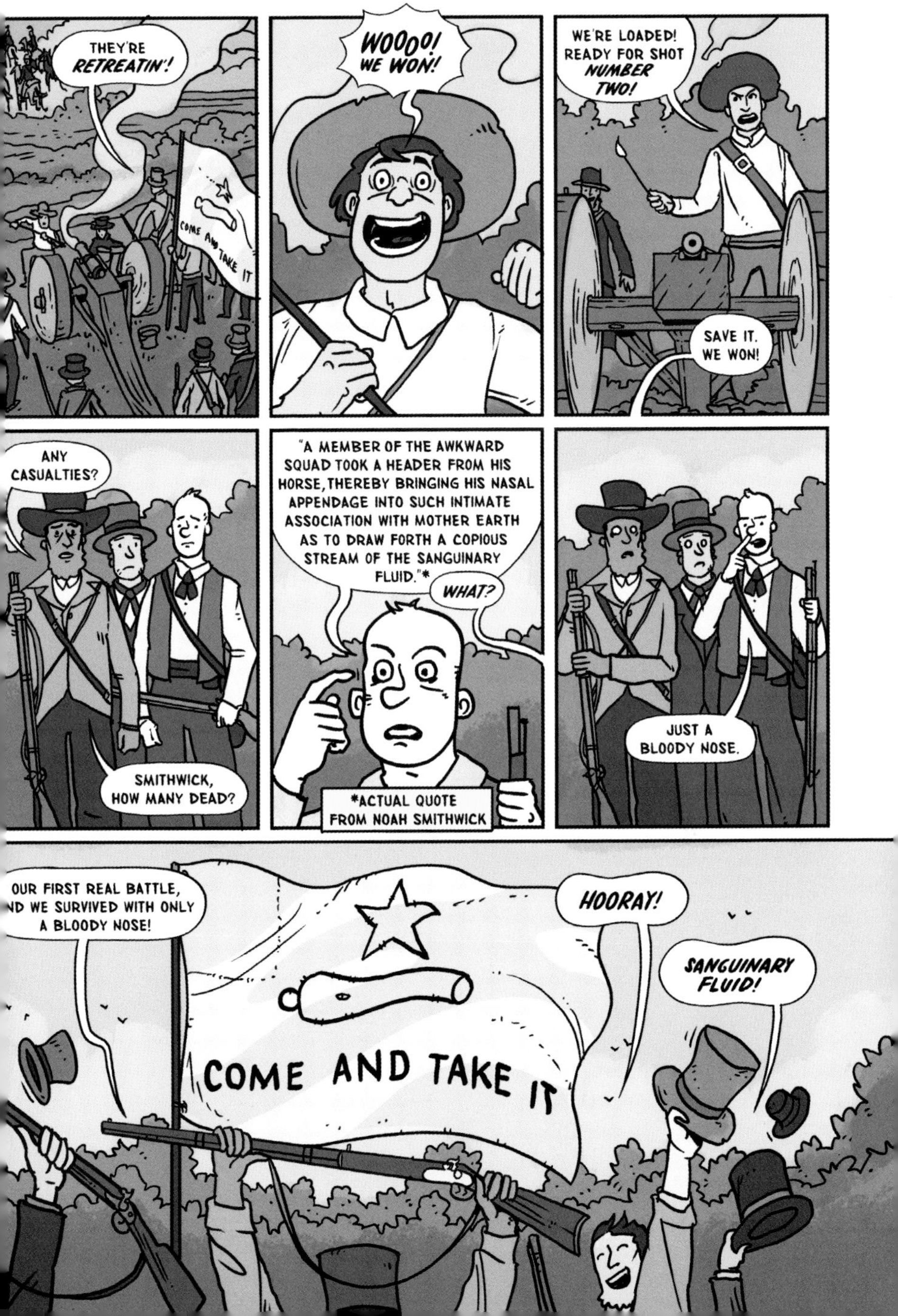
THEY'RE RETREATIN'!
COME AND TAKE IT
WOOOO! WE WON!
WE'RE LOADED! READY FOR SHOT NUMBER TWO!
SAVE IT. WE WON!
ANY CASUALTIES?
SMITHWICK, HOW MANY DEAD?
"A MEMBER OF THE AWKWARD SQUAD TOOK A HEADER FROM HIS HORSE, THEREBY BRINGING HIS NASAL APPENDAGE INTO SUCH INTIMATE ASSOCIATION WITH MOTHER EARTH AS TO DRAW FORTH A COPIOUS STREAM OF THE SANGUINARY FLUID."*
WHAT?
*ACTUAL QUOTE FROM NOAH SMITHWICK
JUST A BLOODY NOSE.
OUR FIRST REAL BATTLE, ND WE SURVIVED WITH ONLY A BLOODY NOSE!
COME AND TAKE IT
HOORAY!
SANGUINARY FLUID!

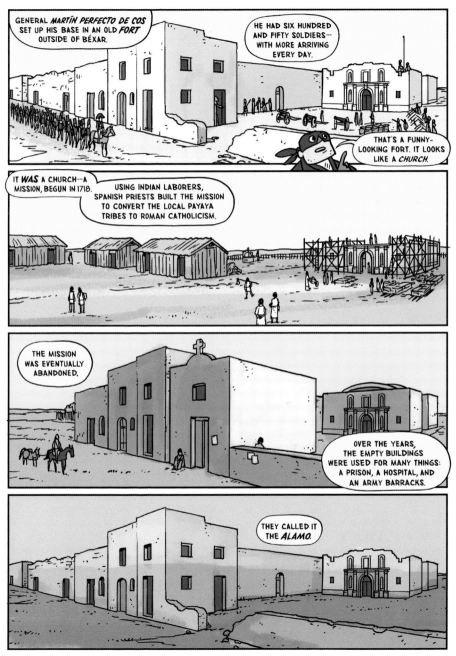

49

50

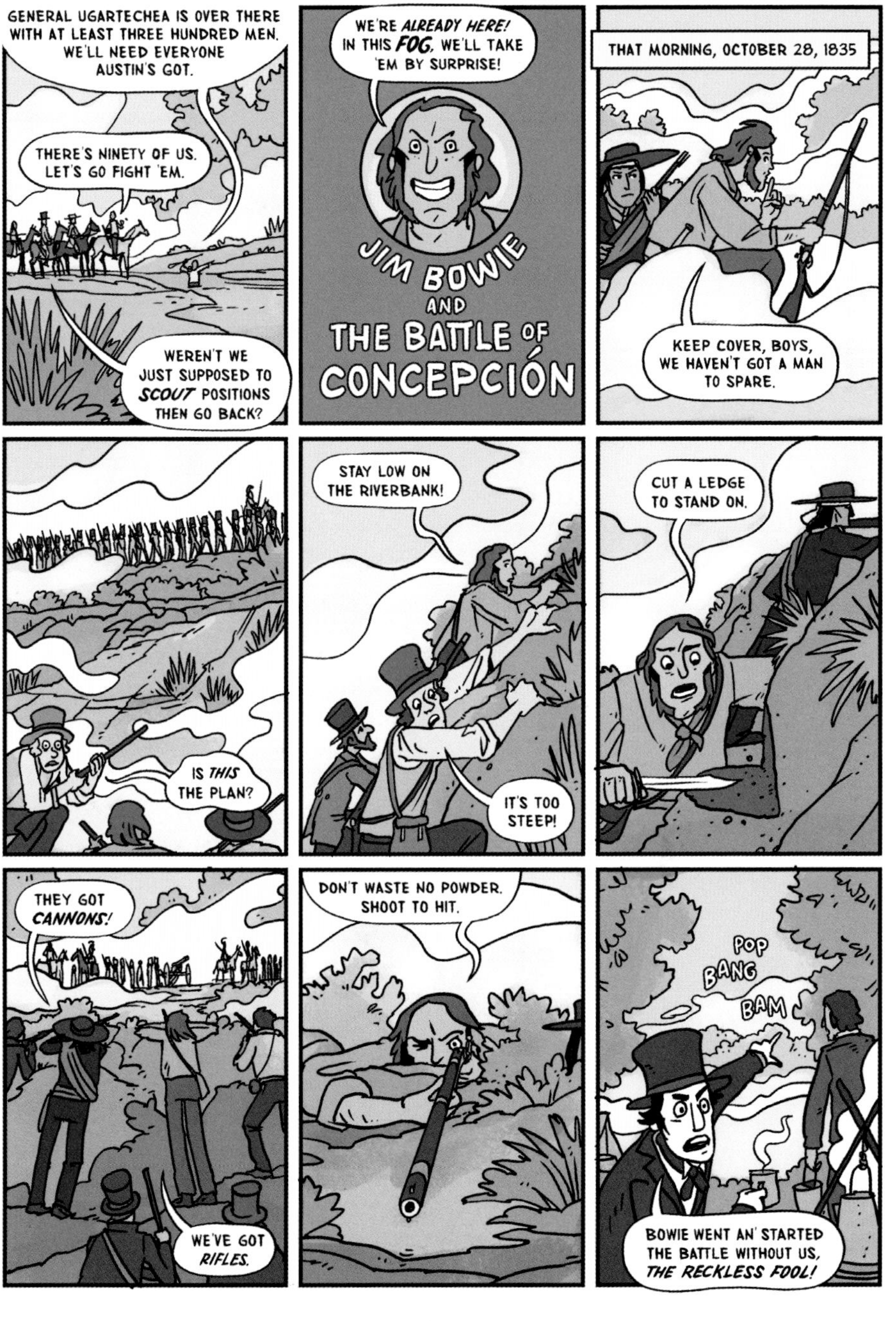

GENERAL UGARTECHEA IS OVER THERE WITH AT LEAST THREE HUNDRED MEN. WE'LL NEED EVERYONE AUSTIN'S GOT.
THERE'S NINETY OF US. LET'S GO FIGHT 'EM.
WEREN'T WE JUST SUPPOSED TO *SCOUT* POSITIONS THEN GO BACK?
WE'RE *ALREADY HERE!* IN THIS *FOG*, WE'LL TAKE 'EM BY SURPRISE!
JIM BOWIE AND THE BATTLE OF CONCEPCIÓN
THAT MORNING, OCTOBER 28, 1835
KEEP COVER, BOYS, WE HAVEN'T GOT A MAN TO SPARE.
IS *THIS* THE PLAN?
STAY LOW ON THE RIVERBANK!
IT'S TOO STEEP!
CUT A LEDGE TO STAND ON.
THEY GOT *CANNONS!*
WE'VE GOT *RIFLES.*
DON'T WASTE NO POWDER. SHOOT TO HIT.
POP
BANG
BAM
BOWIE WENT AN' STARTED THE BATTLE WITHOUT US, *THE RECKLESS FOOL!*

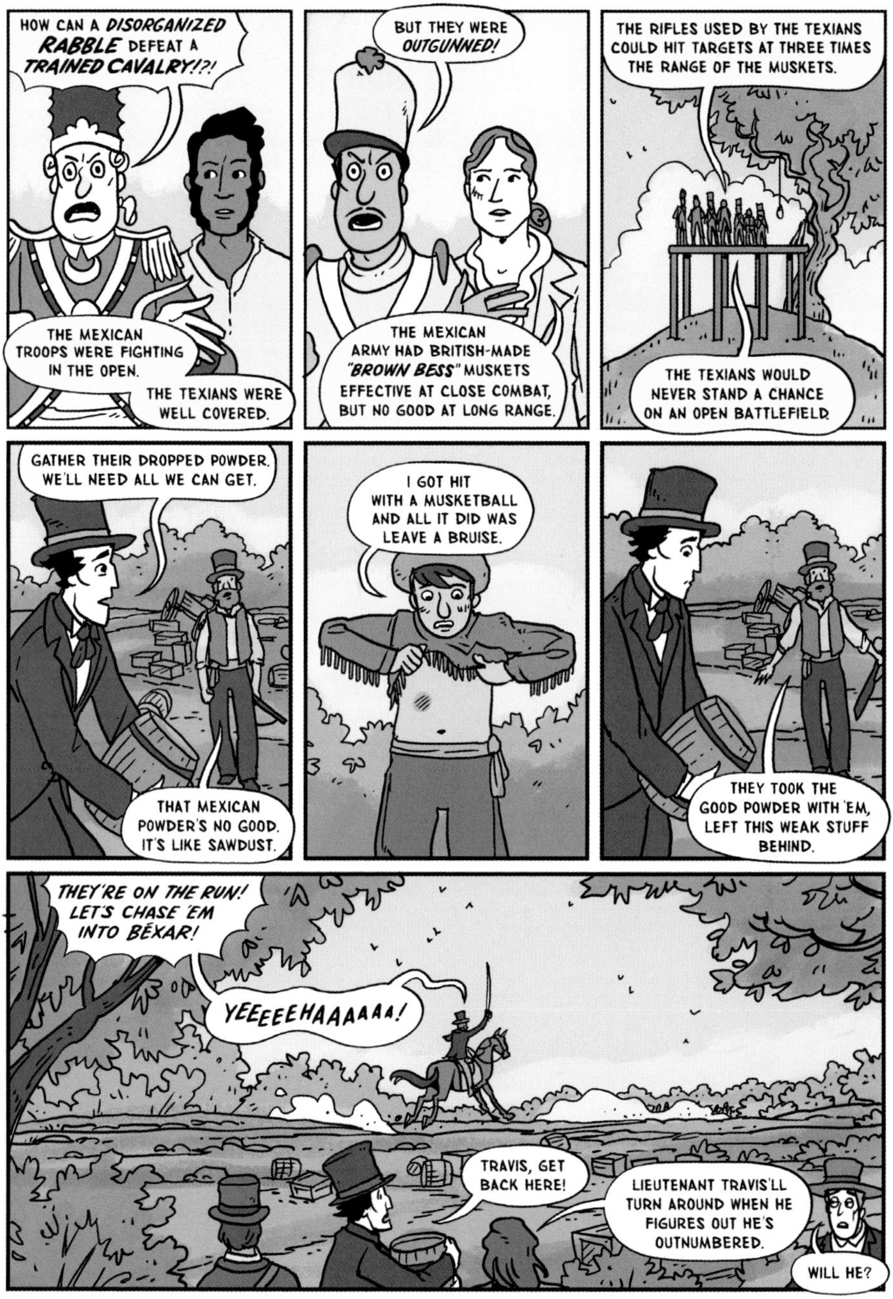
HOW CAN A DISORGANIZED RABBLE DEFEAT A TRAINED CAVALRY!?!
THE MEXICAN TROOPS WERE FIGHTING IN THE OPEN.
THE TEXIANS WERE WELL COVERED.
BUT THEY WERE OUTGUNNED!
THE MEXICAN ARMY HAD BRITISH-MADE "BROWN BESS" MUSKETS EFFECTIVE AT CLOSE COMBAT, BUT NO GOOD AT LONG RANGE.
THE RIFLES USED BY THE TEXIANS COULD HIT TARGETS AT THREE TIMES THE RANGE OF THE MUSKETS.
THE TEXIANS WOULD NEVER STAND A CHANCE ON AN OPEN BATTLEFIELD.
GATHER THEIR DROPPED POWDER. WE'LL NEED ALL WE CAN GET.
THAT MEXICAN POWDER'S NO GOOD. IT'S LIKE SAWDUST.
I GOT HIT WITH A MUSKETBALL AND ALL IT DID WAS LEAVE A BRUISE.
THEY TOOK THE GOOD POWDER WITH 'EM, LEFT THIS WEAK STUFF BEHIND.
THEY'RE ON THE RUN! LET'S CHASE 'EM INTO BÉXAR!
YEEEEEHAAAAAA!
TRAVIS, GET BACK HERE!
LIEUTENANT TRAVIS'LL TURN AROUND WHEN HE FIGURES OUT HE'S OUTNUMBERED.
WILL HE?

57

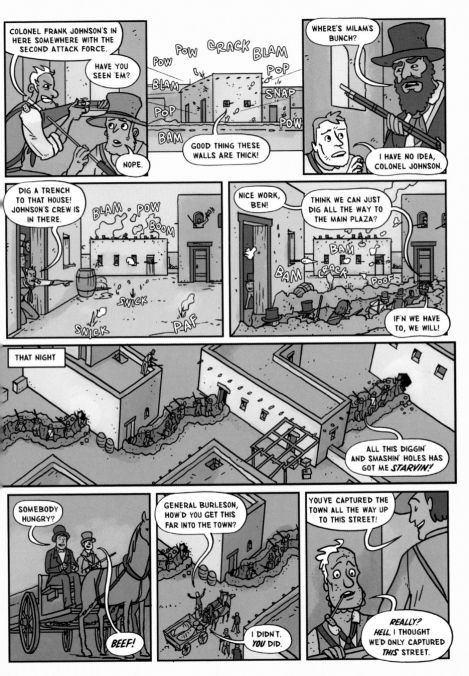

59

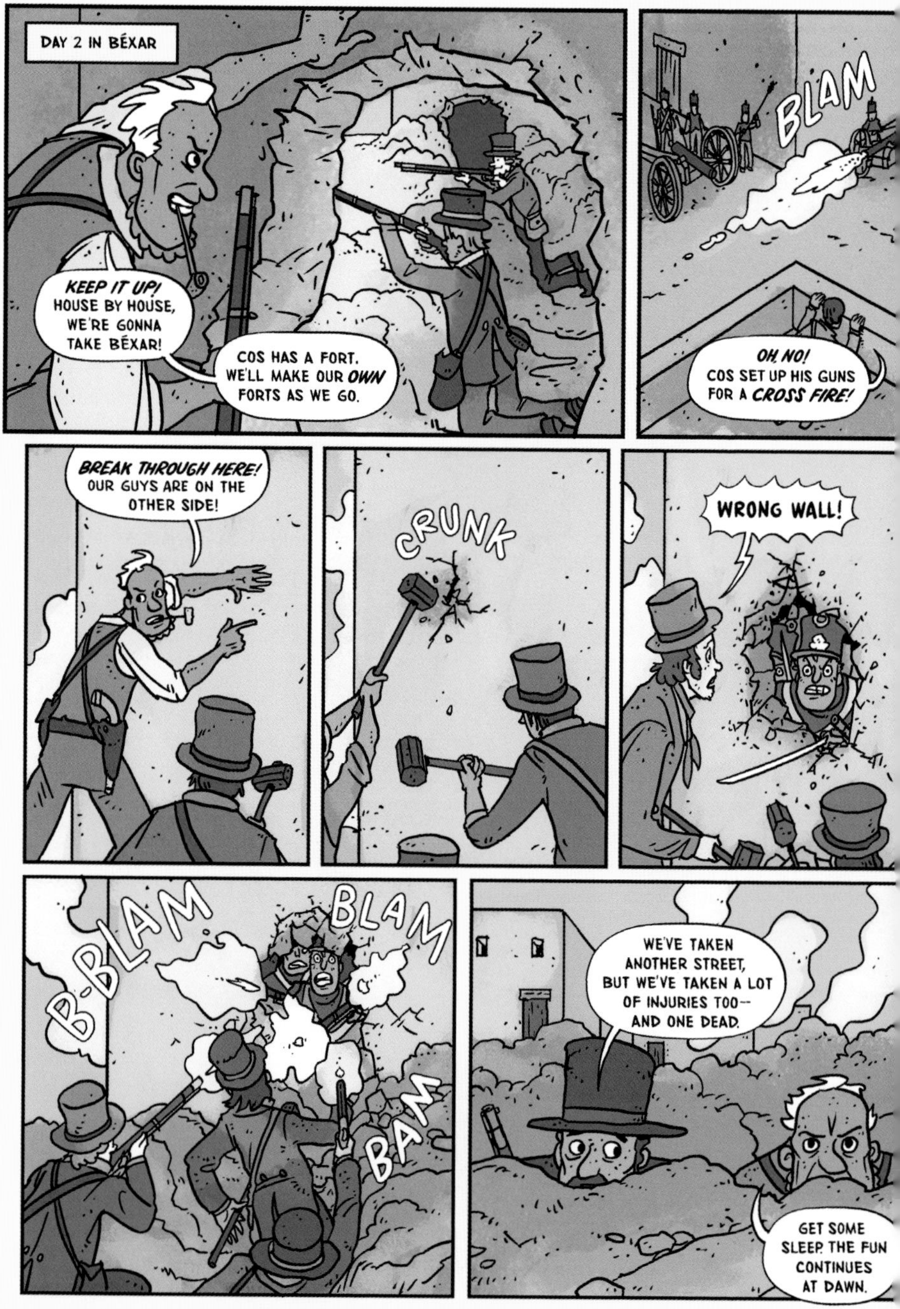
DAY 2 IN BÉXAR
KEEP IT UP! HOUSE BY HOUSE, WE'RE GONNA TAKE BÉXAR!
COS HAS A FORT. WE'LL MAKE OUR OWN FORTS AS WE GO.
BLAM
OH, NO! COS SET UP HIS GUNS FOR A CROSS FIRE!
BREAK THROUGH HERE! OUR GUYS ARE ON THE OTHER SIDE!
CRUNK
WRONG WALL!
B-BLAM
BLAM
BAM
WE'VE TAKEN ANOTHER STREET, BUT WE'VE TAKEN A LOT OF INJURIES TOO-- AND ONE DEAD.
GET SOME SLEEP. THE FUN CONTINUES AT DAWN.

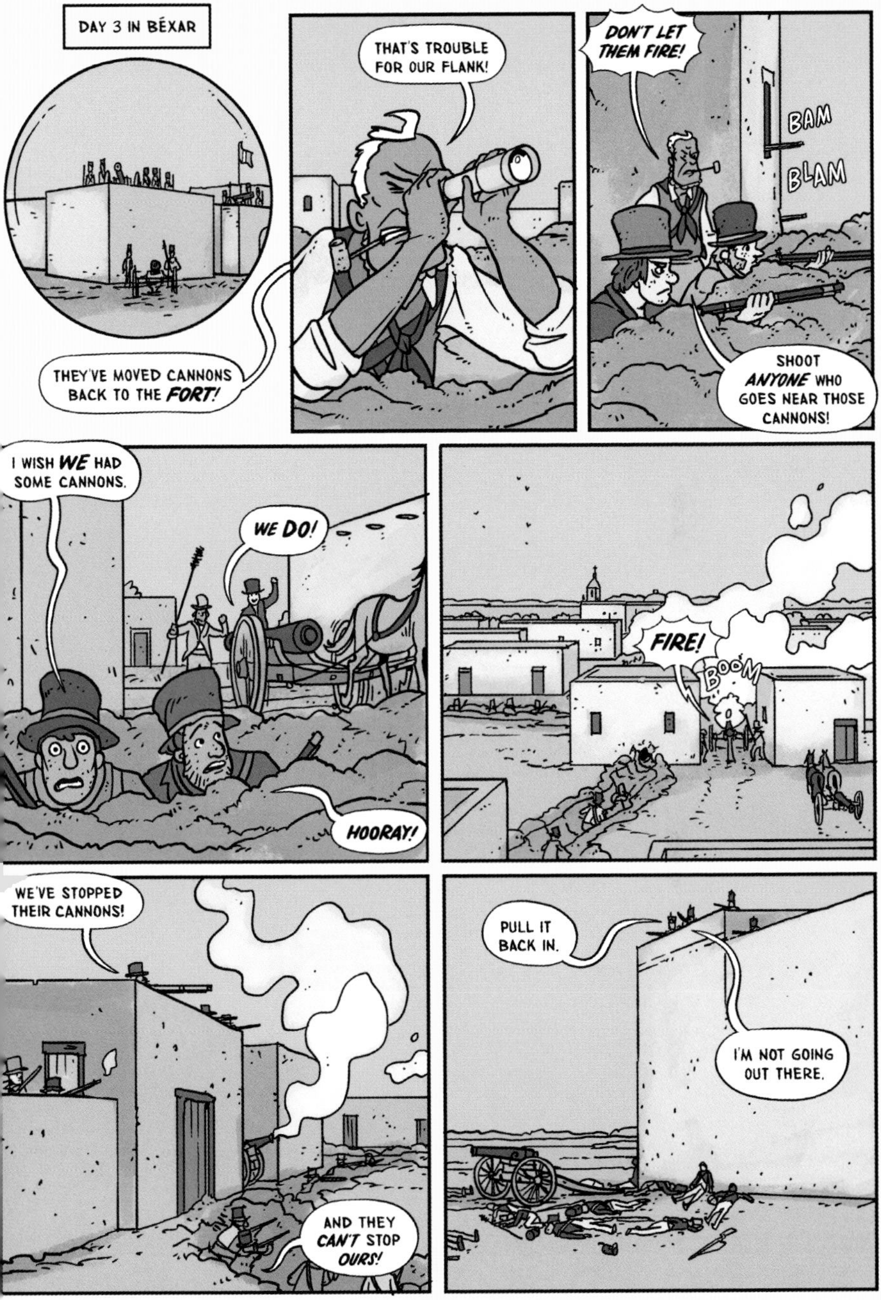
DAY 3 IN BÉXAR
THEY'VE MOVED CANNONS BACK TO THE FORT!
THAT'S TROUBLE FOR OUR FLANK!
DON'T LET THEM FIRE!
BAM
BLAM
SHOOT ANYONE WHO GOES NEAR THOSE CANNONS!
I WISH WE HAD SOME CANNONS.
WE DO!
HOORAY!
FIRE!
BOOM
WE'VE STOPPED THEIR CANNONS!
AND THEY CAN'T STOP OURS!
PULL IT BACK IN.
I'M NOT GOING OUT THERE.

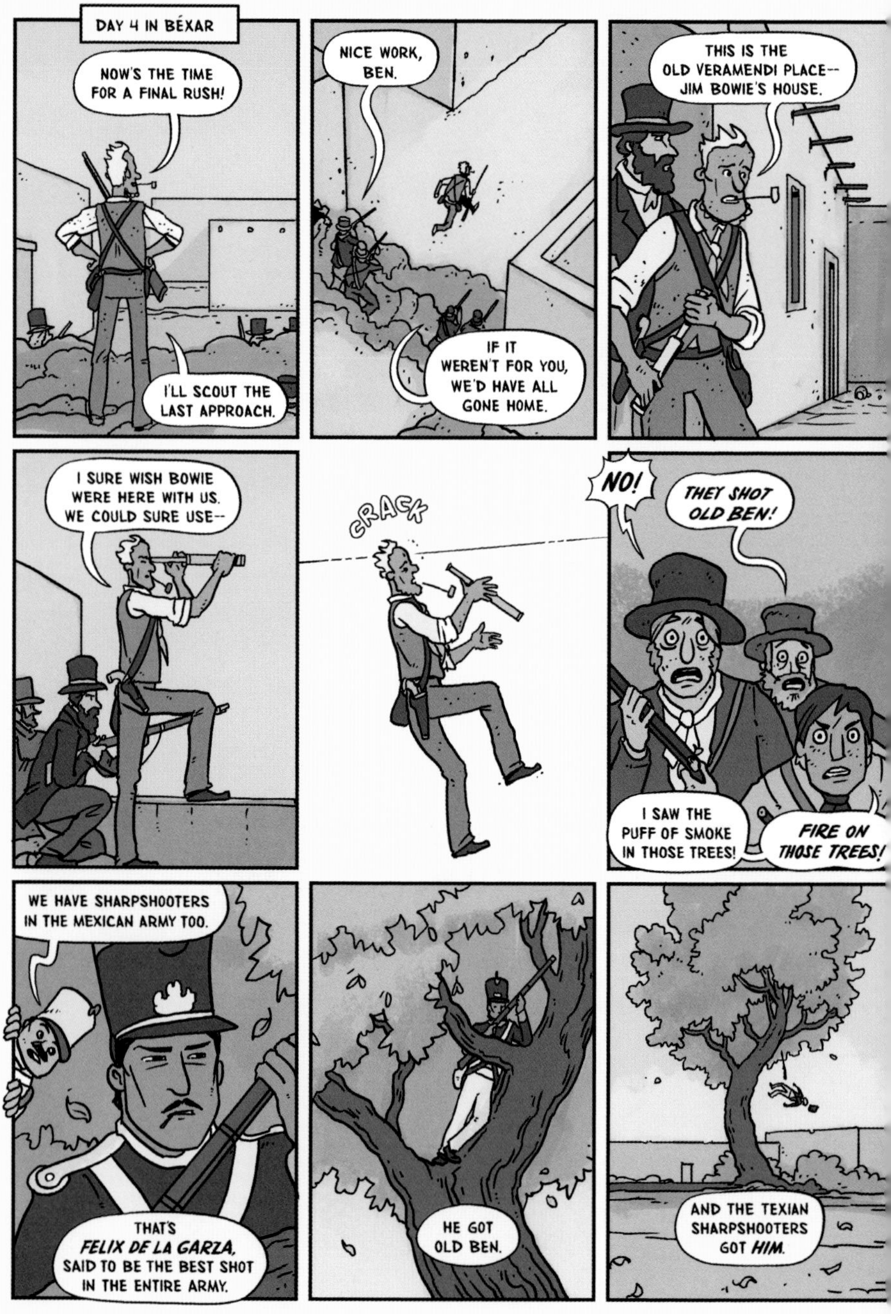
DAY 4 IN BÉXAR
NOW'S THE TIME FOR A FINAL RUSH!
I'LL SCOUT THE LAST APPROACH.
NICE WORK, BEN.
IF IT WEREN'T FOR YOU, WE'D HAVE ALL GONE HOME.
THIS IS THE OLD VERAMENDI PLACE-- JIM BOWIE'S HOUSE.
I SURE WISH BOWIE WERE HERE WITH US. WE COULD SURE USE--
CRACK
NO!
THEY SHOT OLD BEN!
I SAW THE PUFF OF SMOKE IN THOSE TREES!
FIRE ON THOSE TREES!
WE HAVE SHARPSHOOTERS IN THE MEXICAN ARMY TOO.
THAT'S *FELIX DE LA GARZA,* SAID TO BE THE BEST SHOT IN THE ENTIRE ARMY.
HE GOT OLD BEN.
AND THE TEXIAN SHARPSHOOTERS GOT *HIM.*

63

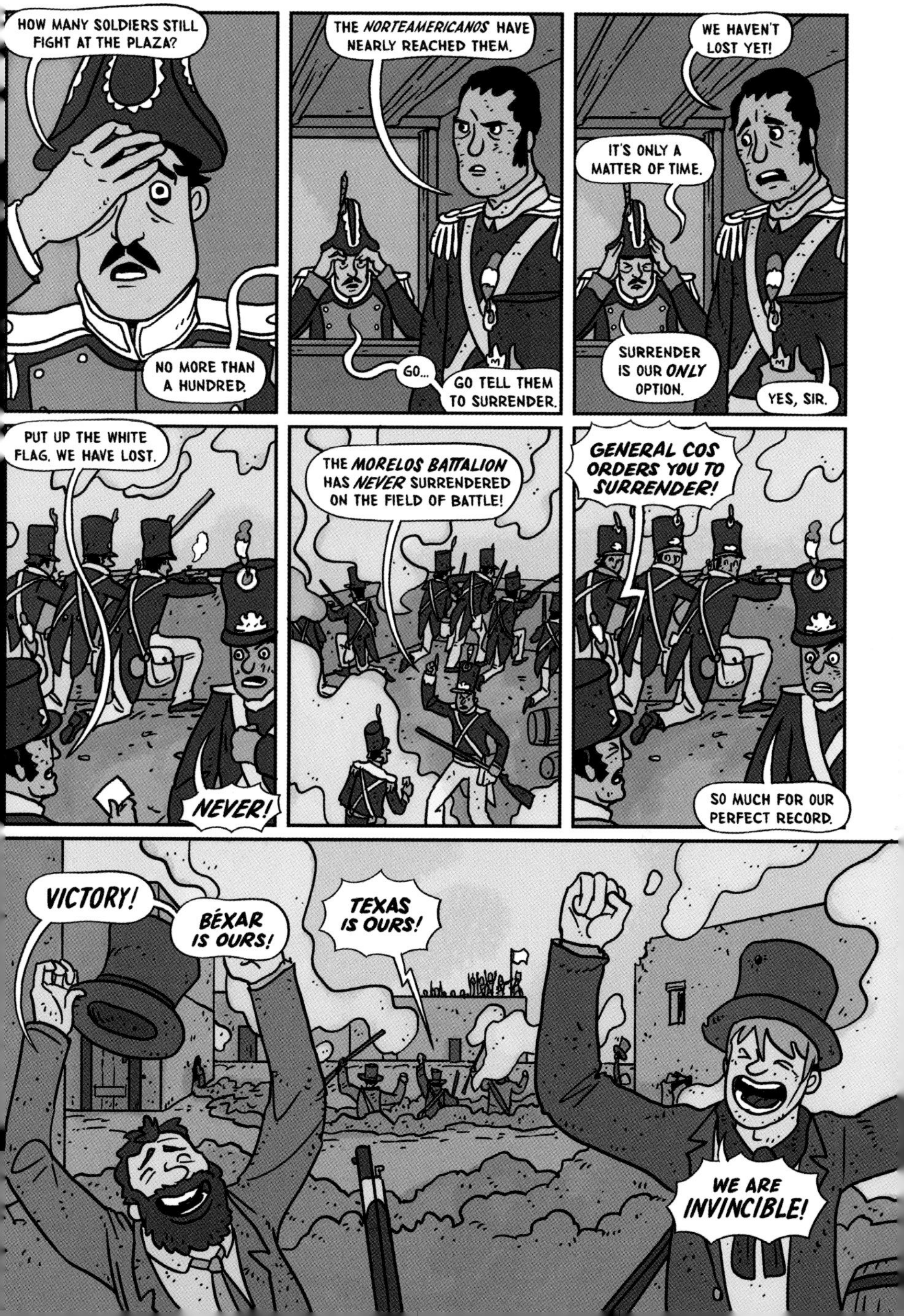
HOW MANY SOLDIERS STILL FIGHT AT THE PLAZA?
NO MORE THAN A HUNDRED.
THE NORTEAMERICANOS HAVE NEARLY REACHED THEM.
GO...
GO TELL THEM TO SURRENDER.
WE HAVEN'T LOST YET!
IT'S ONLY A MATTER OF TIME.
SURRENDER IS OUR ONLY OPTION.
YES, SIR.
PUT UP THE WHITE FLAG. WE HAVE LOST.
NEVER!
THE MORELOS BATTALION HAS NEVER SURRENDERED ON THE FIELD OF BATTLE!
GENERAL COS ORDERS YOU TO SURRENDER!
SO MUCH FOR OUR PERFECT RECORD.
VICTORY!
BÉXAR IS OURS!
TEXAS IS OURS!
WE ARE INVINCIBLE!

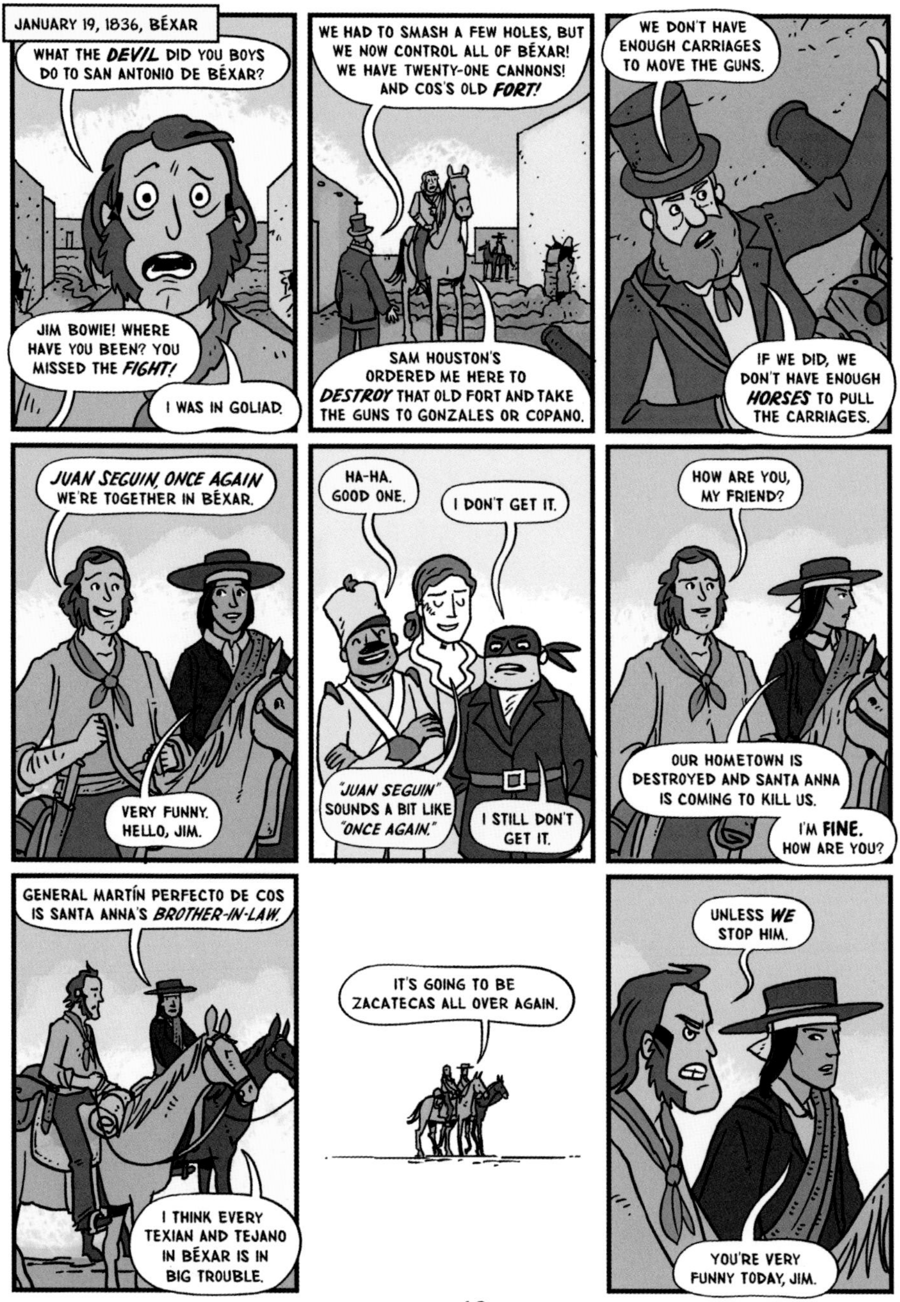

JANUARY 19, 1836, BÉXAR
WHAT THE *DEVIL* DID YOU BOYS DO TO SAN ANTONIO DE BÉXAR?
JIM BOWIE! WHERE HAVE YOU BEEN? YOU MISSED THE *FIGHT!*
I WAS IN GOLIAD.
WE HAD TO SMASH A FEW HOLES, BUT WE NOW CONTROL ALL OF BÉXAR! WE HAVE TWENTY-ONE CANNONS! AND COS'S OLD *FORT!*
SAM HOUSTON'S ORDERED ME HERE TO *DESTROY* THAT OLD FORT AND TAKE THE GUNS TO GONZALES OR COPANO.
WE DON'T HAVE ENOUGH CARRIAGES TO MOVE THE GUNS.
IF WE DID, WE DON'T HAVE ENOUGH *HORSES* TO PULL THE CARRIAGES.
JUAN SEGUIN, ONCE AGAIN WE'RE TOGETHER IN BÉXAR.
VERY FUNNY. HELLO, JIM.
HA-HA. GOOD ONE.
I DON'T GET IT.
"JUAN SEGUIN" SOUNDS A BIT LIKE *"ONCE AGAIN."*
I STILL DON'T GET IT.
HOW ARE YOU, MY FRIEND?
OUR HOMETOWN IS DESTROYED AND SANTA ANNA IS COMING TO KILL US.
I'M **FINE.** HOW ARE YOU?
GENERAL MARTÍN PERFECTO DE COS IS SANTA ANNA'S *BROTHER-IN-LAW.*
I THINK EVERY TEXIAN AND TEJANO IN BÉXAR IS IN BIG TROUBLE.
IT'S GOING TO BE ZACATECAS ALL OVER AGAIN.
UNLESS *WE* STOP HIM.
YOU'RE VERY FUNNY TODAY, JIM.

69

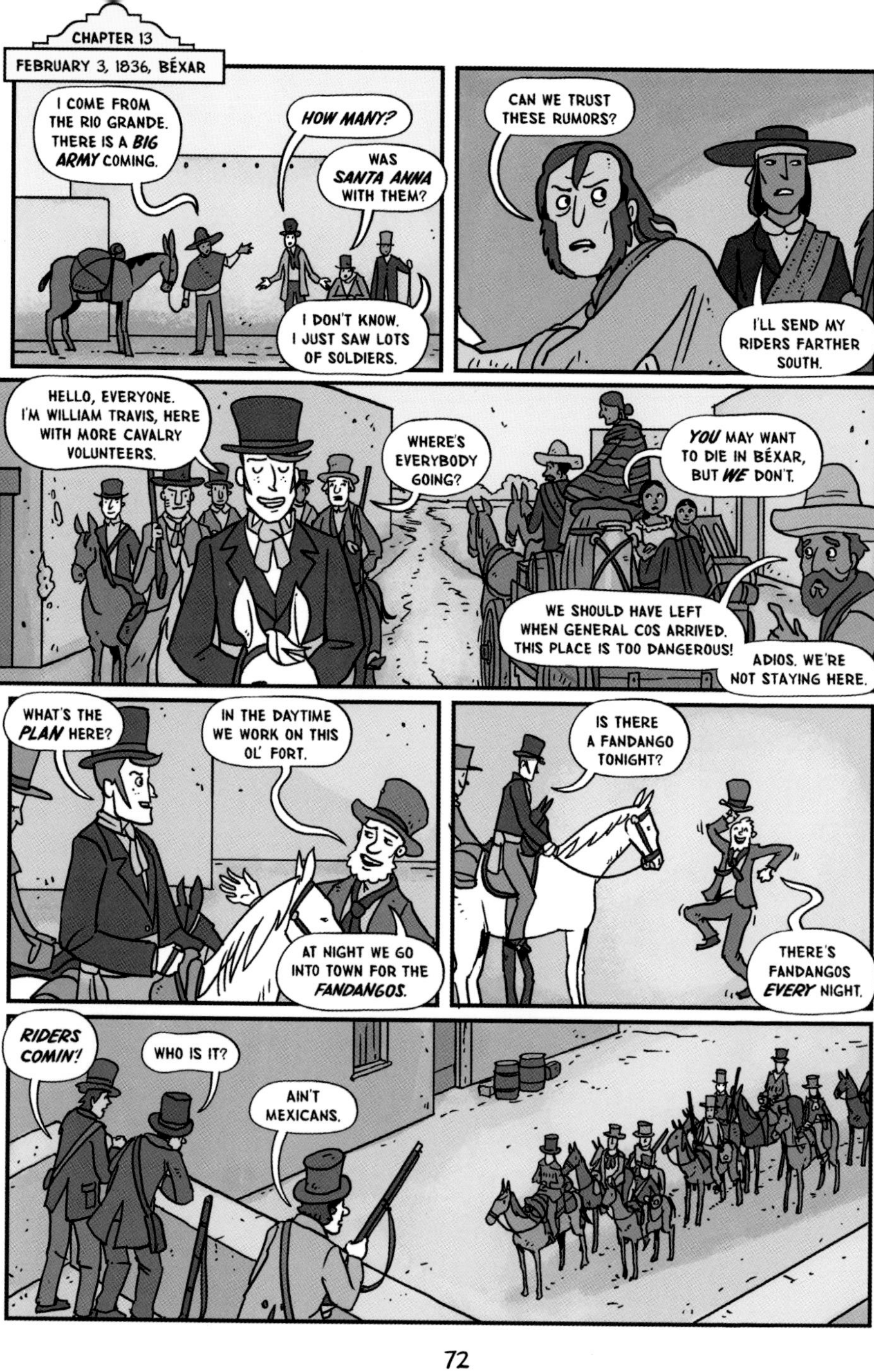
CHAPTER 13
FEBRUARY 3, 1836, BÉXAR
I COME FROM THE RIO GRANDE. THERE IS A *BIG ARMY* COMING.
HOW MANY?
WAS *SANTA ANNA* WITH THEM?
I DON'T KNOW. I JUST SAW LOTS OF SOLDIERS.
CAN WE TRUST THESE RUMORS?
I'LL SEND MY RIDERS FARTHER SOUTH.
HELLO, EVERYONE. I'M WILLIAM TRAVIS, HERE WITH MORE CAVALRY VOLUNTEERS.
WHERE'S EVERYBODY GOING?
YOU MAY WANT TO DIE IN BÉXAR, BUT *WE* DON'T.
WE SHOULD HAVE LEFT WHEN GENERAL COS ARRIVED. THIS PLACE IS TOO DANGEROUS!
ADIOS. WE'RE NOT STAYING HERE.
WHAT'S THE *PLAN* HERE?
IN THE DAYTIME WE WORK ON THIS OL' FORT.
AT NIGHT WE GO INTO TOWN FOR THE *FANDANGOS.*
IS THERE A FANDANGO TONIGHT?
THERE'S FANDANGOS *EVERY* NIGHT.
RIDERS COMIN'!
WHO IS IT?
AIN'T MEXICANS.

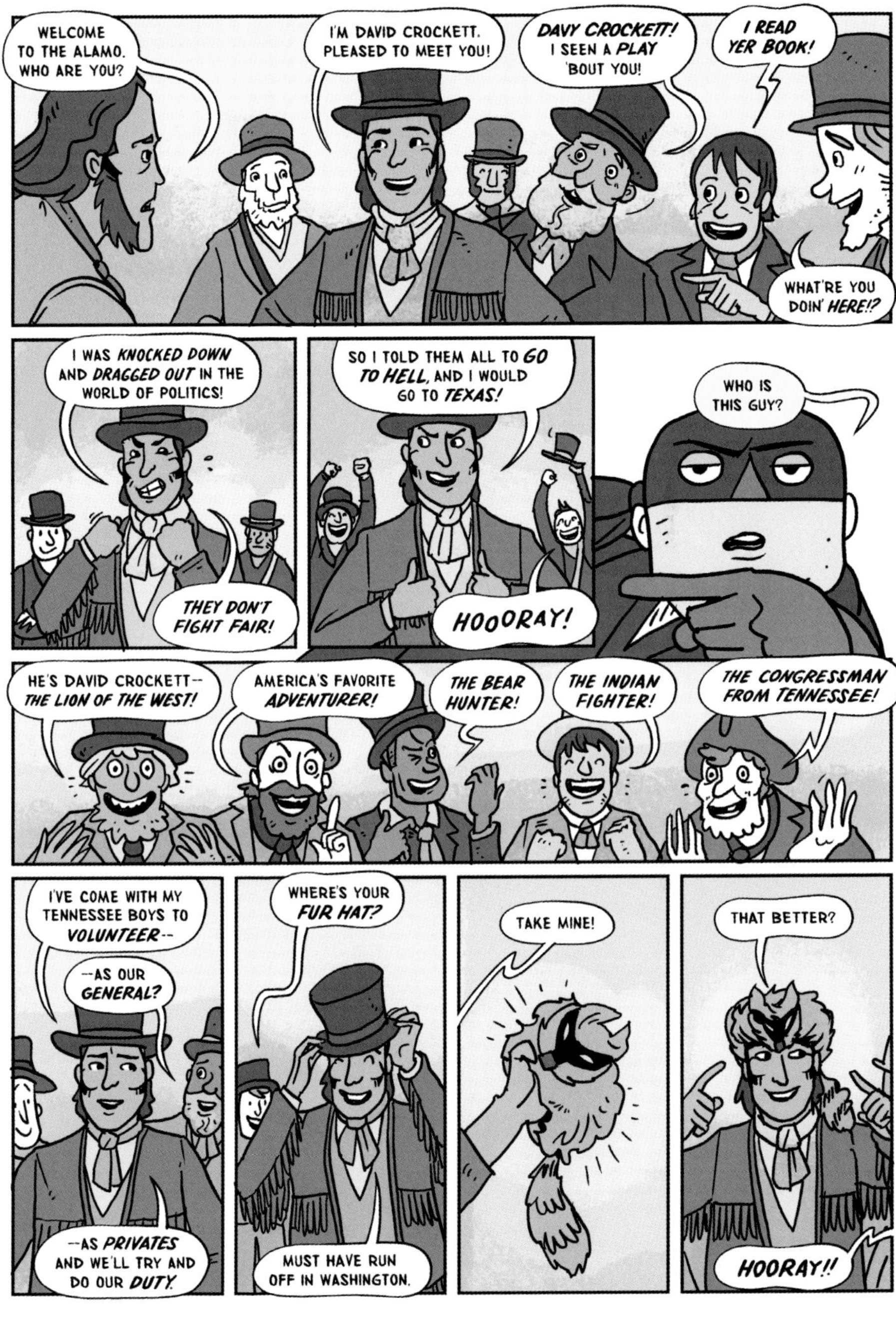
WELCOME TO THE ALAMO. WHO ARE YOU?
I'M DAVID CROCKETT. PLEASED TO MEET YOU!
DAVY CROCKETT! I SEEN A PLAY 'BOUT YOU!
I READ YER BOOK!
WHAT'RE YOU DOIN' HERE!?
I WAS KNOCKED DOWN AND DRAGGED OUT IN THE WORLD OF POLITICS!
THEY DON'T FIGHT FAIR!
SO I TOLD THEM ALL TO GO TO HELL, AND I WOULD GO TO TEXAS!
HOOORAY!
WHO IS THIS GUY?
HE'S DAVID CROCKETT-- THE LION OF THE WEST!
AMERICA'S FAVORITE ADVENTURER!
THE BEAR HUNTER!
THE INDIAN FIGHTER!
THE CONGRESSMAN FROM TENNESSEE!
I'VE COME WITH MY TENNESSEE BOYS TO VOLUNTEER--
--AS OUR GENERAL?
--AS PRIVATES AND WE'LL TRY AND DO OUR DUTY.
WHERE'S YOUR FUR HAT?
MUST HAVE RUN OFF IN WASHINGTON.
TAKE MINE!
THAT BETTER?
HOORAY!!

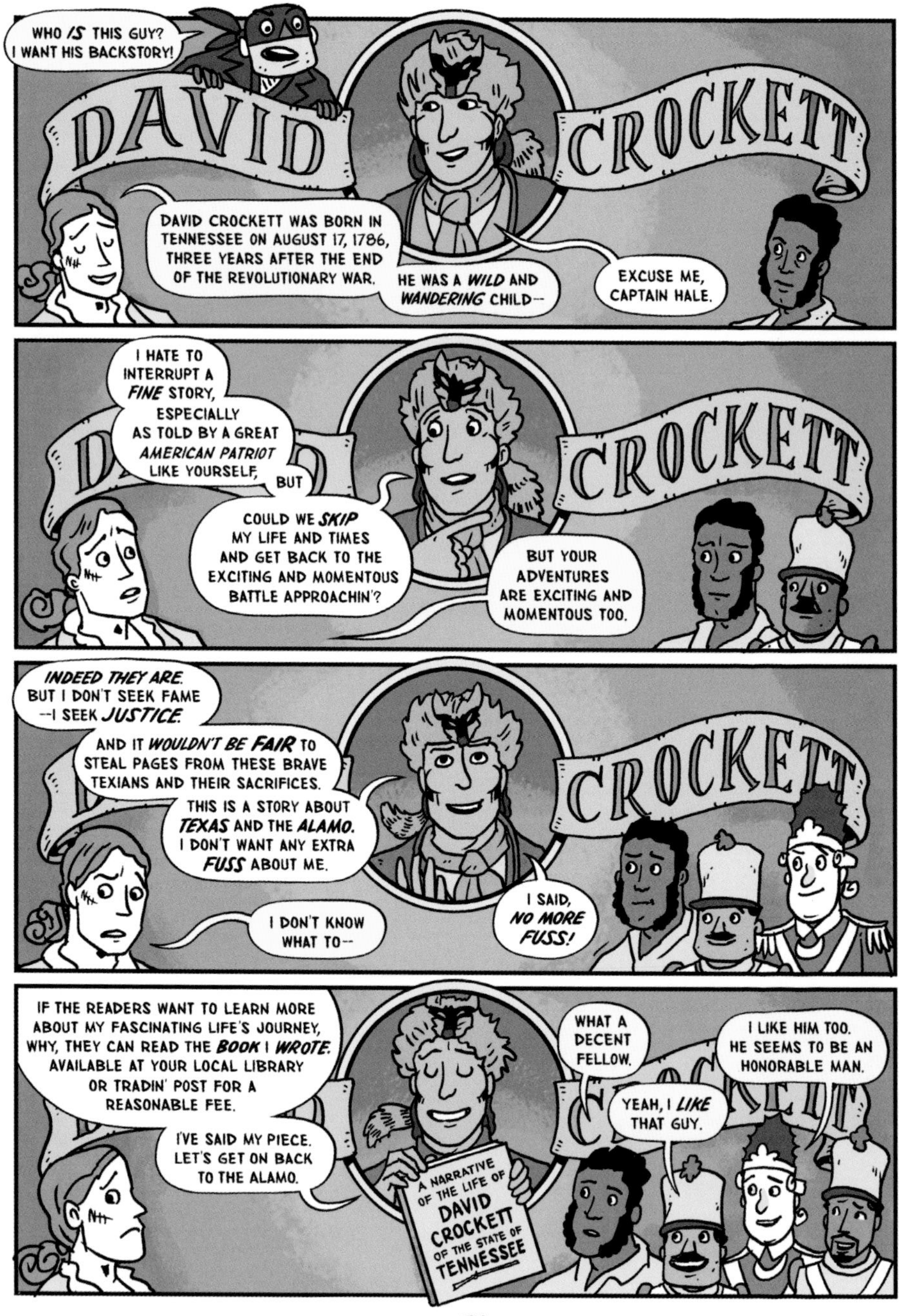
WHO *IS* THIS GUY? I WANT HIS BACKSTORY!
DAVID CROCKETT
DAVID CROCKETT WAS BORN IN TENNESSEE ON AUGUST 17, 1786, THREE YEARS AFTER THE END OF THE REVOLUTIONARY WAR.
HE WAS A *WILD* AND *WANDERING* CHILD--
EXCUSE ME, CAPTAIN HALE.
I HATE TO INTERRUPT A *FINE* STORY, ESPECIALLY AS TOLD BY A GREAT *AMERICAN PATRIOT* LIKE YOURSELF,
BUT
COULD WE *SKIP* MY LIFE AND TIMES AND GET BACK TO THE EXCITING AND MOMENTOUS BATTLE APPROACHIN'?
BUT YOUR ADVENTURES ARE EXCITING AND MOMENTOUS TOO.
INDEED THEY ARE. BUT I DON'T SEEK FAME --I SEEK *JUSTICE.*
AND IT *WOULDN'T BE FAIR* TO STEAL PAGES FROM THESE BRAVE TEXIANS AND THEIR SACRIFICES.
THIS IS A STORY ABOUT *TEXAS* AND THE *ALAMO.* I DON'T WANT ANY EXTRA *FUSS* ABOUT ME.
I DON'T KNOW WHAT TO--
I SAID, *NO MORE FUSS!*
IF THE READERS WANT TO LEARN MORE ABOUT MY FASCINATING LIFE'S JOURNEY, WHY, THEY CAN READ THE *BOOK* I *WROTE.* AVAILABLE AT YOUR LOCAL LIBRARY OR TRADIN' POST FOR A REASONABLE FEE.
I'VE SAID MY PIECE. LET'S GET ON BACK TO THE ALAMO.
A NARRATIVE OF THE LIFE OF DAVID CROCKETT OF THE STATE OF TENNESSEE
WHAT A DECENT FELLOW.
YEAH, I *LIKE* THAT GUY.
I LIKE HIM TOO. HE SEEMS TO BE AN HONORABLE MAN.

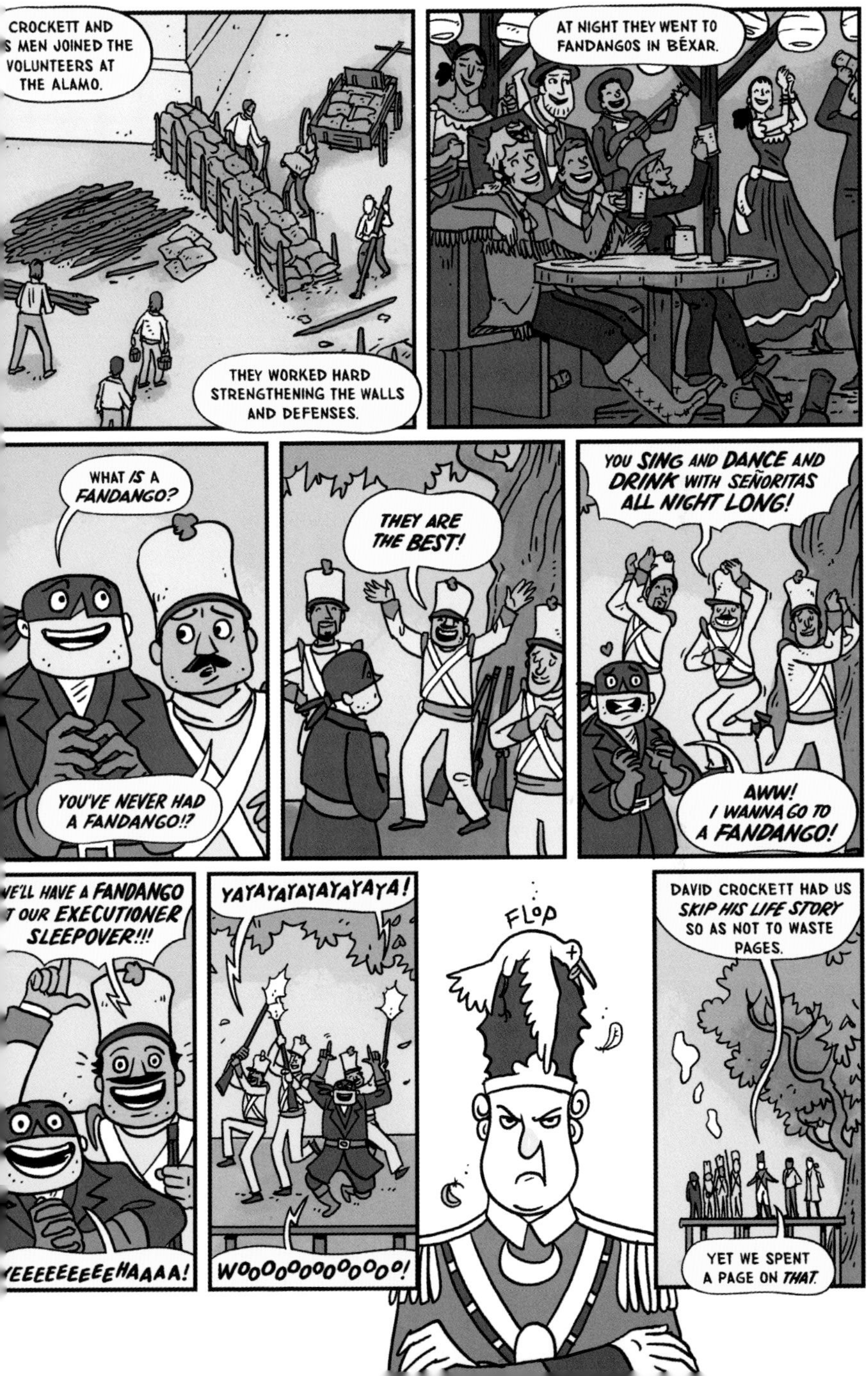
CROCKETT AND
S MEN JOINED THE
VOLUNTEERS AT
THE ALAMO.
THEY WORKED HARD
STRENGTHENING THE WALLS
AND DEFENSES.
AT NIGHT THEY WENT TO
FANDANGOS IN BÉXAR.
WHAT IS A
FANDANGO?
YOU'VE NEVER HAD
A FANDANGO!?
THEY ARE
THE BEST!
YOU SING AND DANCE AND
DRINK WITH SEÑORITAS
ALL NIGHT LONG!
AWW!
I WANNA GO TO
A FANDANGO!
E'LL HAVE A FANDANGO
T OUR EXECUTIONER
SLEEPOVER!!!
EEEEEEEEEEHAAAA!
YAYAYAYAYAYAYAYA!
WOOOOOOOOOOOO!
FLOP
DAVID CROCKETT HAD US
SKIP HIS LIFE STORY
SO AS NOT TO WASTE
PAGES.
YET WE SPENT
A PAGE ON THAT.

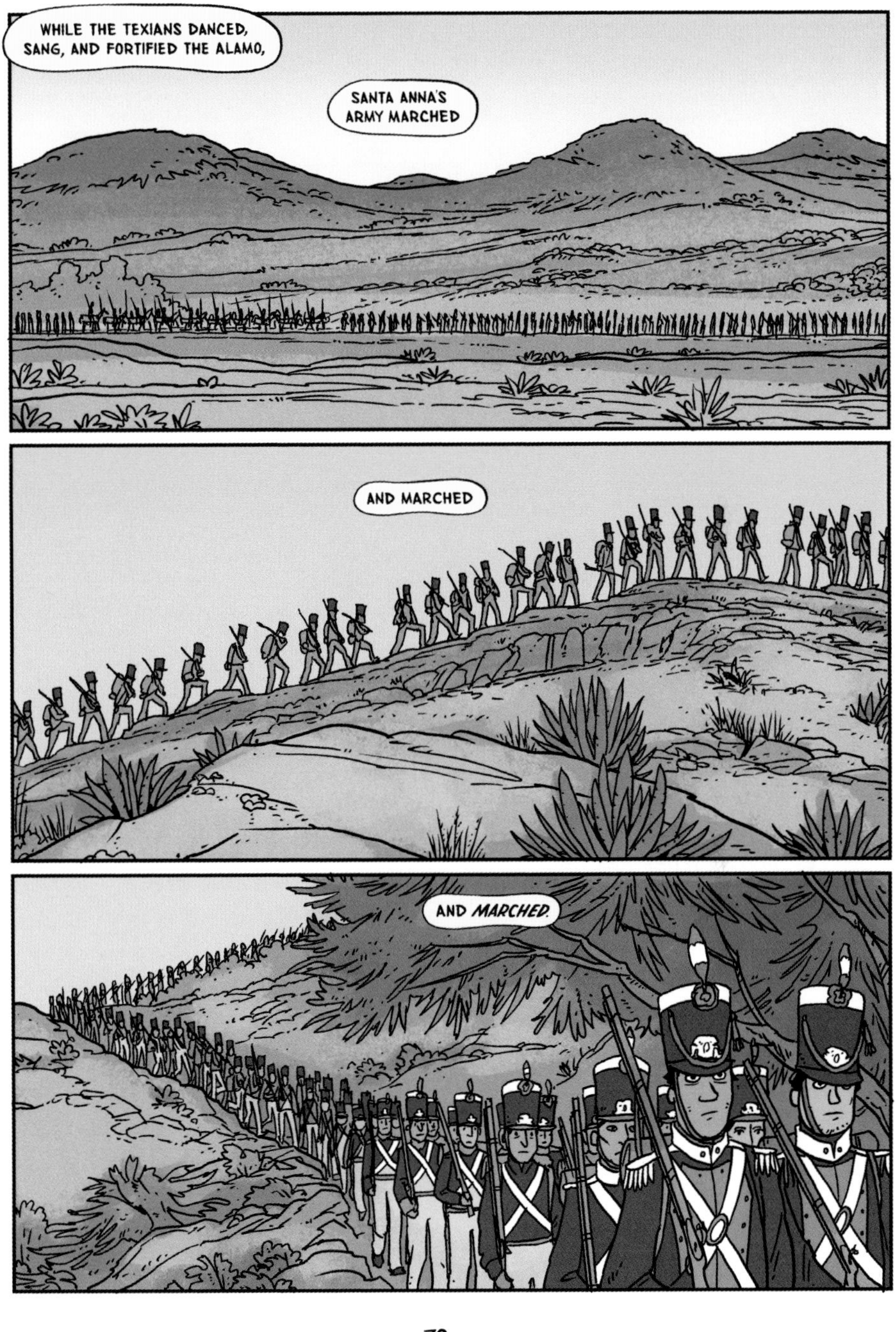
WHILE THE TEXIANS DANCED, SANG, AND FORTIFIED THE ALAMO,
SANTA ANNA'S ARMY MARCHED
AND MARCHED
AND *MARCHED*.

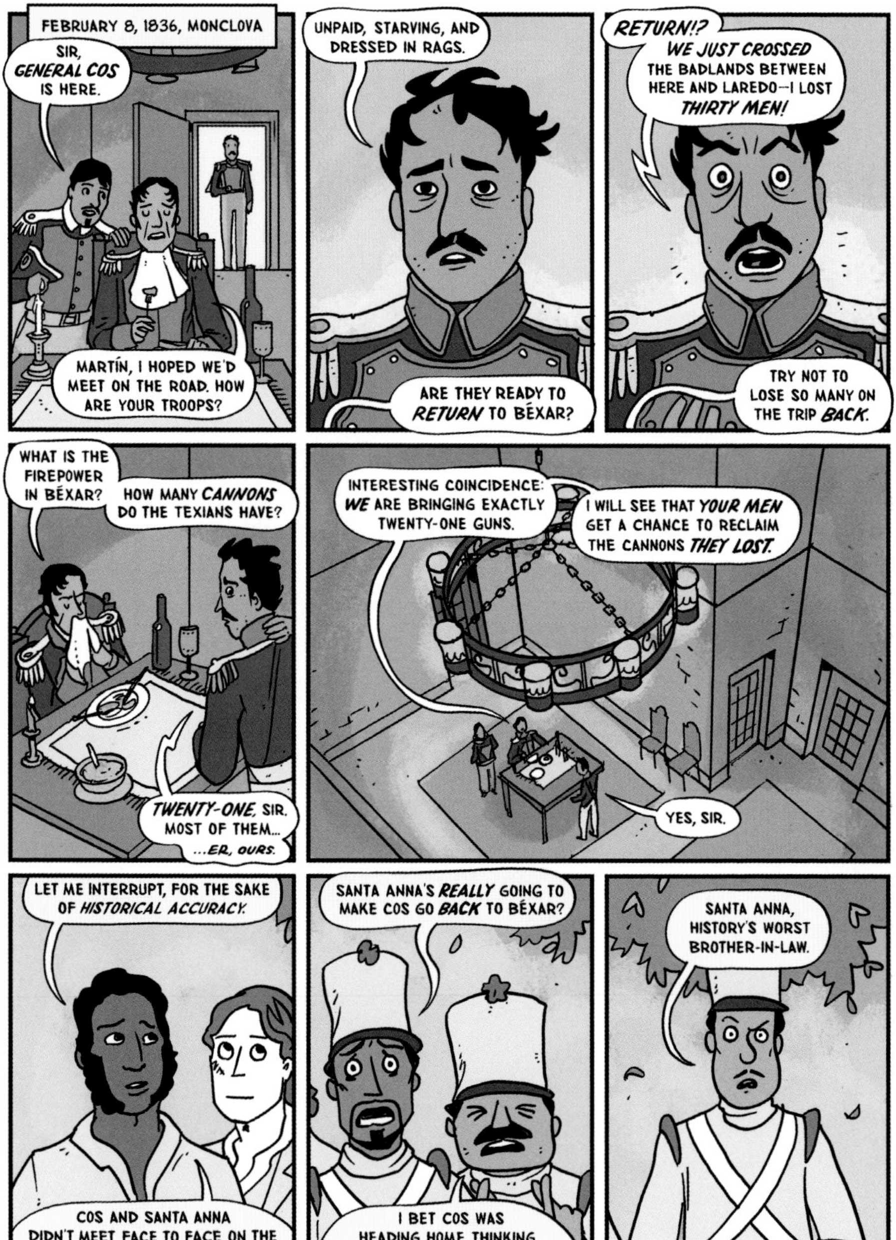
FEBRUARY 8, 1836, MONCLOVA
SIR, GENERAL COS IS HERE.
MARTÍN, I HOPED WE'D MEET ON THE ROAD. HOW ARE YOUR TROOPS?
UNPAID, STARVING, AND DRESSED IN RAGS.
ARE THEY READY TO RETURN TO BÉXAR?
RETURN!? WE JUST CROSSED THE BADLANDS BETWEEN HERE AND LAREDO—I LOST THIRTY MEN!
TRY NOT TO LOSE SO MANY ON THE TRIP BACK.
WHAT IS THE FIREPOWER IN BÉXAR?
HOW MANY CANNONS DO THE TEXIANS HAVE?
TWENTY-ONE, SIR. MOST OF THEM... ...ER, OURS.
INTERESTING COINCIDENCE: WE ARE BRINGING EXACTLY TWENTY-ONE GUNS.
I WILL SEE THAT YOUR MEN GET A CHANCE TO RECLAIM THE CANNONS THEY LOST.
YES, SIR.
LET ME INTERRUPT, FOR THE SAKE OF HISTORICAL ACCURACY.
COS AND SANTA ANNA DIDN'T MEET FACE TO FACE ON THE ROAD. THEY DID EXCHANGE THESE MESSAGES, JUST NOT IN PERSON.
SANTA ANNA'S REALLY GOING TO MAKE COS GO BACK TO BÉXAR?
I BET COS WAS HEADING HOME THINKING, "DON'T RUN INTO SANTA ANNA, DON'T RUN INTO SANTA ANNA..."
SANTA ANNA, HISTORY'S WORST BROTHER-IN-LAW.

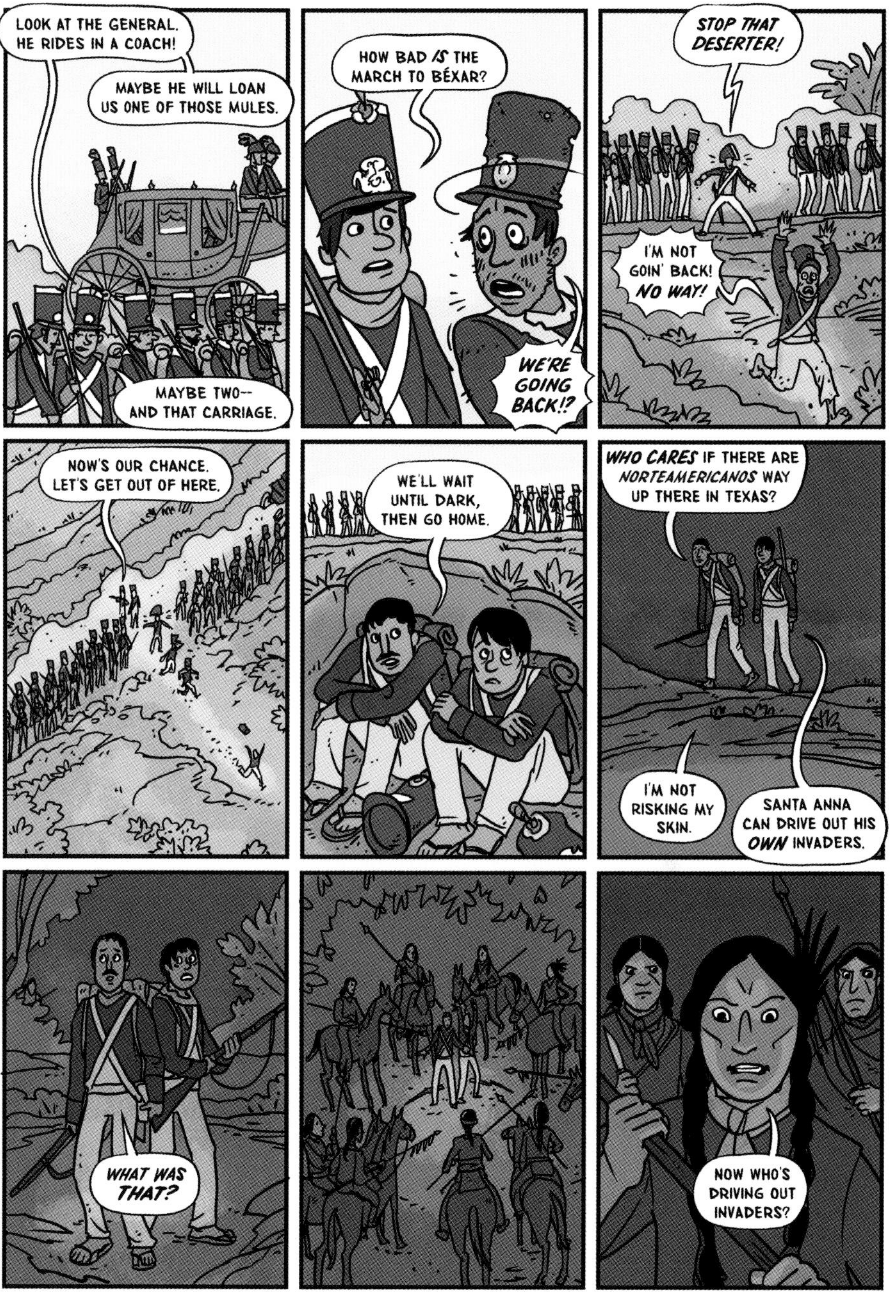
LOOK AT THE GENERAL. HE RIDES IN A COACH!
MAYBE HE WILL LOAN US ONE OF THOSE MULES.
MAYBE TWO-- AND THAT CARRIAGE.
HOW BAD *IS* THE MARCH TO BÉXAR?
WE'RE GOING BACK!?
STOP THAT DESERTER!
I'M NOT GOIN' BACK! *NO WAY!*
NOW'S OUR CHANCE. LET'S GET OUT OF HERE.
WE'LL WAIT UNTIL DARK, THEN GO HOME.
WHO CARES IF THERE ARE *NORTEAMERICANOS* WAY UP THERE IN TEXAS?
I'M NOT RISKING MY SKIN.
SANTA ANNA CAN DRIVE OUT HIS *OWN* INVADERS.
WHAT WAS THAT?
NOW WHO'S DRIVING OUT INVADERS?

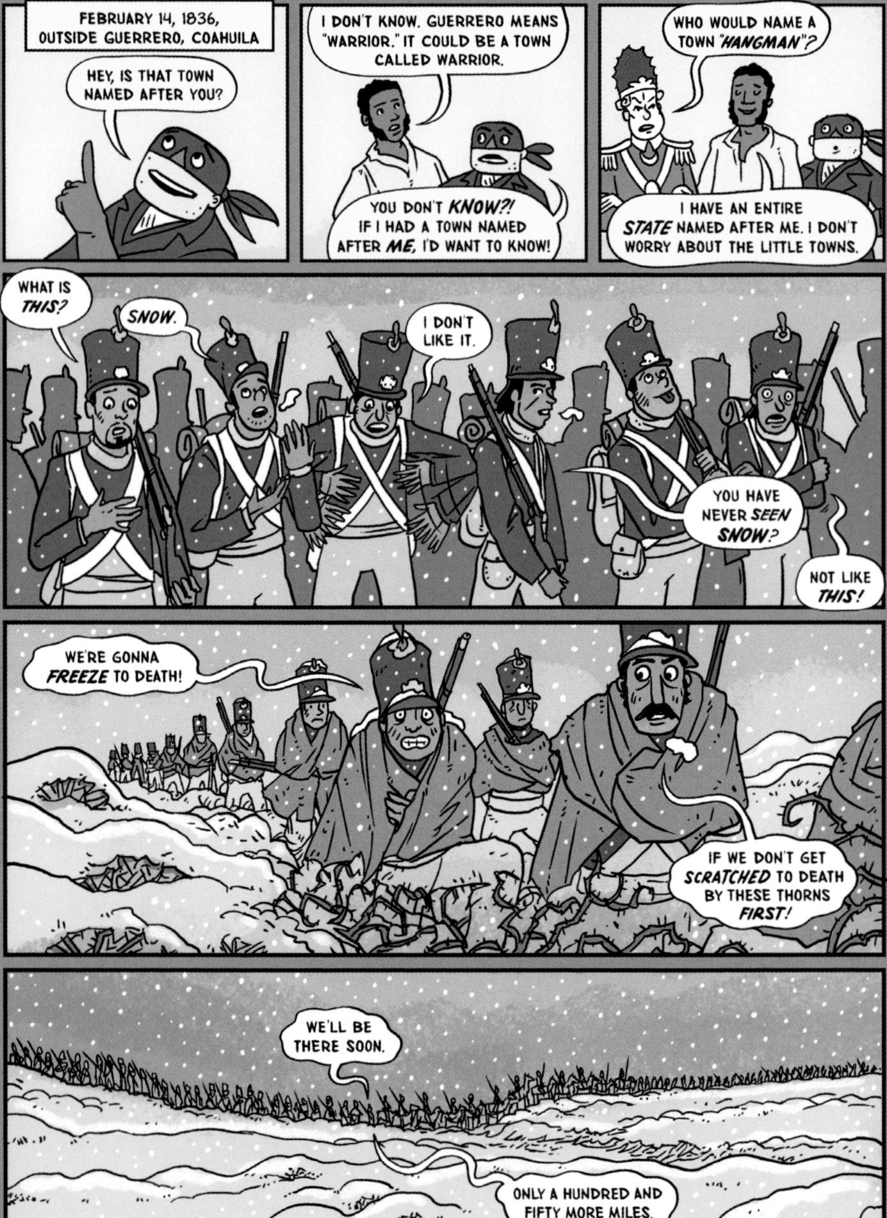
FEBRUARY 14, 1836,
OUTSIDE GUERRERO, COAHUILA
HEY, IS THAT TOWN NAMED AFTER YOU?
I DON'T KNOW. GUERRERO MEANS "WARRIOR." IT COULD BE A TOWN CALLED WARRIOR.
YOU DON'T *KNOW?!* IF I HAD A TOWN NAMED AFTER *ME*, I'D WANT TO KNOW!
WHO WOULD NAME A TOWN *"HANGMAN"*?
I HAVE AN ENTIRE *STATE* NAMED AFTER ME. I DON'T WORRY ABOUT THE LITTLE TOWNS.
WHAT IS *THIS?*
SNOW.
I DON'T LIKE IT.
YOU HAVE NEVER *SEEN SNOW?*
NOT LIKE *THIS!*
WE'RE GONNA *FREEZE* TO DEATH!
IF WE DON'T GET *SCRATCHED* TO DEATH BY THESE THORNS *FIRST!*
WE'LL BE THERE SOON.
ONLY A HUNDRED AND FIFTY MORE MILES.

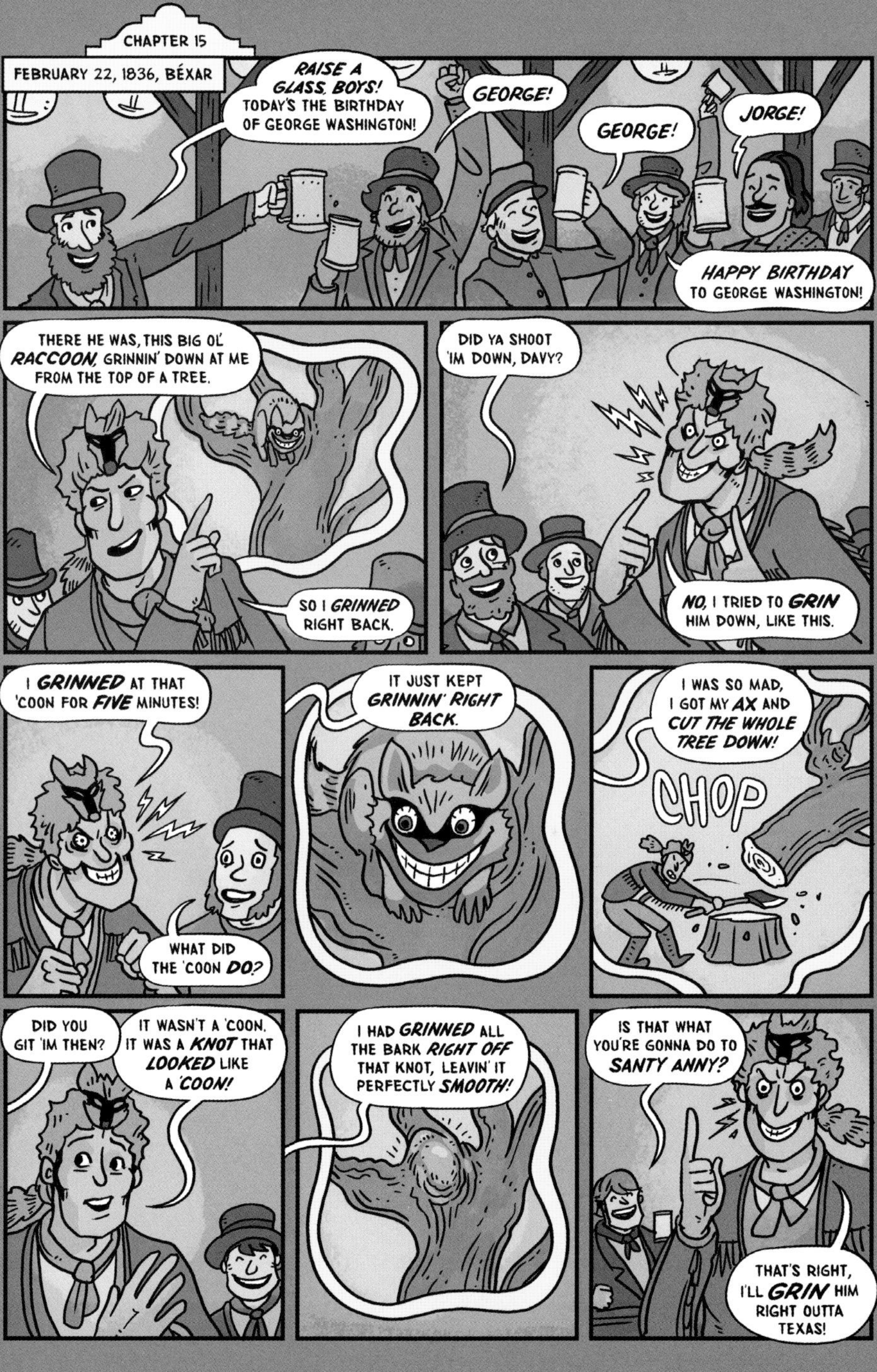
CHAPTER 15
FEBRUARY 22, 1836, BÉXAR
RAISE A GLASS, BOYS! TODAY'S THE BIRTHDAY OF GEORGE WASHINGTON!
GEORGE!
GEORGE!
JORGE!
HAPPY BIRTHDAY TO GEORGE WASHINGTON!
THERE HE WAS, THIS BIG OL' RACCOON, GRINNIN' DOWN AT ME FROM THE TOP OF A TREE.
SO I GRINNED RIGHT BACK.
DID YA SHOOT 'IM DOWN, DAVY?
NO, I TRIED TO GRIN HIM DOWN, LIKE THIS.
I GRINNED AT THAT 'COON FOR FIVE MINUTES!
WHAT DID THE 'COON DO?
IT JUST KEPT GRINNIN' RIGHT BACK.
I WAS SO MAD, I GOT MY AX AND CUT THE WHOLE TREE DOWN!
CHOP
DID YOU GIT 'IM THEN?
IT WASN'T A 'COON. IT WAS A KNOT THAT LOOKED LIKE A 'COON!
I HAD GRINNED ALL THE BARK RIGHT OFF THAT KNOT, LEAVIN' IT PERFECTLY SMOOTH!
IS THAT WHAT YOU'RE GONNA DO TO SANTY ANNY?
THAT'S RIGHT, I'LL GRIN HIM RIGHT OUTTA TEXAS!

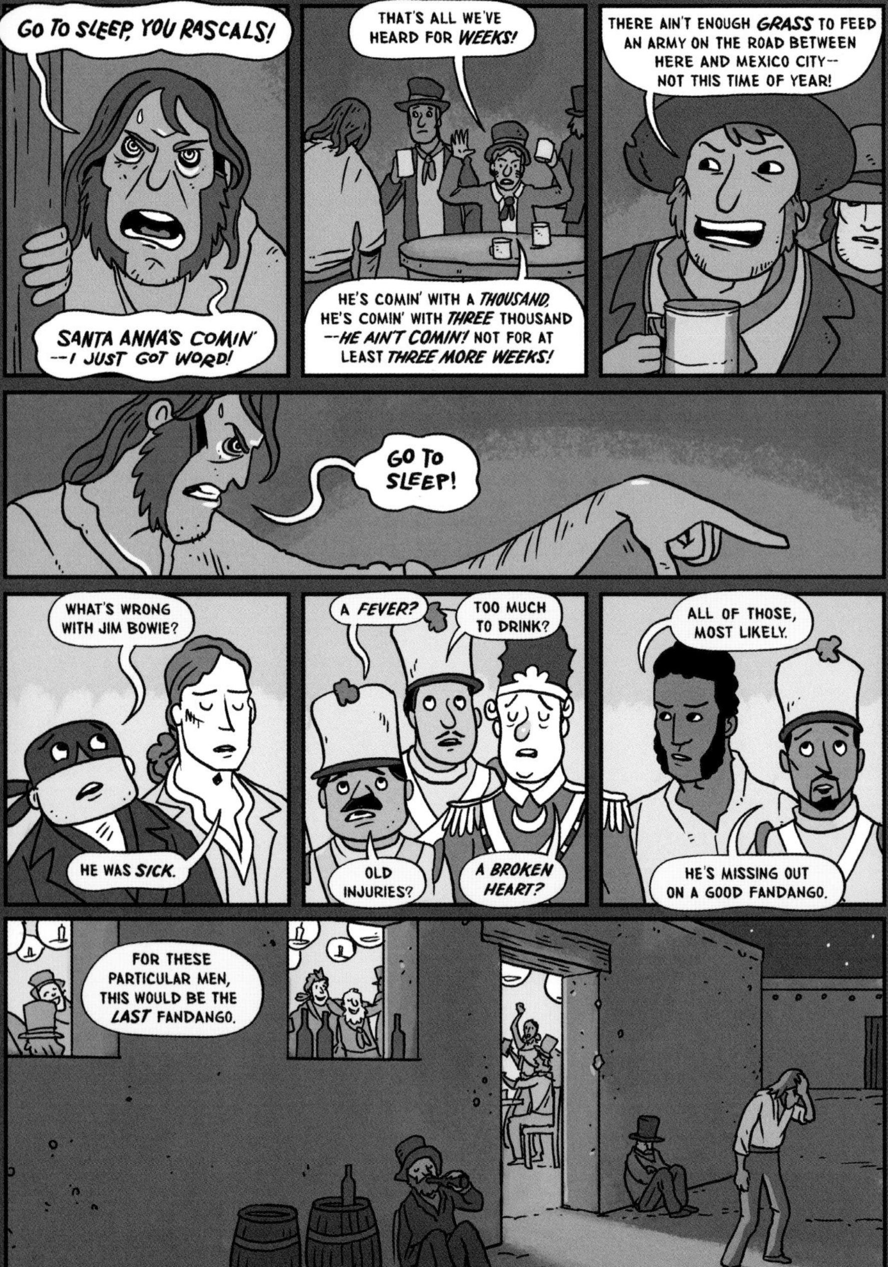
GO TO SLEEP, YOU RASCALS!
SANTA ANNA'S COMIN' --I JUST GOT WORD!
THAT'S ALL WE'VE HEARD FOR *WEEKS!*
HE'S COMIN' WITH A *THOUSAND,* HE'S COMIN' WITH *THREE* THOUSAND --*HE AIN'T COMIN'!* NOT FOR AT LEAST *THREE MORE WEEKS!*
THERE AIN'T ENOUGH *GRASS* TO FEED AN ARMY ON THE ROAD BETWEEN HERE AND MEXICO CITY-- NOT THIS TIME OF YEAR!
GO TO SLEEP!
WHAT'S WRONG WITH JIM BOWIE?
HE WAS *SICK.*
A *FEVER?*
TOO MUCH TO DRINK?
OLD INJURIES?
A *BROKEN HEART?*
ALL OF THOSE, MOST LIKELY.
HE'S MISSING OUT ON A GOOD FANDANGO.
FOR THESE PARTICULAR MEN, THIS WOULD BE THE *LAST* FANDANGO.

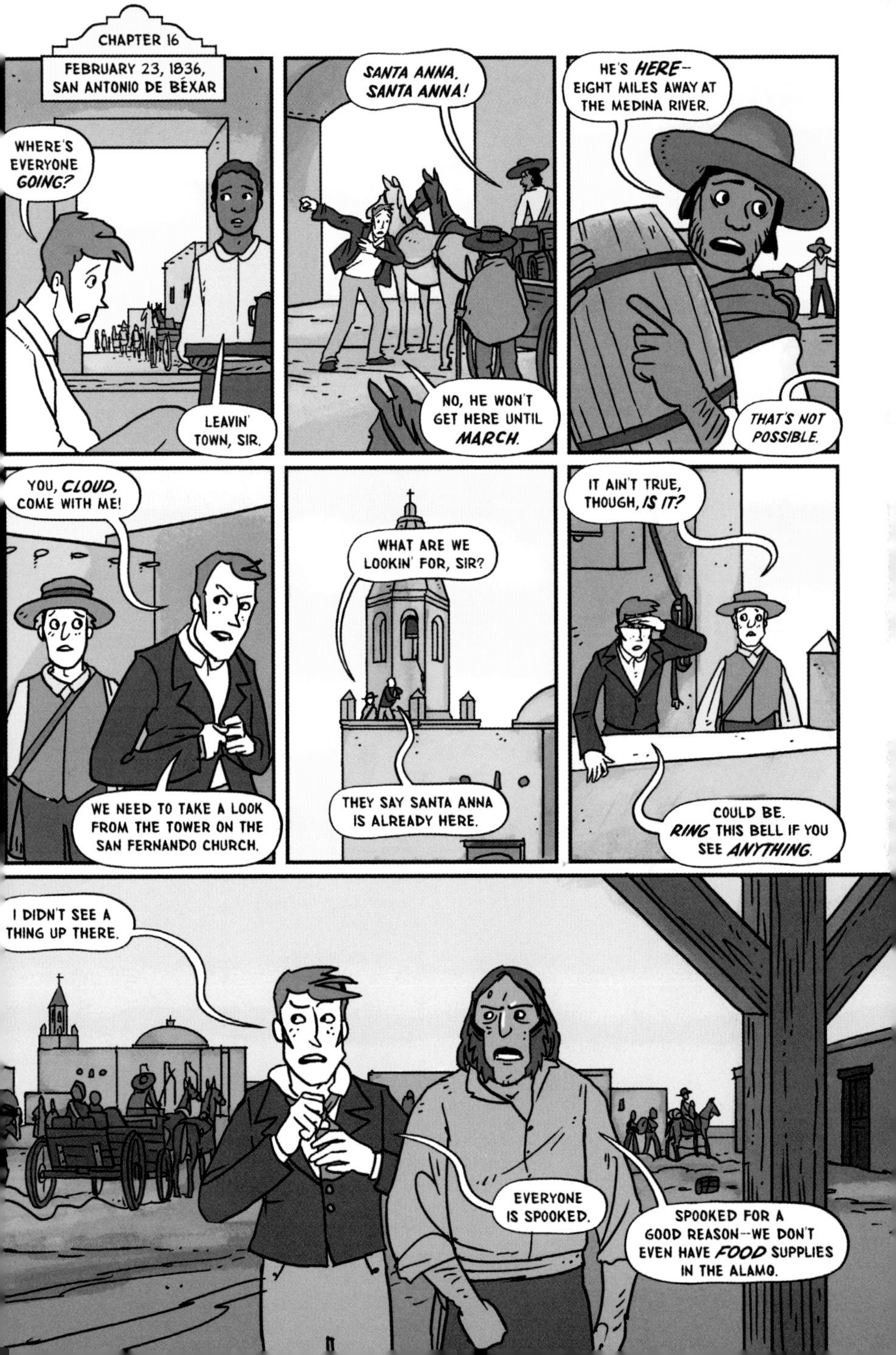

CHAPTER 16
FEBRUARY 23, 1836, SAN ANTONIO DE BÉXAR
WHERE'S EVERYONE *GOING?*
LEAVIN' TOWN, SIR.
SANTA ANNA. SANTA ANNA!
NO, HE WON'T GET HERE UNTIL *MARCH*.
HE'S *HERE*--EIGHT MILES AWAY AT THE MEDINA RIVER.
THAT'S NOT POSSIBLE.
YOU, *CLOUD,* COME WITH ME!
WE NEED TO TAKE A LOOK FROM THE TOWER ON THE SAN FERNANDO CHURCH.
WHAT ARE WE LOOKIN' FOR, SIR?
THEY SAY SANTA ANNA IS ALREADY HERE.
IT AIN'T TRUE, THOUGH, *IS IT?*
COULD BE. *RING* THIS BELL IF YOU SEE *ANYTHING*.
I DIDN'T SEE A THING UP THERE.
EVERYONE IS SPOOKED.
SPOOKED FOR A GOOD REASON--WE DON'T EVEN HAVE *FOOD* SUPPLIES IN THE ALAMO.

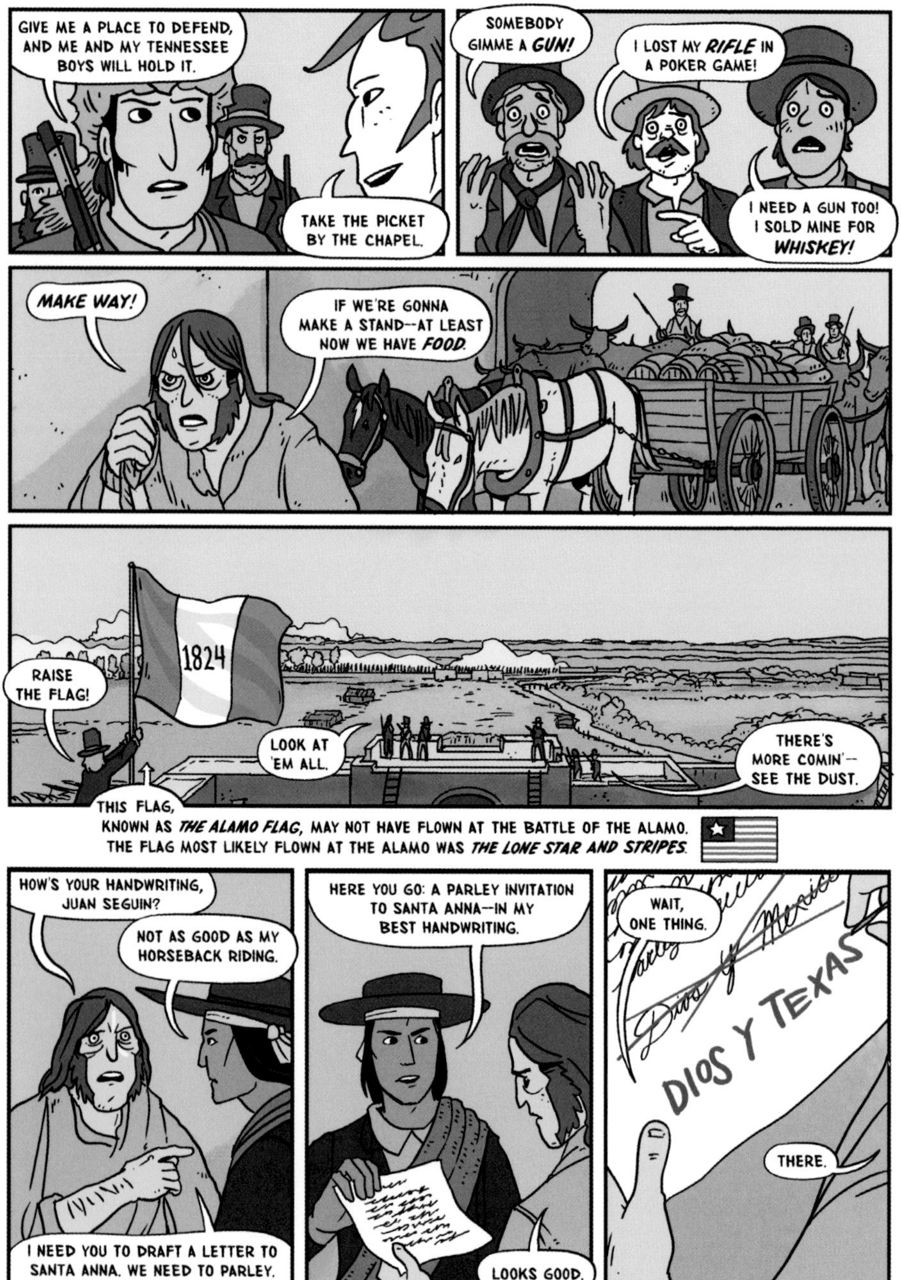
GIVE ME A PLACE TO DEFEND, AND ME AND MY TENNESSEE BOYS WILL HOLD IT.
TAKE THE PICKET BY THE CHAPEL.
SOMEBODY GIMME A *GUN!*
I LOST MY *RIFLE* IN A POKER GAME!
I NEED A GUN TOO! I SOLD MINE FOR *WHISKEY!*
MAKE WAY!
IF WE'RE GONNA MAKE A STAND--AT LEAST NOW WE HAVE *FOOD.*
1824
RAISE THE FLAG!
LOOK AT 'EM ALL.
THERE'S MORE COMIN'-- SEE THE DUST.
THIS FLAG, KNOWN AS *THE ALAMO FLAG*, MAY NOT HAVE FLOWN AT THE BATTLE OF THE ALAMO. THE FLAG MOST LIKELY FLOWN AT THE ALAMO WAS *THE LONE STAR AND STRIPES.*
HOW'S YOUR HANDWRITING, JUAN SEGUIN?
NOT AS GOOD AS MY HORSEBACK RIDING.
I NEED YOU TO DRAFT A LETTER TO SANTA ANNA. WE NEED TO PARLEY.
HERE YOU GO: A PARLEY INVITATION TO SANTA ANNA--IN MY BEST HANDWRITING.
LOOKS GOOD.
WAIT, ONE THING.
Dios y Mexico
DIOS Y TEXAS
THERE.

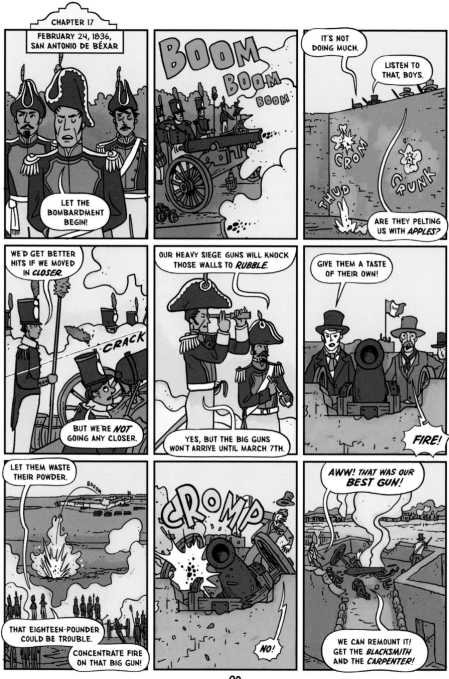

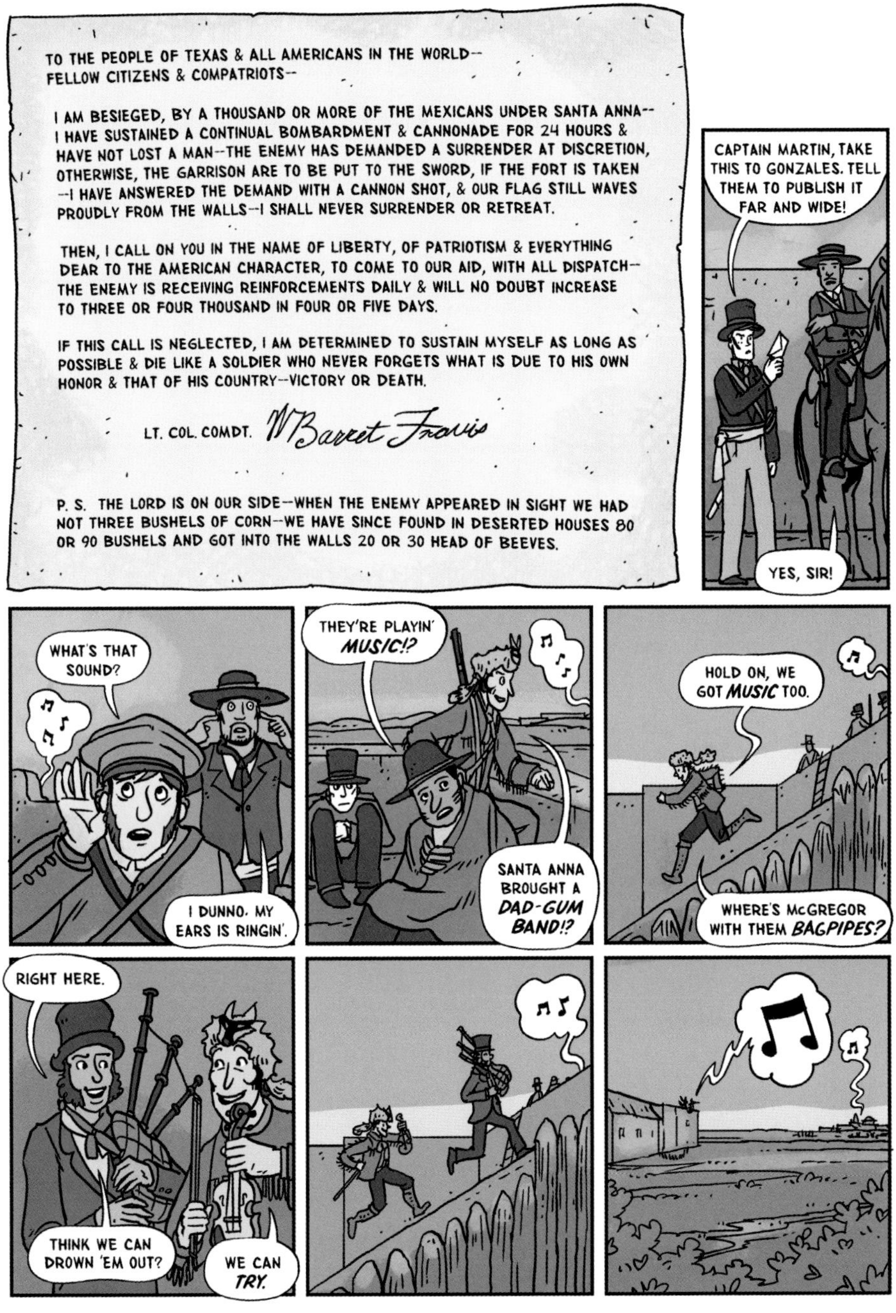
TO THE PEOPLE OF TEXAS & ALL AMERICANS IN THE WORLD--
FELLOW CITIZENS & COMPATRIOTS--
I AM BESIEGED, BY A THOUSAND OR MORE OF THE MEXICANS UNDER SANTA ANNA-- I HAVE SUSTAINED A CONTINUAL BOMBARDMENT & CANNONADE FOR 24 HOURS & HAVE NOT LOST A MAN--THE ENEMY HAS DEMANDED A SURRENDER AT DISCRETION, OTHERWISE, THE GARRISON ARE TO BE PUT TO THE SWORD, IF THE FORT IS TAKEN --I HAVE ANSWERED THE DEMAND WITH A CANNON SHOT, & OUR FLAG STILL WAVES PROUDLY FROM THE WALLS--I SHALL NEVER SURRENDER OR RETREAT.
THEN, I CALL ON YOU IN THE NAME OF LIBERTY, OF PATRIOTISM & EVERYTHING DEAR TO THE AMERICAN CHARACTER, TO COME TO OUR AID, WITH ALL DISPATCH-- THE ENEMY IS RECEIVING REINFORCEMENTS DAILY & WILL NO DOUBT INCREASE TO THREE OR FOUR THOUSAND IN FOUR OR FIVE DAYS.
IF THIS CALL IS NEGLECTED, I AM DETERMINED TO SUSTAIN MYSELF AS LONG AS POSSIBLE & DIE LIKE A SOLDIER WHO NEVER FORGETS WHAT IS DUE TO HIS OWN HONOR & THAT OF HIS COUNTRY--VICTORY OR DEATH.
LT. COL. COMDT. W Barret Travis
P. S. THE LORD IS ON OUR SIDE--WHEN THE ENEMY APPEARED IN SIGHT WE HAD NOT THREE BUSHELS OF CORN--WE HAVE SINCE FOUND IN DESERTED HOUSES 80 OR 90 BUSHELS AND GOT INTO THE WALLS 20 OR 30 HEAD OF BEEVES.
CAPTAIN MARTIN, TAKE THIS TO GONZALES. TELL THEM TO PUBLISH IT FAR AND WIDE!
YES, SIR!
WHAT'S THAT SOUND?
I DUNNO. MY EARS IS RINGIN'.
THEY'RE PLAYIN' *MUSIC!?*
SANTA ANNA BROUGHT A *DAD-GUM BAND!?*
HOLD ON, WE GOT *MUSIC* TOO.
WHERE'S McGREGOR WITH THEM *BAGPIPES?*
RIGHT HERE.
THINK WE CAN DROWN 'EM OUT?
WE CAN *TRY.*

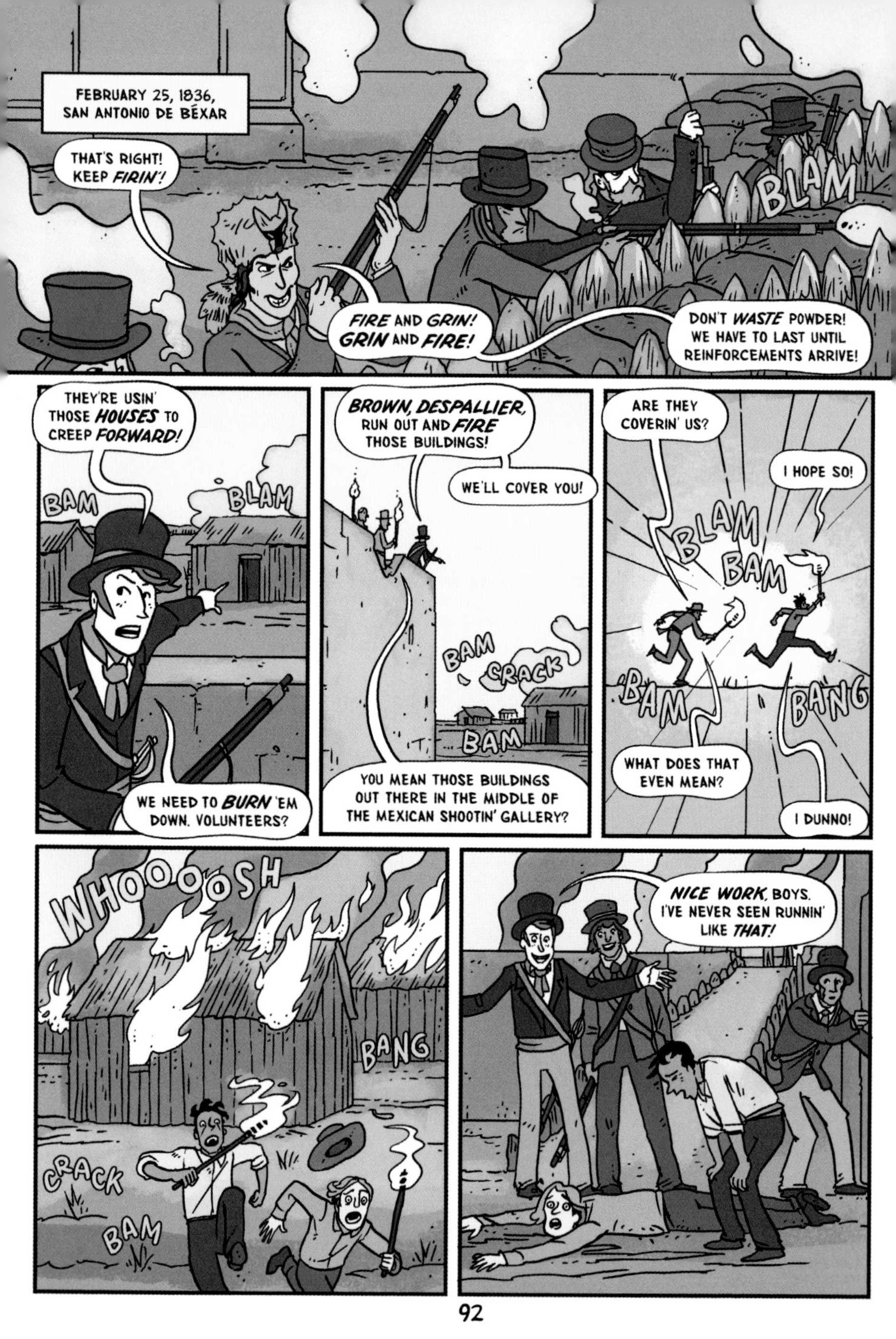
FEBRUARY 25, 1836, SAN ANTONIO DE BÉXAR
THAT'S RIGHT! KEEP *FIRIN'*!
FIRE AND *GRIN*! *GRIN* AND *FIRE*!
DON'T *WASTE* POWDER! WE HAVE TO LAST UNTIL REINFORCEMENTS ARRIVE!
BLAM
THEY'RE USIN' THOSE *HOUSES* TO CREEP *FORWARD*!
BAM
BLAM
WE NEED TO *BURN* 'EM DOWN. VOLUNTEERS?
BROWN, DESPALLIER, RUN OUT AND *FIRE* THOSE BUILDINGS!
WE'LL COVER YOU!
BAM
CRACK
BAM
YOU MEAN THOSE BUILDINGS OUT THERE IN THE MIDDLE OF THE MEXICAN SHOOTIN' GALLERY?
ARE THEY COVERIN' US?
I HOPE SO!
BLAM
BAM
BAM
BANG
WHAT DOES THAT EVEN MEAN?
I DUNNO!
WHOOOOSH
BANG
CRACK
BAM
NICE WORK, BOYS. I'VE NEVER SEEN RUNNIN' LIKE *THAT*!

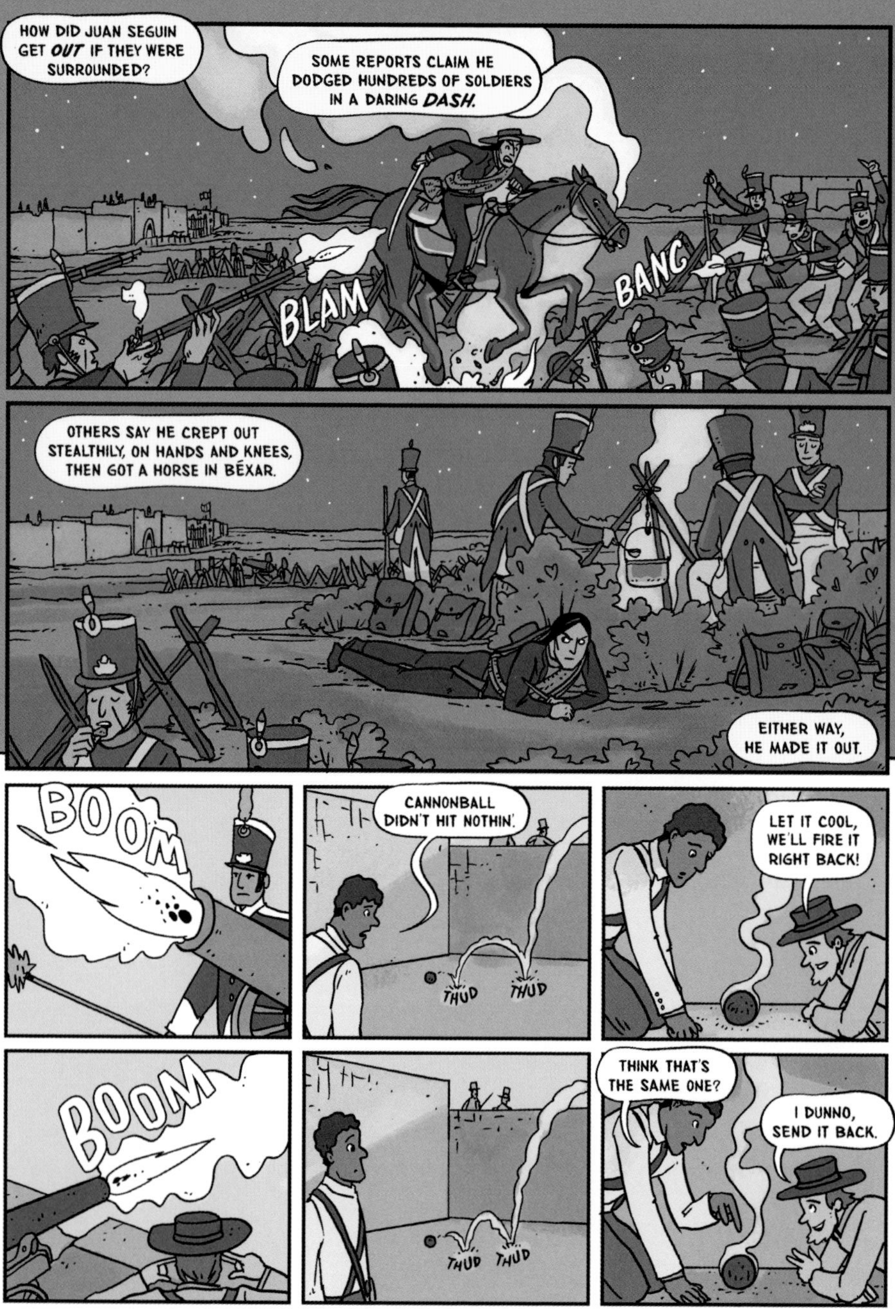
HOW DID JUAN SEGUIN GET OUT IF THEY WERE SURROUNDED?
SOME REPORTS CLAIM HE DODGED HUNDREDS OF SOLDIERS IN A DARING DASH.
BLAM
BANG
OTHERS SAY HE CREPT OUT STEALTHILY, ON HANDS AND KNEES, THEN GOT A HORSE IN BÉXAR.
EITHER WAY, HE MADE IT OUT.
BOOM
CANNONBALL DIDN'T HIT NOTHIN'.
THUD THUD
LET IT COOL, WE'LL FIRE IT RIGHT BACK!
BOOM
THUD THUD
THINK THAT'S THE SAME ONE?
I DUNNO, SEND IT BACK.

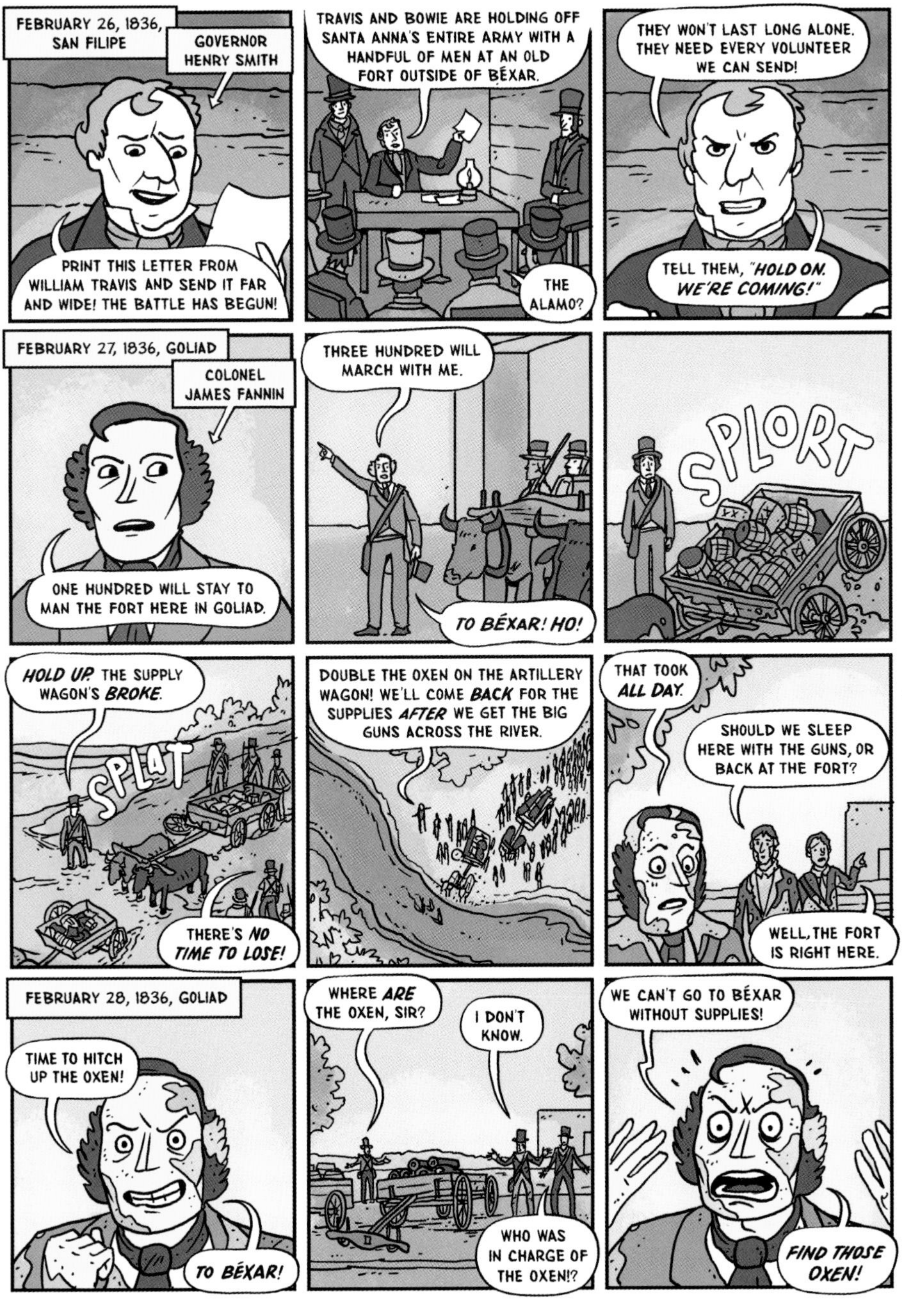
FEBRUARY 26, 1836, SAN FILIPE
GOVERNOR HENRY SMITH
PRINT THIS LETTER FROM WILLIAM TRAVIS AND SEND IT FAR AND WIDE! THE BATTLE HAS BEGUN!
TRAVIS AND BOWIE ARE HOLDING OFF SANTA ANNA'S ENTIRE ARMY WITH A HANDFUL OF MEN AT AN OLD FORT OUTSIDE OF BÉXAR.
THE ALAMO?
THEY WON'T LAST LONG ALONE. THEY NEED EVERY VOLUNTEER WE CAN SEND!
TELL THEM, "HOLD ON. WE'RE COMING!"
FEBRUARY 27, 1836, GOLIAD
COLONEL JAMES FANNIN
ONE HUNDRED WILL STAY TO MAN THE FORT HERE IN GOLIAD.
THREE HUNDRED WILL MARCH WITH ME.
TO BÉXAR! HO!
SPLORT
HOLD UP. THE SUPPLY WAGON'S BROKE.
SPLAT
THERE'S NO TIME TO LOSE!
DOUBLE THE OXEN ON THE ARTILLERY WAGON! WE'LL COME BACK FOR THE SUPPLIES AFTER WE GET THE BIG GUNS ACROSS THE RIVER.
THAT TOOK ALL DAY.
SHOULD WE SLEEP HERE WITH THE GUNS, OR BACK AT THE FORT?
WELL, THE FORT IS RIGHT HERE.
FEBRUARY 28, 1836, GOLIAD
TIME TO HITCH UP THE OXEN!
TO BÉXAR!
WHERE ARE THE OXEN, SIR?
I DON'T KNOW.
WHO WAS IN CHARGE OF THE OXEN!?
WE CAN'T GO TO BÉXAR WITHOUT SUPPLIES!
FIND THOSE OXEN!

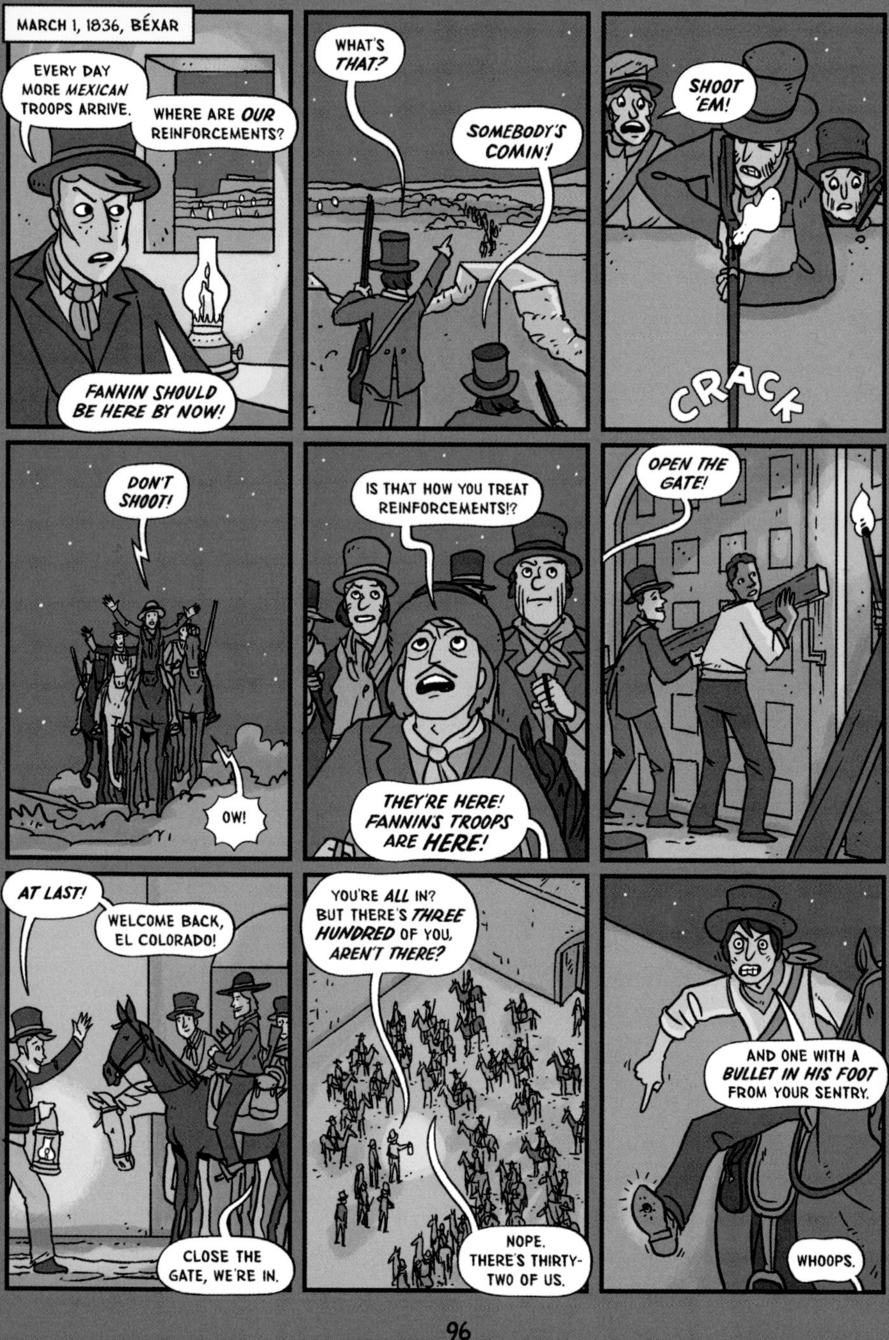
MARCH 1, 1836, BÉXAR
EVERY DAY MORE *MEXICAN* TROOPS ARRIVE.
WHERE ARE *OUR* REINFORCEMENTS?
FANNIN SHOULD BE HERE BY NOW!
WHAT'S *THAT?*
SOMEBODY'S COMIN'!
SHOOT 'EM!
CRACK
DON'T SHOOT!
OW!
IS THAT HOW YOU TREAT REINFORCEMENTS!?
*THEY'RE HERE! FANNIN'S TROOPS ARE **HERE**!*
OPEN THE GATE!
AT LAST!
WELCOME BACK, EL COLORADO!
CLOSE THE GATE, WE'RE IN.
YOU'RE *ALL* IN? BUT THERE'S *THREE HUNDRED* OF YOU, *AREN'T THERE?*
NOPE. THERE'S THIRTY-TWO OF US.
AND ONE WITH A ***BULLET IN HIS FOOT*** FROM YOUR SENTRY.
WHOOPS.

100

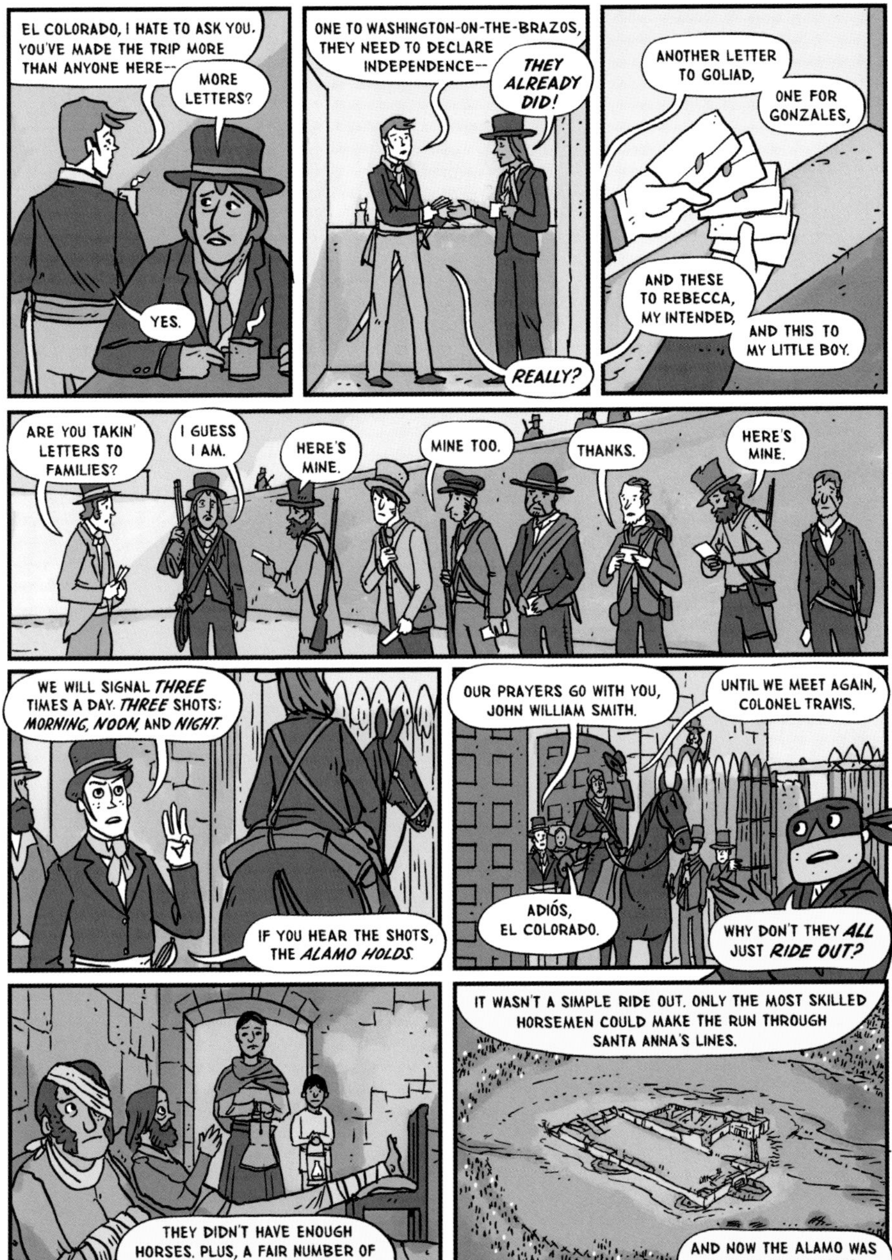
EL COLORADO, I HATE TO ASK YOU. YOU'VE MADE THE TRIP MORE THAN ANYONE HERE--
MORE LETTERS?
YES.
ONE TO WASHINGTON-ON-THE-BRAZOS, THEY NEED TO DECLARE INDEPENDENCE--
THEY ALREADY DID!
REALLY?
ANOTHER LETTER TO GOLIAD,
ONE FOR GONZALES,
AND THESE TO REBECCA, MY INTENDED,
AND THIS TO MY LITTLE BOY.
ARE YOU TAKIN' LETTERS TO FAMILIES?
I GUESS I AM.
HERE'S MINE.
MINE TOO.
THANKS.
HERE'S MINE.
WE WILL SIGNAL THREE TIMES A DAY. THREE SHOTS: MORNING, NOON, AND NIGHT.
IF YOU HEAR THE SHOTS, THE ALAMO HOLDS.
OUR PRAYERS GO WITH YOU, JOHN WILLIAM SMITH.
UNTIL WE MEET AGAIN, COLONEL TRAVIS.
ADIÓS, EL COLORADO.
WHY DON'T THEY ALL JUST RIDE OUT?
THEY DIDN'T HAVE ENOUGH HORSES. PLUS, A FAIR NUMBER OF THE MEN WERE SICK OR INJURED.
IT WASN'T A SIMPLE RIDE OUT. ONLY THE MOST SKILLED HORSEMEN COULD MAKE THE RUN THROUGH SANTA ANNA'S LINES.
AND NOW THE ALAMO WAS NEARLY SURROUNDED.

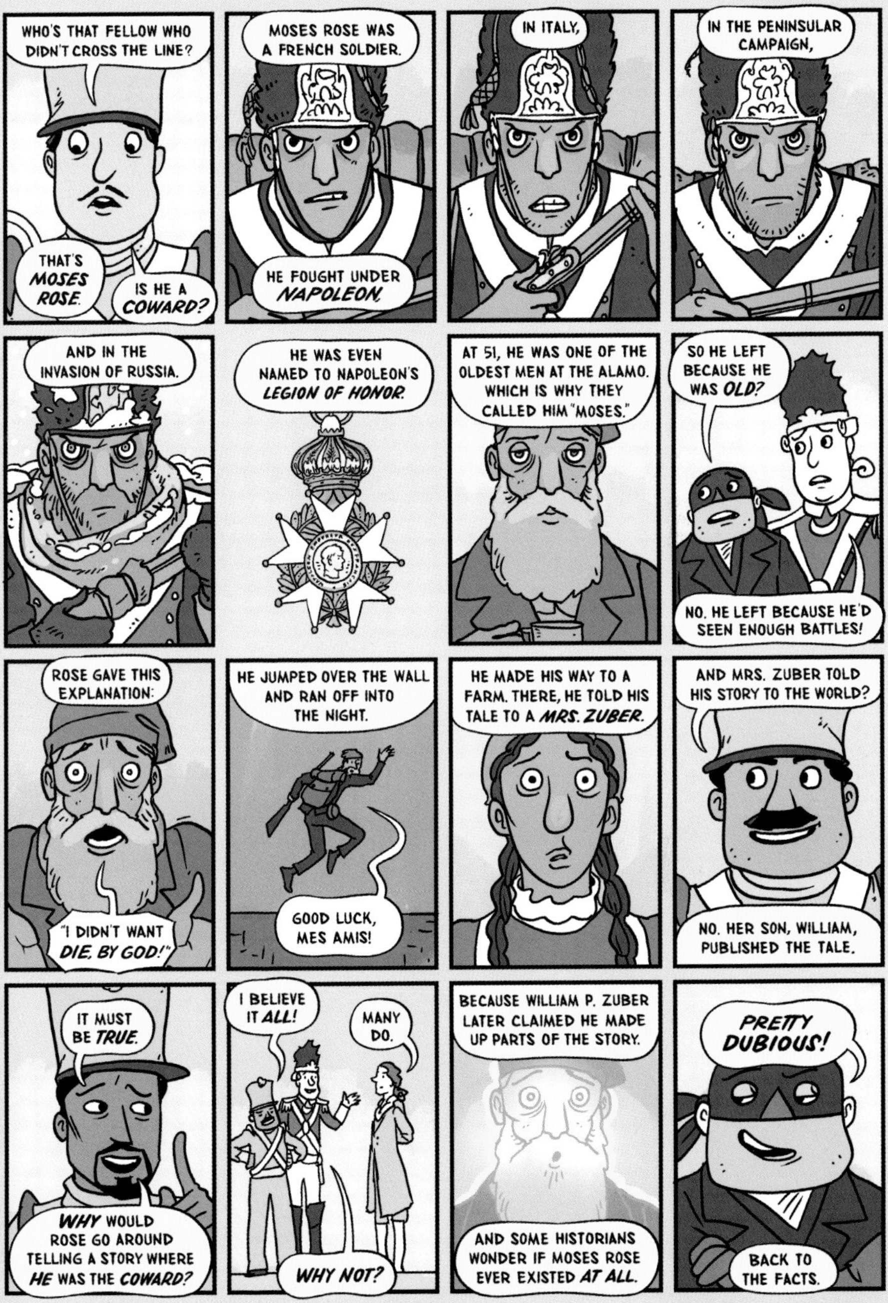
WHO'S THAT FELLOW WHO DIDN'T CROSS THE LINE?
THAT'S *MOSES ROSE*.
IS HE A *COWARD?*
MOSES ROSE WAS A FRENCH SOLDIER.
HE FOUGHT UNDER *NAPOLEON*,
IN ITALY,
IN THE PENINSULAR CAMPAIGN,
AND IN THE INVASION OF RUSSIA.
HE WAS EVEN NAMED TO NAPOLEON'S *LEGION OF HONOR*.
AT 51, HE WAS ONE OF THE OLDEST MEN AT THE ALAMO. WHICH IS WHY THEY CALLED HIM "MOSES."
SO HE LEFT BECAUSE HE WAS *OLD?*
NO. HE LEFT BECAUSE HE'D SEEN ENOUGH BATTLES!
ROSE GAVE THIS EXPLANATION:
"I DIDN'T WANT *DIE, BY GOD!*"
HE JUMPED OVER THE WALL AND RAN OFF INTO THE NIGHT.
GOOD LUCK, MES AMIS!
HE MADE HIS WAY TO A FARM. THERE, HE TOLD HIS TALE TO A *MRS. ZUBER*.
AND MRS. ZUBER TOLD HIS STORY TO THE WORLD?
NO. HER SON, WILLIAM, PUBLISHED THE TALE.
IT MUST BE *TRUE*.
WHY WOULD ROSE GO AROUND TELLING A STORY WHERE *HE* WAS THE *COWARD?*
I BELIEVE IT *ALL!*
MANY DO.
WHY NOT?
BECAUSE WILLIAM P. ZUBER LATER CLAIMED HE MADE UP PARTS OF THE STORY.
AND SOME HISTORIANS WONDER IF MOSES ROSE EVER EXISTED *AT ALL*.
PRETTY DUBIOUS!
BACK TO THE FACTS.

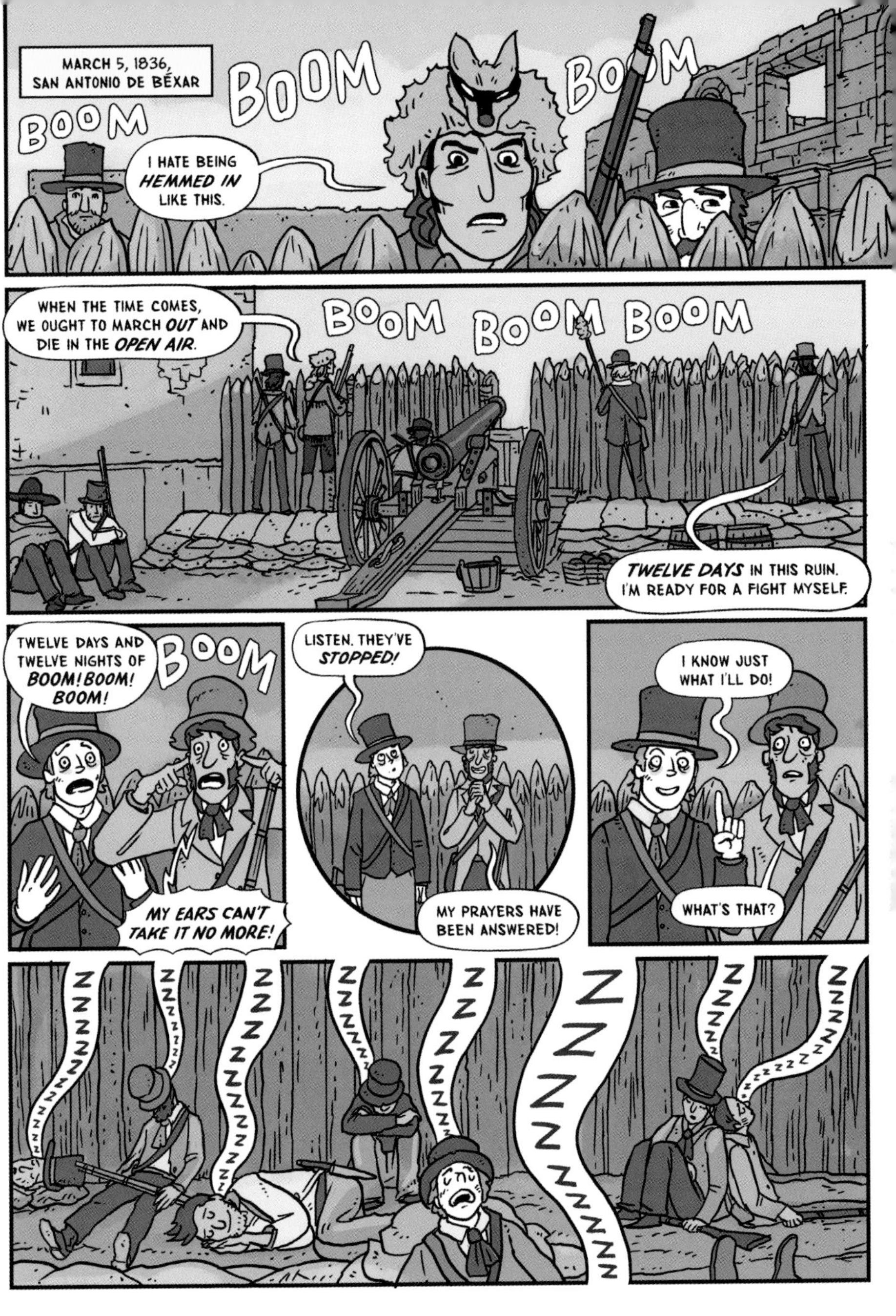
MARCH 5, 1836,
SAN ANTONIO DE BÉXAR
BOOM
BOOM
BOOM
I HATE BEING *HEMMED IN* LIKE THIS.
WHEN THE TIME COMES, WE OUGHT TO MARCH *OUT* AND DIE IN THE *OPEN AIR*.
BOOM BOOM BOOM
TWELVE DAYS IN THIS RUIN. I'M READY FOR A FIGHT MYSELF.
TWELVE DAYS AND TWELVE NIGHTS OF *BOOM! BOOM! BOOM!*
BOOM
MY EARS CAN'T TAKE IT NO MORE!
LISTEN. THEY'VE *STOPPED!*
MY PRAYERS HAVE BEEN ANSWERED!
I KNOW JUST WHAT I'LL DO!
WHAT'S THAT?
ZZZZZZZZ

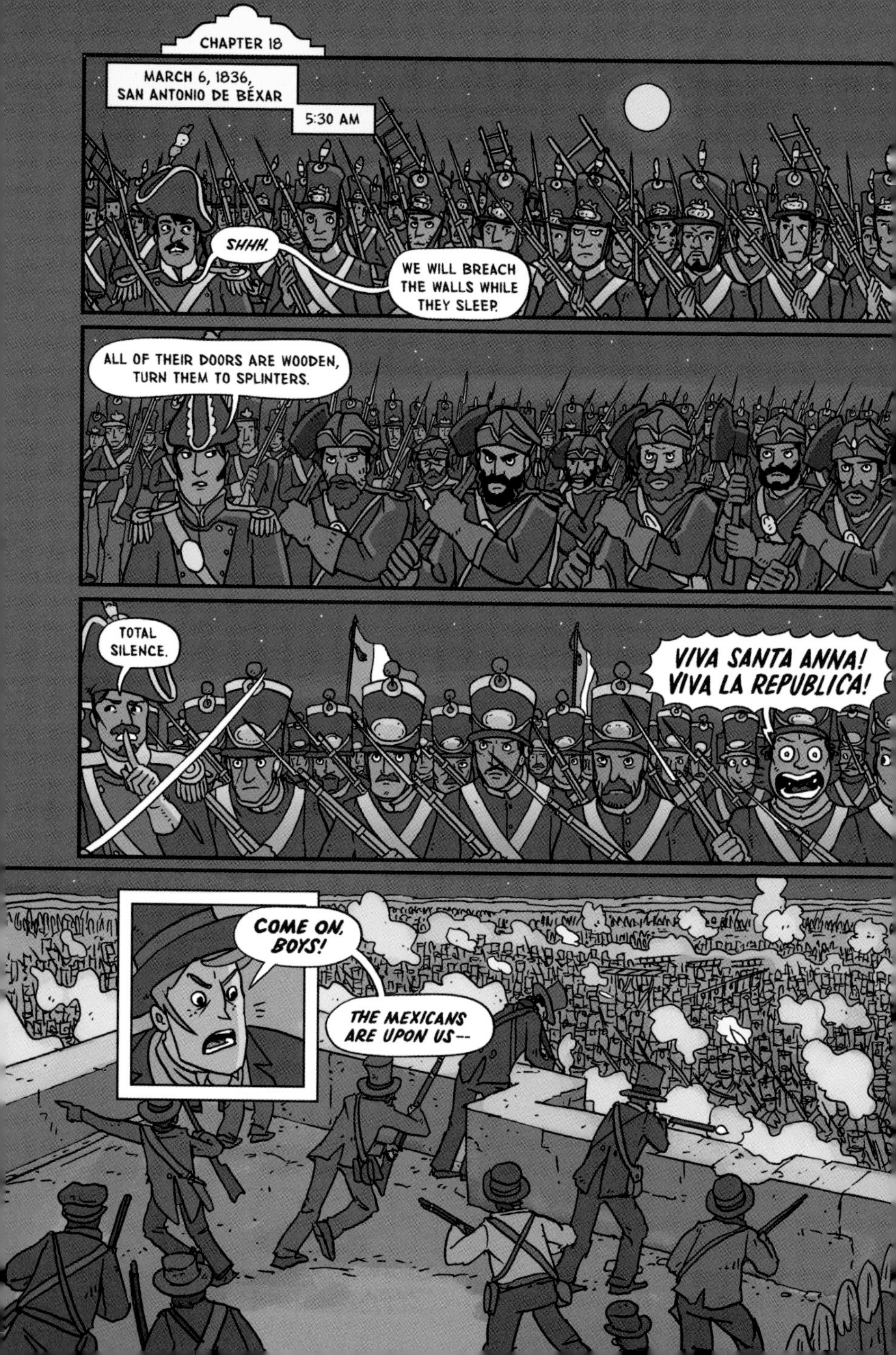
CHAPTER 18
MARCH 6, 1836,
SAN ANTONIO DE BÉXAR
5:30 AM
SHHH.
WE WILL BREACH THE WALLS WHILE THEY SLEEP.
ALL OF THEIR DOORS ARE WOODEN, TURN THEM TO SPLINTERS.
TOTAL SILENCE.
VIVA SANTA ANNA! VIVA LA REPUBLICA!
COME ON, BOYS!
THE MEXICANS ARE UPON US--

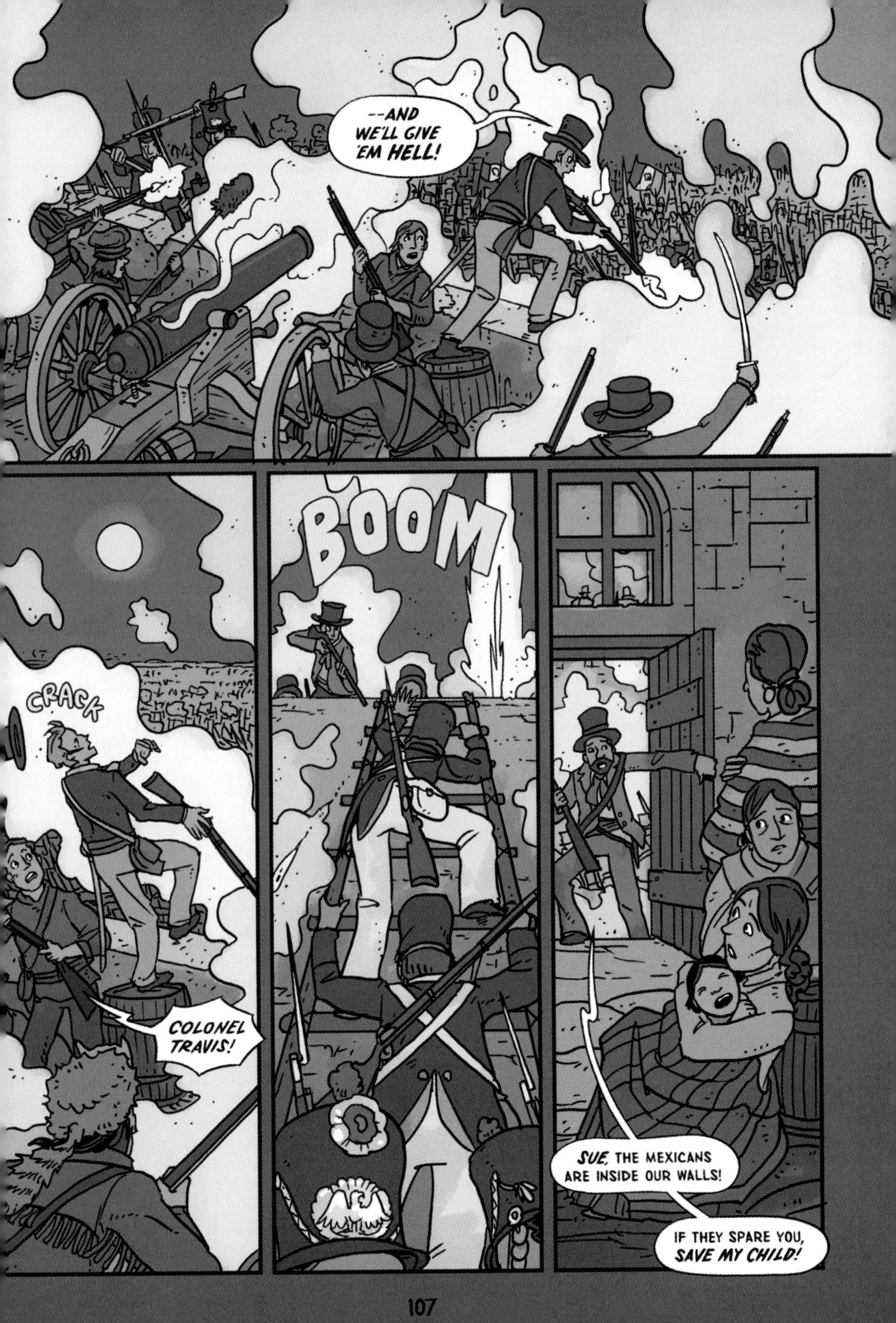
--AND WE'LL GIVE 'EM HELL!
CRACK
COLONEL TRAVIS!
BOOM
SUE, THE MEXICANS ARE INSIDE OUR WALLS!
IF THEY SPARE YOU, SAVE MY CHILD!

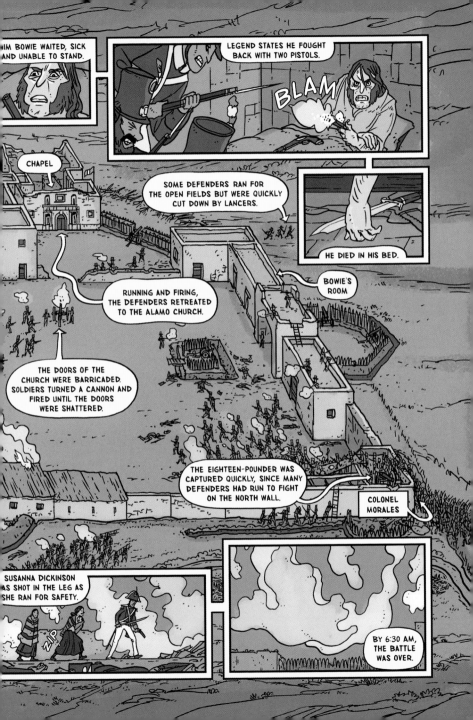

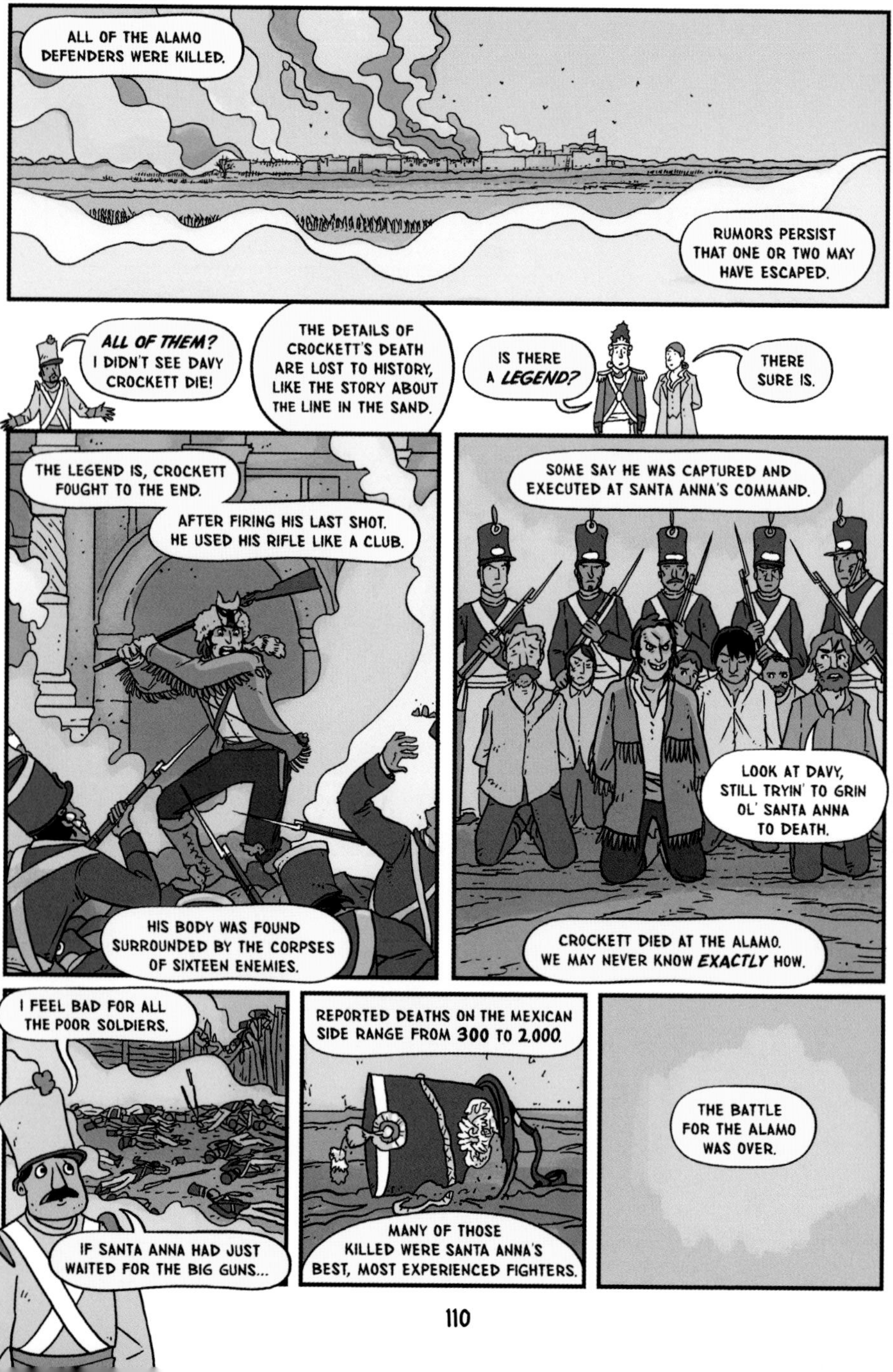

ALL OF THE ALAMO DEFENDERS WERE KILLED.
RUMORS PERSIST THAT ONE OR TWO MAY HAVE ESCAPED.
ALL OF THEM? I DIDN'T SEE DAVY CROCKETT DIE!
THE DETAILS OF CROCKETT'S DEATH ARE LOST TO HISTORY, LIKE THE STORY ABOUT THE LINE IN THE SAND.
IS THERE A LEGEND?
THERE SURE IS.
THE LEGEND IS, CROCKETT FOUGHT TO THE END.
AFTER FIRING HIS LAST SHOT, HE USED HIS RIFLE LIKE A CLUB.
HIS BODY WAS FOUND SURROUNDED BY THE CORPSES OF SIXTEEN ENEMIES.
SOME SAY HE WAS CAPTURED AND EXECUTED AT SANTA ANNA'S COMMAND.
LOOK AT DAVY, STILL TRYIN' TO GRIN OL' SANTA ANNA TO DEATH.
CROCKETT DIED AT THE ALAMO. WE MAY NEVER KNOW EXACTLY HOW.
I FEEL BAD FOR ALL THE POOR SOLDIERS.
IF SANTA ANNA HAD JUST WAITED FOR THE BIG GUNS...
REPORTED DEATHS ON THE MEXICAN SIDE RANGE FROM 300 TO 2,000.
MANY OF THOSE KILLED WERE SANTA ANNA'S BEST, MOST EXPERIENCED FIGHTERS.
THE BATTLE FOR THE ALAMO WAS OVER.

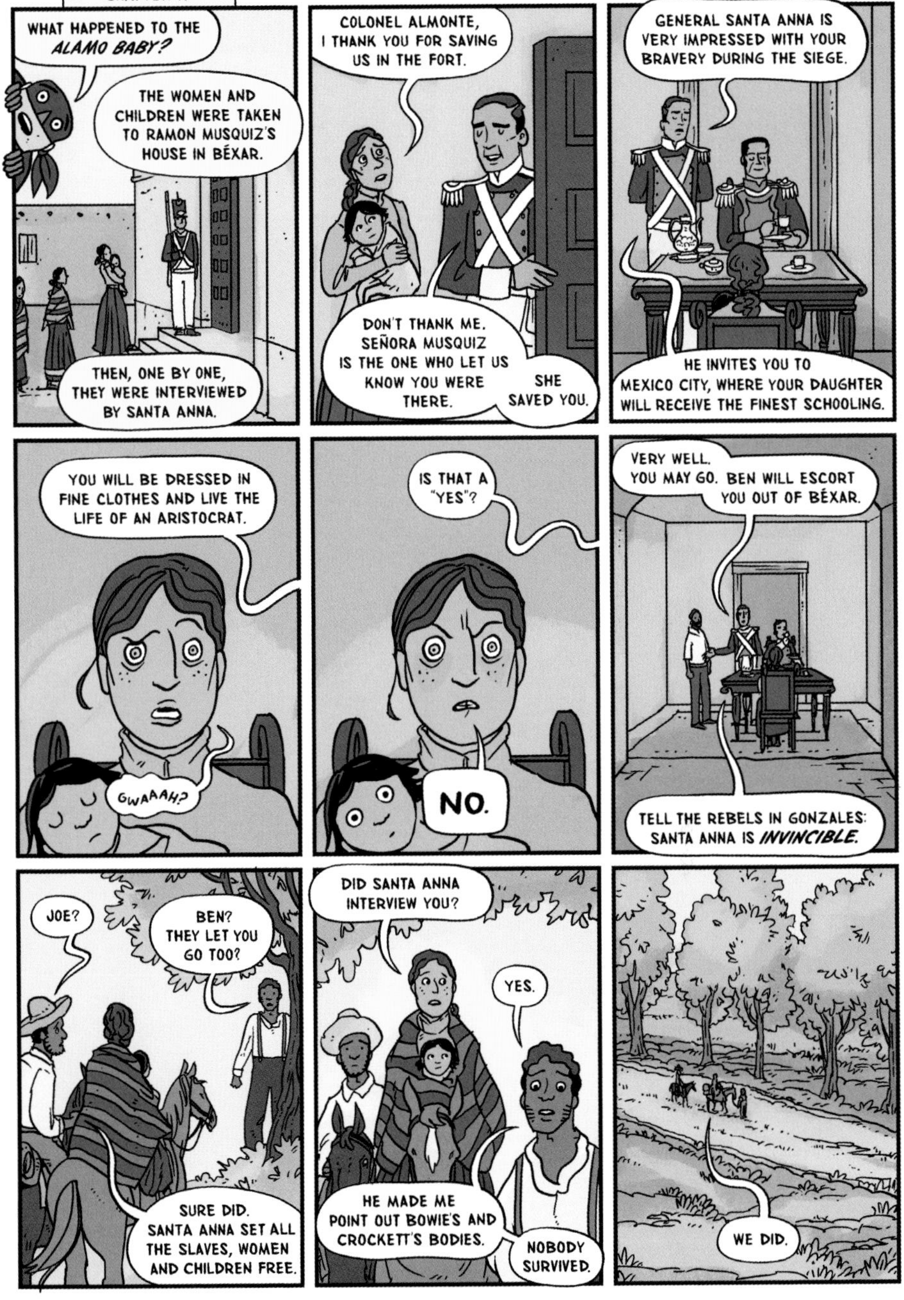
WHAT HAPPENED TO THE *ALAMO BABY?*
THE WOMEN AND CHILDREN WERE TAKEN TO RAMON MUSQUIZ'S HOUSE IN BÉXAR.
THEN, ONE BY ONE, THEY WERE INTERVIEWED BY SANTA ANNA.
COLONEL ALMONTE, I THANK YOU FOR SAVING US IN THE FORT.
DON'T THANK ME. SEÑORA MUSQUIZ IS THE ONE WHO LET US KNOW YOU WERE THERE.
SHE SAVED YOU.
GENERAL SANTA ANNA IS VERY IMPRESSED WITH YOUR BRAVERY DURING THE SIEGE.
HE INVITES YOU TO MEXICO CITY, WHERE YOUR DAUGHTER WILL RECEIVE THE FINEST SCHOOLING.
YOU WILL BE DRESSED IN FINE CLOTHES AND LIVE THE LIFE OF AN ARISTOCRAT.
GWAAAH?
IS THAT A "YES"?
NO.
VERY WELL. YOU MAY GO. BEN WILL ESCORT YOU OUT OF BÉXAR.
TELL THE REBELS IN GONZALES: SANTA ANNA IS *INVINCIBLE.*
JOE?
BEN? THEY LET YOU GO TOO?
SURE DID. SANTA ANNA SET ALL THE SLAVES, WOMEN AND CHILDREN FREE.
DID SANTA ANNA INTERVIEW YOU?
YES.
HE MADE ME POINT OUT BOWIE'S AND CROCKETT'S BODIES.
NOBODY SURVIVED.
WE DID.

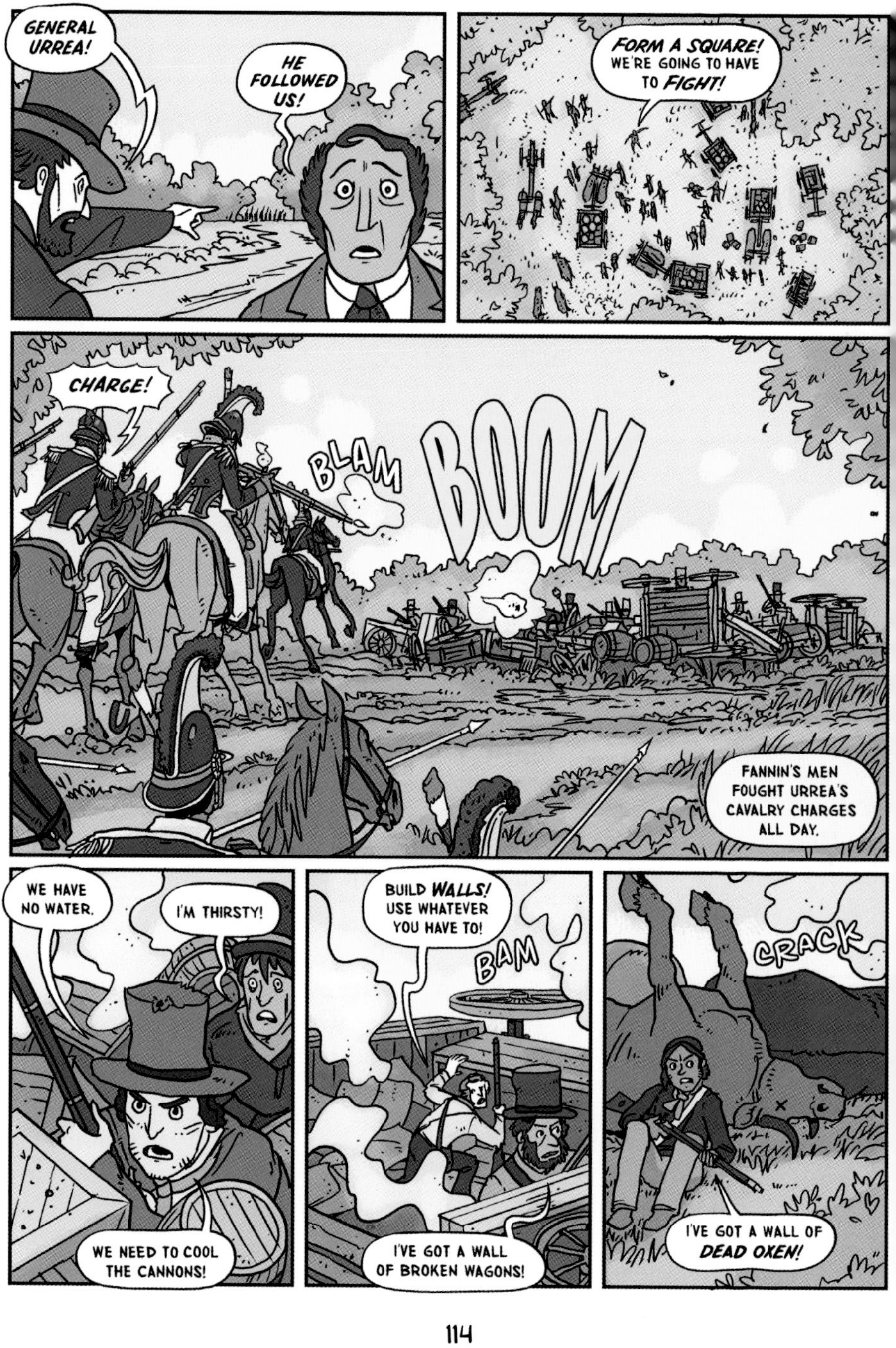
GENERAL URREA!
HE FOLLOWED US!
FORM A SQUARE! WE'RE GOING TO HAVE TO FIGHT!
CHARGE!
BLAM
BOOM
FANNIN'S MEN FOUGHT URREA'S CAVALRY CHARGES ALL DAY.
WE HAVE NO WATER.
I'M THIRSTY!
WE NEED TO COOL THE CANNONS!
BUILD WALLS! USE WHATEVER YOU HAVE TO!
BAM
I'VE GOT A WALL OF BROKEN WAGONS!
CRACK
I'VE GOT A WALL OF DEAD OXEN!

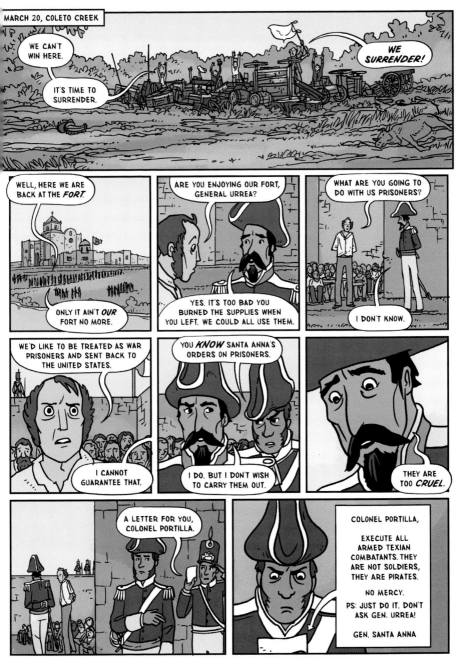

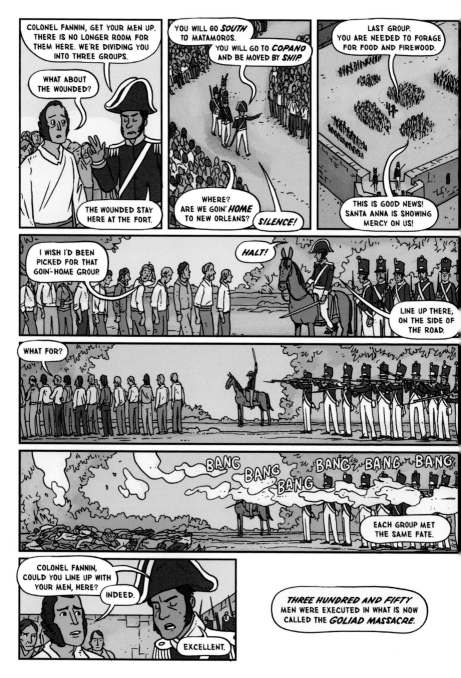

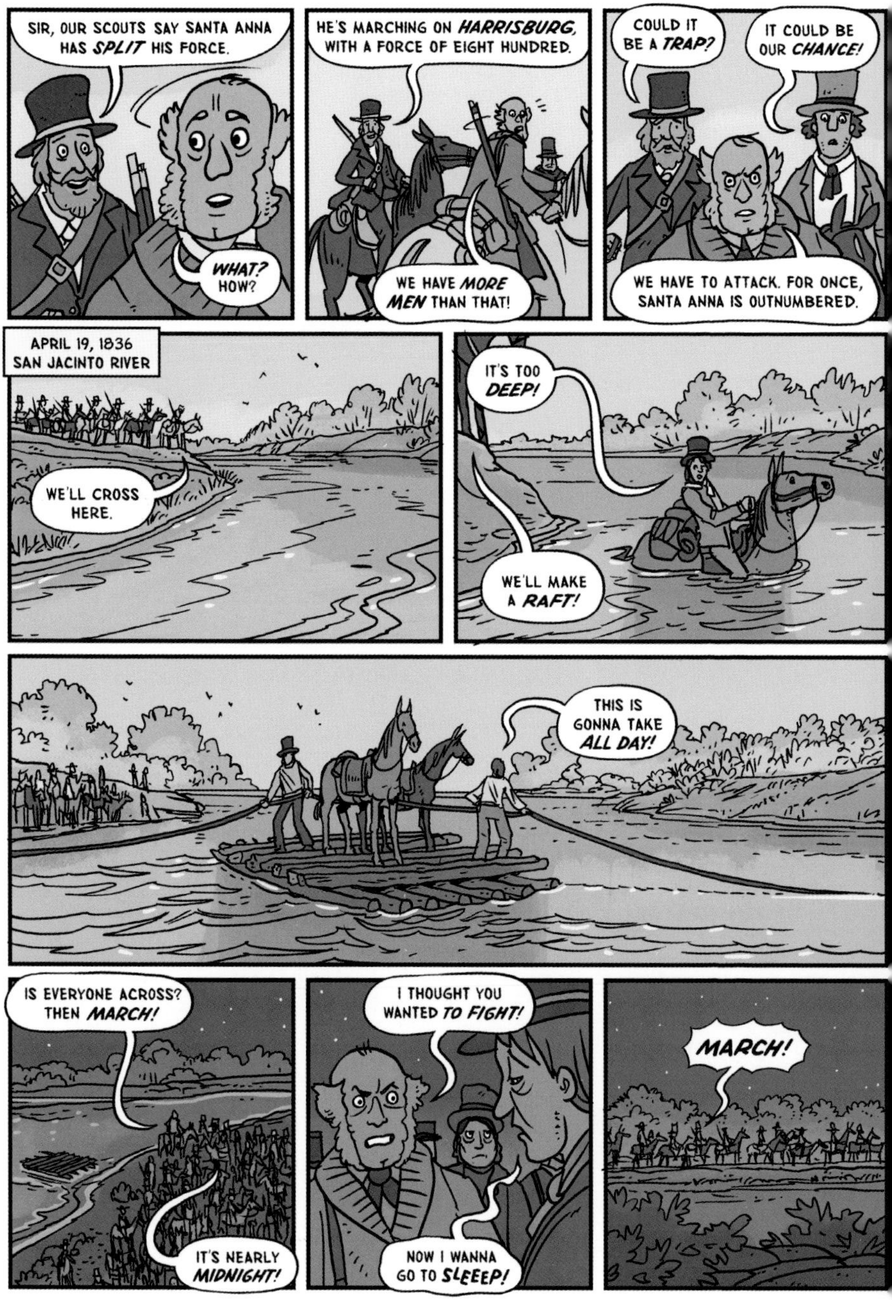
SIR, OUR SCOUTS SAY SANTA ANNA HAS SPLIT HIS FORCE.
WHAT? HOW?
HE'S MARCHING ON HARRISBURG, WITH A FORCE OF EIGHT HUNDRED.
WE HAVE MORE MEN THAN THAT!
COULD IT BE A TRAP?
IT COULD BE OUR CHANCE!
WE HAVE TO ATTACK. FOR ONCE, SANTA ANNA IS OUTNUMBERED.
APRIL 19, 1836
SAN JACINTO RIVER
WE'LL CROSS HERE.
IT'S TOO DEEP!
WE'LL MAKE A RAFT!
THIS IS GONNA TAKE ALL DAY!
IS EVERYONE ACROSS? THEN MARCH!
IT'S NEARLY MIDNIGHT!
I THOUGHT YOU WANTED TO FIGHT!
NOW I WANNA GO TO SLEEEP!
MARCH!

119

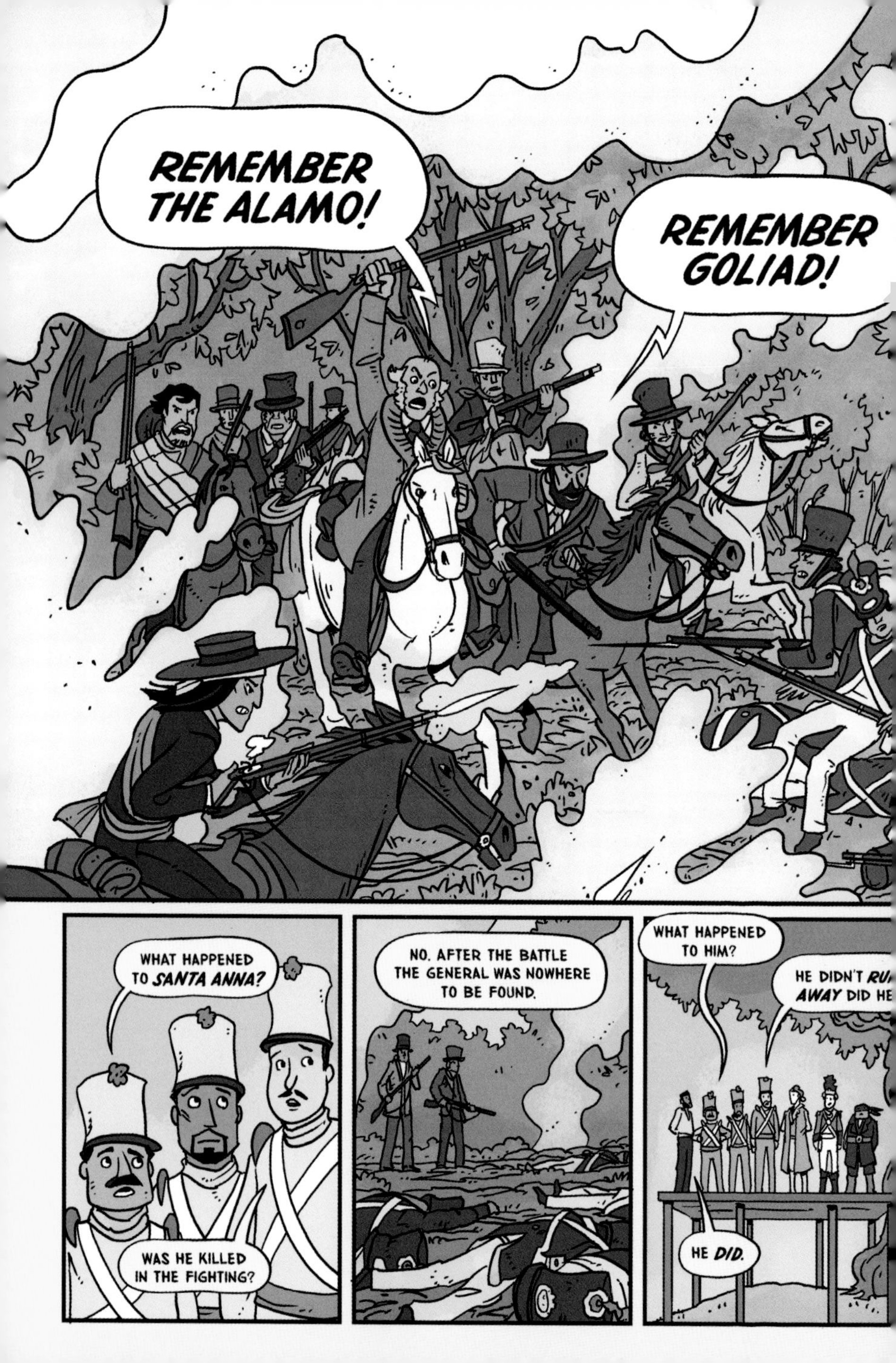
REMEMBER THE ALAMO!
REMEMBER GOLIAD!
WHAT HAPPENED TO SANTA ANNA?
WAS HE KILLED IN THE FIGHTING?
NO. AFTER THE BATTLE THE GENERAL WAS NOWHERE TO BE FOUND.
WHAT HAPPENED TO HIM?
HE DIDN'T
AWAY DID HE
HE DID.

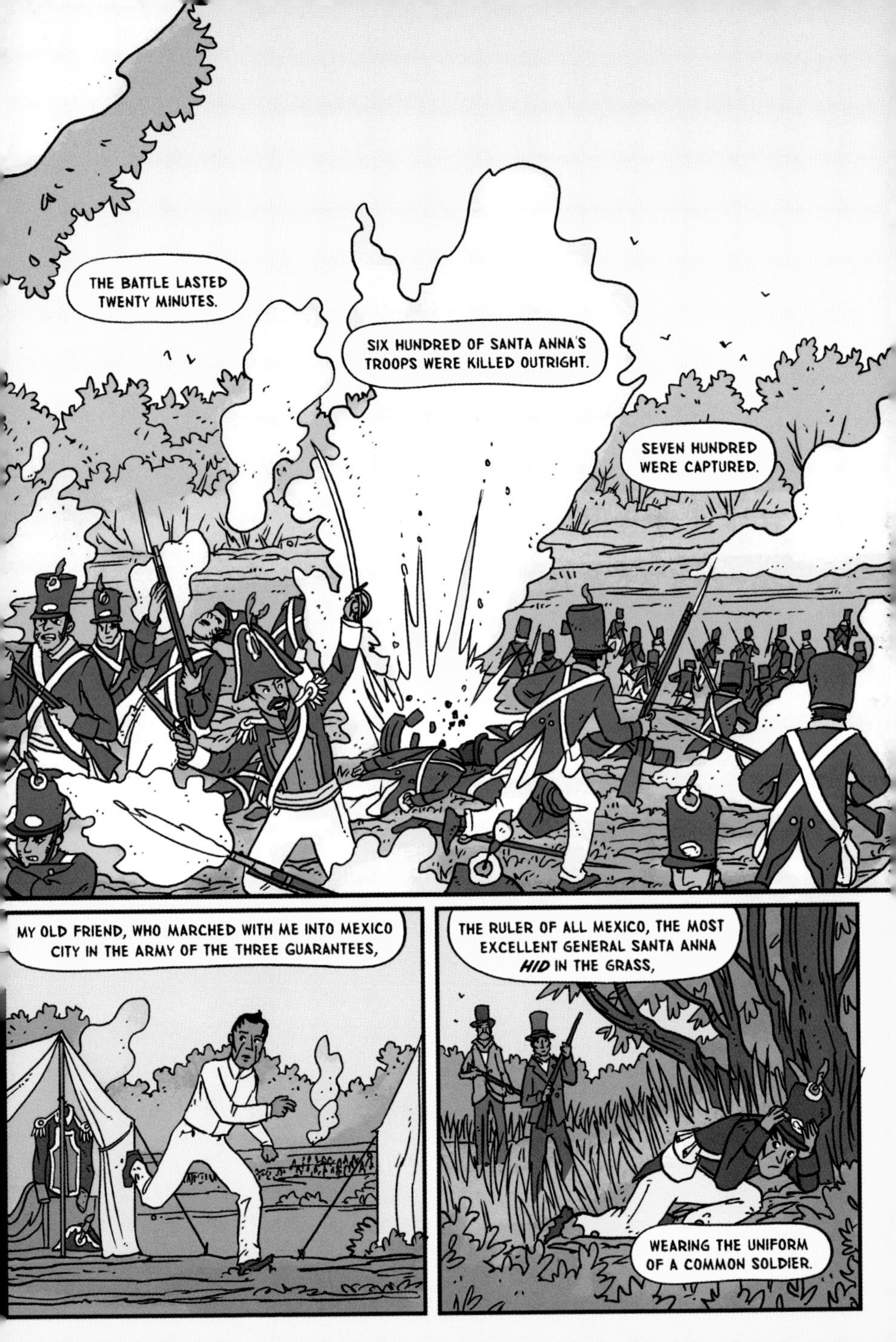
THE BATTLE LASTED TWENTY MINUTES.
SIX HUNDRED OF SANTA ANNA'S TROOPS WERE KILLED OUTRIGHT.
SEVEN HUNDRED WERE CAPTURED.
MY OLD FRIEND, WHO MARCHED WITH ME INTO MEXICO CITY IN THE ARMY OF THE THREE GUARANTEES,
THE RULER OF ALL MEXICO, THE MOST EXCELLENT GENERAL SANTA ANNA *HID* IN THE GRASS,
WEARING THE UNIFORM OF A COMMON SOLDIER.

NH
HT
NATHAN · HALE'S · HAZARDOUS · TALES

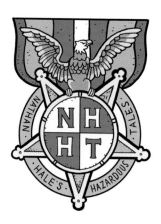

THE SURRENDER OF SANTA ANNA, BY WILLIAM HENRY HUDDLE

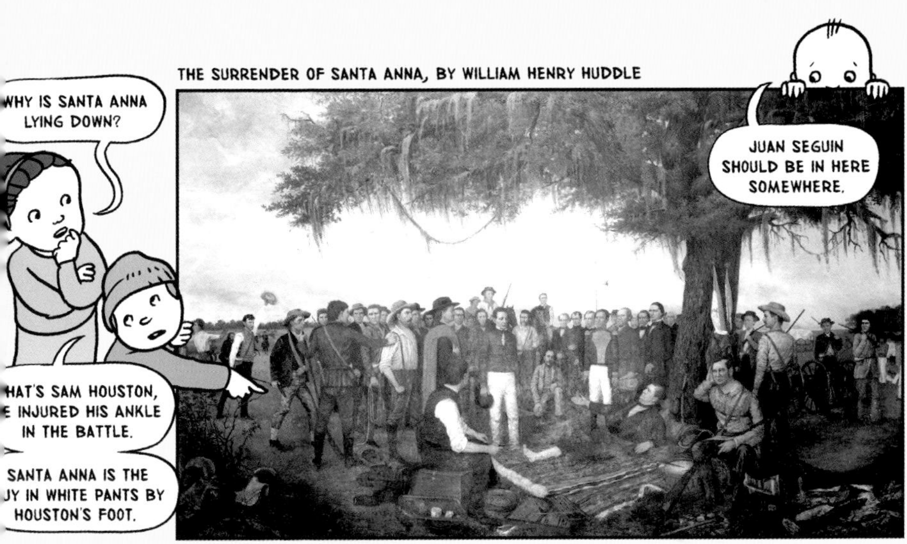
WHY IS SANTA ANNA LYING DOWN?
JUAN SEGUIN SHOULD BE IN HERE SOMEWHERE.
HAT'S SAM HOUSTON, E INJURED HIS ANKLE IN THE BATTLE.
SANTA ANNA IS THE JY IN WHITE PANTS BY HOUSTON'S FOOT.

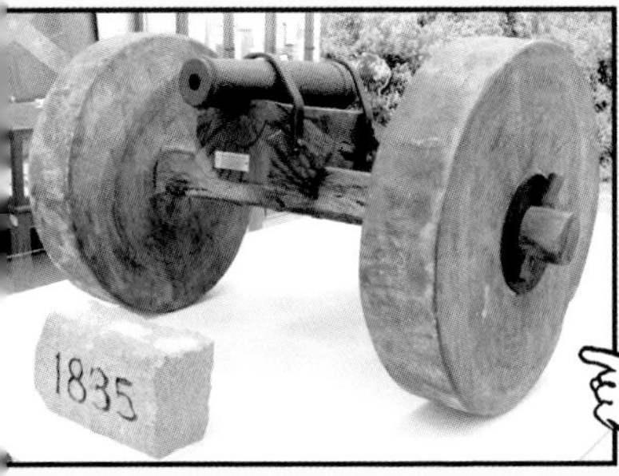
1835

E "COME AND TAKE IT" CANNON, ON DISPLAY AT THE ONZALES MEMORIAL MUSEUM IN GONZALES, TEXAS

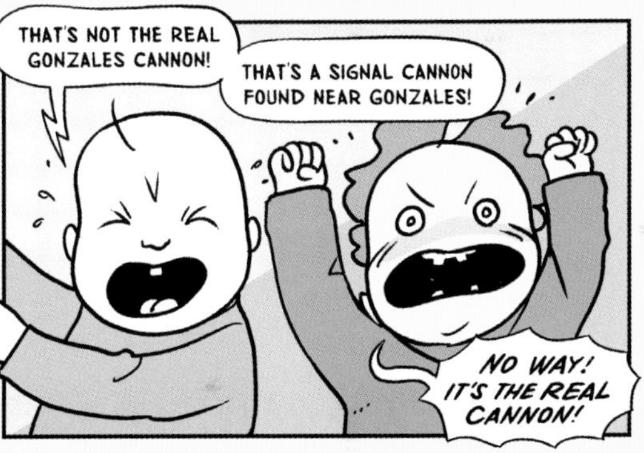
THAT'S NOT THE REAL GONZALES CANNON!
THAT'S A SIGNAL CANNON FOUND NEAR GONZALES!
NO WAY! IT'S THE REAL CANNON!

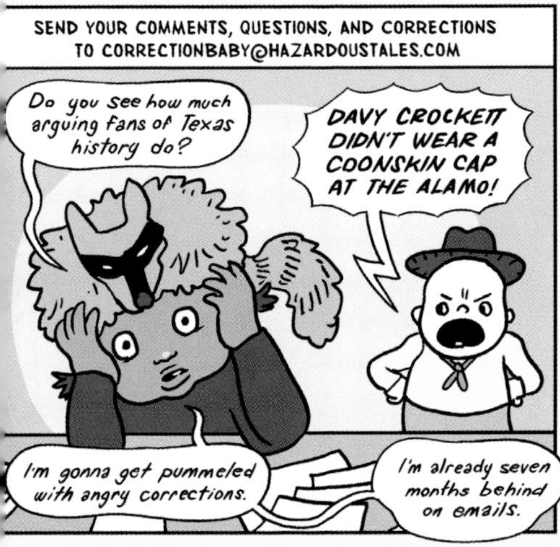
SEND YOUR COMMENTS, QUESTIONS, AND CORRECTIONS TO CORRECTIONBABY@HAZARDOUSTALES.COM
Do you see how much arguing fans of Texas history do?
DAVY CROCKETT DIDN'T WEAR A COONSKIN CAP AT THE ALAMO!
I'm gonna get pummeled with angry corrections.
I'm already seven months behind on emails.

THANKS—

SPECIAL THANKS TO CHRIS SCHWEIZER FOR THE ONCE AGAIN/JUAN SEGUIN JOKE. IF YOU DON'T KNOW MR. SCHWEIZER'S HISTORICAL FICTION COMIC, THE CROGAN ADVENTURES, YOU SHOULD. SUPER FUN SWASHBUCKLING BOOKS FOR READERS OF ALL AGES.

BIG THANKS TO THE MANY TEXAS LIBRARIANS WHO HOSTED ME AT THEIR SCHOOLS DURING THE WRITING AND RESEARCHING OF THIS BOOK, AND TO THE MANY STUDENTS WHO EXPRESSED THIER ENTHUSIASM FOR HISTORY AND SUGGESTED NEW SUBJECTS FOR FUTURE HAZARDOUS TALES BOOKS.

I CAN EASILY SAY I'VE VISITED MORE SCHOOLS IN TEXAS THAN ANY OTHER STATE!

AND THANK ***YOU*** FOR BEING A HISTORY READER, A COMICS READER, AND THE TYPE OF READER WHO READS THIS KIND OF INFORMATION IN THE BACK OF BOOKS. YOU ARE SERIOUSLY AN OUTSTANDING READER.

—NATHAN HALE, 2015

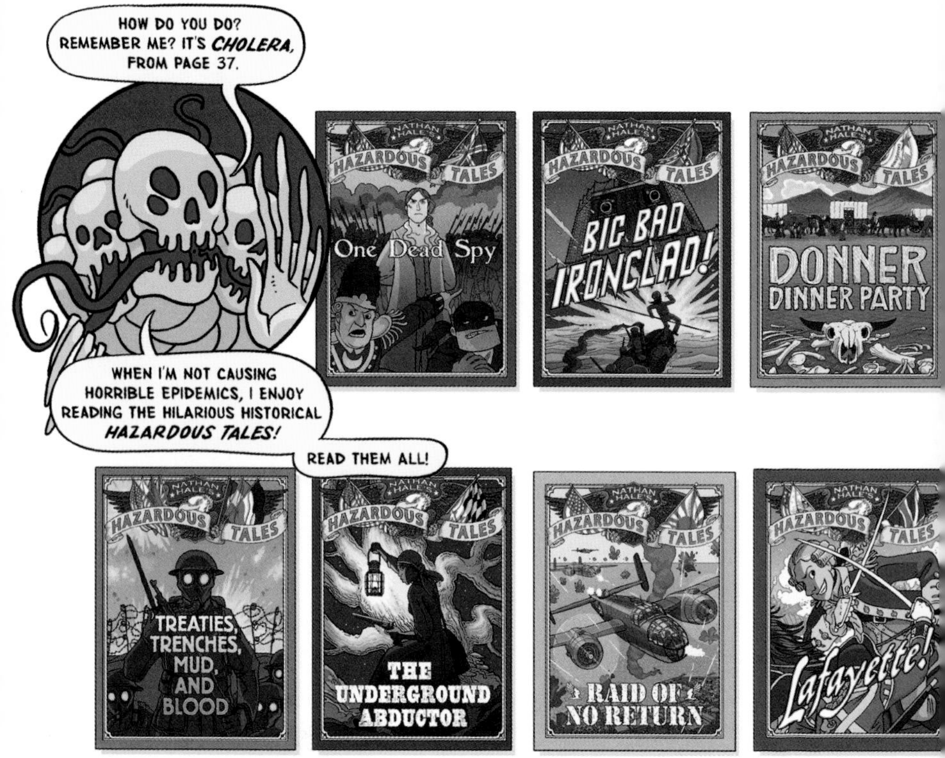
HOW DO YOU DO? REMEMBER ME? IT'S *CHOLERA*, FROM PAGE 37.
WHEN I'M NOT CAUSING HORRIBLE EPIDEMICS, I ENJOY READING THE HILARIOUS HISTORICAL *HAZARDOUS TALES!*
READ THEM ALL!
NATHAN HALE'S HAZARDOUS TALES
One Dead Spy
NATHAN HALE'S HAZARDOUS TALES
BIG BAD IRONCLAD!
NATHAN HALE'S HAZARDOUS TALES
DONNER DINNER PARTY
NATHAN HALE'S HAZARDOUS TALES
TREATIES, TRENCHES, MUD, AND BLOOD
NATHAN HALE'S HAZARDOUS TALES
THE UNDERGROUND ABDUCTOR
NATHAN HALE'S HAZARDOUS TALES
RAID OF NO RETURN
NATHAN HALE'S HAZARDOUS TALES
Lafayette!

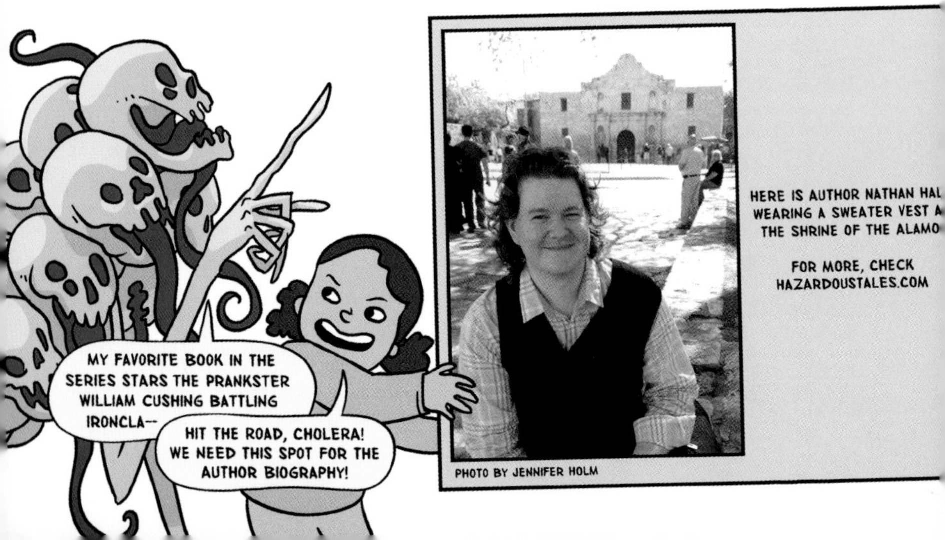
MY FAVORITE BOOK IN THE SERIES STARS THE PRANKSTER WILLIAM CUSHING BATTLING IRONCLA--
HIT THE ROAD, CHOLERA! WE NEED THIS SPOT FOR THE AUTHOR BIOGRAPHY!
HERE IS AUTHOR NATHAN HAL
WEARING A SWEATER VEST A
THE SHRINE OF THE ALAMO
FOR MORE, CHECK HAZARDOUSTALES.COM
PHOTO BY JENNIFER HOLM

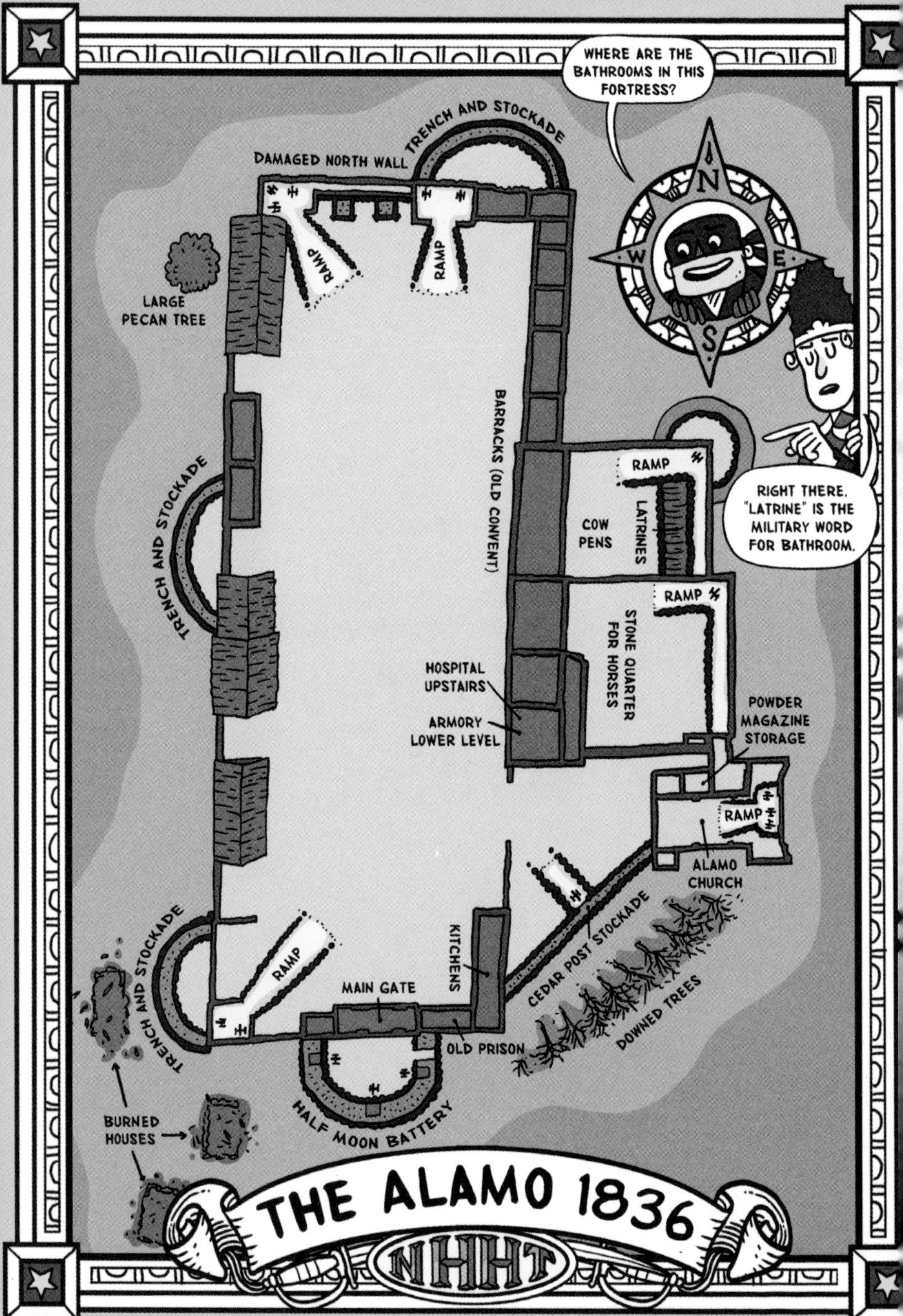
WHERE ARE THE BATHROOMS IN THIS FORTRESS?
RIGHT THERE. "LATRINE" IS THE MILITARY WORD FOR BATHROOM.
N
E
S
W
TRENCH AND STOCKADE
DAMAGED NORTH WALL
LARGE PECAN TREE
RAMP
RAMP
BARRACKS (OLD CONVENT)
RAMP
LATRINES
COW PENS
RAMP
STONE QUARTER FOR HORSES
TRENCH AND STOCKADE
HOSPITAL UPSTAIRS
ARMORY LOWER LEVEL
POWDER MAGAZINE STORAGE
RAMP
ALAMO CHURCH
KITCHENS
CEDAR POST STOCKADE
DOWNED TREES
TRENCH AND STOCKADE
RAMP
MAIN GATE
OLD PRISON
HALF MOON BATTERY
BURNED HOUSES
THE ALAMO 1836
NHHT